digital
underground
SEX
PACKETS
digital
underground
THE
HUMPTY
DANCE
digital
underground
HUMPTY
SKYY

Keep It Beautiful

WHAT'S THE MATTER?
CAN'T CONCENT

KEEP IT BEAUTIFUL

Inside the Funkyverse of Shock G and Digital Underground

ALEXIS WOLFE MBASSA
AND GREGORY E. JACOBS

Clarkson Potter/Publishers
New York

HUMP
WAS
HERE

CONTENTS

OAKLAND

TOPANGA CANYON

NEW YORK CITY

TAMPA

RACKADELIC '89

FOREWORD

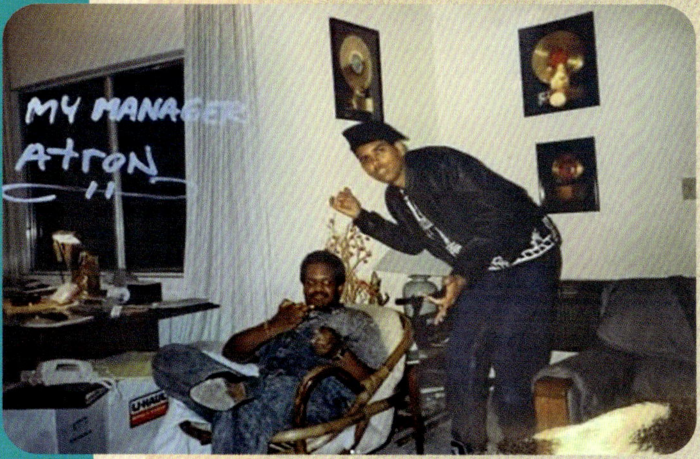

I met Gregory "Shock G" Jacobs in 1988. Our journey spanned over three decades, ending in a final exchange on April 20, 2021, at 11:37 AM. The last thing he texted me was, "Love u back!" I believe I was the last member of his "family" to communicate with him prior to his unfortunate passing.

Back in 1988, I heard music that was unlike anything else—creative, infectious, and deeply layered. I heard songs like "Underwater Rhymes" and "Your Life's Cartoon," where Shock rapped as himself and as a character called MC Blowfish. He didn't just produce the music; he drew the cover art to go with it. When you listened closely, his lyrics were thought-provoking and socially conscious. Like the work of most prophetic artists, Shock's message still resonates today. You can hear his heart for humanity in the early lines of Doowutchyalike:

"Now, red, white, black, tan, yellow, or brown, / It really doesn't matter, we can all get down."

Shock was more than a producer or a rapper; he was a radio DJ, a drummer, a pianist, and a brilliant visual artist. He was meticulous in every sense of the word. I remember once someone showed him a cover sketch that looked nearly identical to his own style. To my eyes, the lines were the same, but not to Shock. He pointed out that the width of the lines was off—they weren't "his" lines. He told me he never would have approved that sketch for public consumption. He was that particular about what he released to the world.

That level of integrity is why this book exists. Shock sought out a partner to help share his art and his story, and he settled on Alexis Wolfe.

Over the years, I have grown to know Alexis well. I saw firsthand why Shock not only chose her but trusted her with his legacy. They spent years putting this book together, traveling to places that were important to him, including his childhood home. As an accomplished photographer, Alexis shares Shock's obsession with integrity in art. He recognized that in her. He knew she would treat his work like her own and make sure it kept the standard he always sought.

This book is the culmination of interviews with others, conversations they had, and the art and pictures he shared with her.

The title, *Keep It Beautiful,* says it all. Shock always wanted the best for everyone he knew, but more importantly, he wanted the best for mankind—especially for those who faced challenges. He saw the beauty in the struggle and the art in the everyday. I believe this book is the truest representation to date of who Gregory "Shock G" Jacobs really was.

—Atron Gregory

From an Insider, On what it was like to be a hip hopper before rap records:

In the late 1970s, before there was such a thing as a rap record or a published graffiti image of any kind, hip hop thrived as an organized underground cult, oblivious to the media and to the rest of the music industry, or to the traditional musicians' community. Most adults, and even most kids, didn't yet know what the word "hip hop" meant, or what scratching on a turntable was; only an elite 1 or 2 percent of the northeastern United States were in the know. I say "elite" of course not for any superiority or material wealth (most of us were poor), but because in hindsight it was such a blessed privilege to be one of the lucky few who lived that scene. Such a great feeling it was too; we felt like artistic outlaws, or like musical aliens with our own coded language. Words like "chill," "def," "dope," "wack," "fresh," "ill," "scratchin," "b-boy," "breakdance," "bomb," and "tag" were "in effect" and only spoken by this small group of maybe fifteen to twenty thousand people total (deejay crews and fans combined), who were sprinkled here and there throughout New York's population of twelve million in the five-borough area (Bronx, Manhattan, Brooklyn, Queens, Staten Island), including a few heads from New Jersey and surrounding cities. Imagine it; only twenty thousand people in the entire world, most of whom were teens, using these words regularly, all with a common understanding of their new hip hop meanings, and circulating this new sound on cassette tapes in the neighborhoods and schools. These tapes featured acts that were already considered hip hop royalty by us loyal fans; Kool Herc, Africa Bambaataa, DJ Hollywood, Grandmaster Flash & the Furious Five MCs, The Chief Rocker Busy Bee, Cold Crush Four, DJ Charlie Chase, Grand Wizard Theodore (aka Theodore With Cuts Galore) & the Fantastic Five were the big names. Other schoolyard legends were MC Woody Wood from Brooklyn, The Disco Brothas from Astoria Queens, MC Cartwright, The Albino Brothers featuring MC Good Lookin' Lance & DJ Prince from Queens Village, and emcees Shah Born and Shock-Dell from Far Rockaway just to name a few, but there were hundreds more.

This exclusive subculture lasted for about four years between 1976 and 1980. And trust me, *we knew*. All of us, whether breakdancer, graffiti artist, deejay, emcee, promoter, or just listener, we all knew we were a part of something that was artistically heavy, unique, intelligent, different, as creatively rich as jazz or classical music, and completely brand-new to the Universe. If you were a hip hopper in those years, it felt similar to how an X-Man with shape-shifting abilities might feel among regular human beings; it was the *SHIIIIIT*.

Then in late 1979 a historic event happened that blew the door open and allowed the rest of the world to pour into the hip hop community; "Rappers Delight" by the Sugarhill Gang came out. It was released nationwide, and received massive and immediate radio airplay. And that was all it took. The floodgates were open, and the people came pouring in. Fans, new artists, businesspeople, radio, TV, film, advertising; everybody wanted a piece of the action. From that point on, as we all witnessed, hip hop began a steady climb toward revolutionizing world culture and replacing rock 'n' roll as the dominant popular music of the planet.

Bravo hip hop, I tip my Kangol to you.

Shock-G

Rackadelic, 1979

Background pulled from original artwork for the album, "Fear of a Mixed Planet."

PHOTOGRAPH INSERT: Shock storytelling on a porch in Olympia, WA, with Eddie Sumlin and friend.

AUTHOR'S NOTE

Spokane, Washington

Summer of 2004

We were sitting with a group of people on somebody's rickety front porch, late-night after another digital underground show. A spill-out of fans were huddled around Shock pulling puffs off their cigarettes, eyes wide open, not wanting to miss a thing while he told a story about going after the Flavor Unit with boiling hot water. It was all part of a major water fight between digital underground and the 3rd Bass crew versus the Flavor Unit, which escalated city after city on tour with Public Enemy back in 1990. Shock felt like they had gone too far after holding Tupac upside down, stripping him and beating him with water guns:

Pac came storming back to the hotel all tore up and pissed, "Look what they did to me!" He was foaming at the mouth! So we ended up making a plan to ambush the entire Flavor Unit with liters of scorching hot water. I remember Queen Latifah and I noticed each other first from about a block away. She was like, "Hey, what's up, Shock? Yo, they got black beans and rice over there." It was nervous small talk. I was walking at the time and then that turned into a run. I yelled out "It's an ambush!" and we all came after them out from bushes and all corners, causing Queen Latifah, her road manager, her DJ, Treach, and Apache to all fling their to-go plates of Jamaican food into the air screaming and rolling around like they were on fire.

As Shock spoke, I stilled the porch swing for a minute and listened. I'd heard this one before, but in that moment, watching everyone else, I realized the stories he told needed to be heard by more than just those who crossed paths directly with him. He had a unique power to pull people in while he created a scene that engaged your imagination and senses. I remember thinking he should create a book, but I never imagined I'd eventually be the one to write it with him. On March 24, 2011, he wrote me an email: "Lex, how much living expen$e do I need to give u for a 2-ta-3 month live-in period to do my book? A big fat everything-Shock G book. Then we translate it into every language and every technology, including iPads and digital book readers, and release it worldwide!" I was excited, humbled, honored, and ready to pack my bags.

This book, written by and with Greg Jacobs, aka Shock G, over the course of ten years between 2011 and 2021, is largely the manuscript he reviewed and approved before he passed away suddenly in April of 2021. The process took many years, with numerous twists and turns along the way. While there are more stories and interviews I could gather, I chose to leave it as close as possible to how he last saw it. This is the book we created together.

Working on this project with Shock was an adventure. His freedom of thought and the stories he told created worlds of fun. There was humor in everything, and everything was a movie or comic playing out in his mind. There was color, texture, creativity. But Shock's various personas and outlandish ideas could also be a challenge. Sometimes he was filled with a quick and natural spontaneity, and other times he was hyper-focused and precise—it was his paradox. I was impressed by the care he put into his work, but it caused the project to draw out.

In the summer of 2017, Shock gave the book to me to complete, calling me a "lucky blessing" and writing: "Do ur book with my blessings. I'll approve and cooperate in any/all ways—whatever you need, use whatever you wish." At that point he truly handed me the ball. When Shock left the project with me, it was still very much a scrapbook filled with random images. The pieces of the story were there but mismatched and all over the place. It didn't reflect that meticulous order and careful thought that Shock put into so much of what he did.

In the final draft, before sending it out to agents in 2020, I included my own voice among his stories and interviews with others in his world. This enabled me to give background information from other sources and provided a broader picture of Shock. He looked it over and sent back a video message. "Setsi Letsi. Hi mama. How y'all doing? Yeah send it! . . . Yeah! Let's see what it do! . . . Love you, Lexi! Imma holla at you soon." Shock's texted videos were always super-long. Even that one. He would divide them into parts. They would be labeled one of seven, two of seven. And you had to wait until all seven parts came through, before you could text back. He got mad at me once because I didn't wait: "Okay, go 'head, you text, i'll wait & finish my text series later when ur done."

We sent the manuscript out to agents in August of 2020, and Greg passed eight months later. He did not live to meet the spectacular agent, editors, and publisher that our project found. He won't be there to celebrate or hold the finished book in his own two hands. That is and will forever be painful for me. I would have loved for Greg to feel the acknowledgment and recognition; I wish he could see his community coming together throughout the world in honor of him.

The format of the book follows our making of it. We started the interview process in Topanga Canyon, and the book traces our journey in conversation through Hollywood, Los Angeles, Oakland, back to Topanga Canyon, New York City, and finally to Tampa, where we visited Greg's family and old friends from where he grew up. These cities were pivotal in his life—they shaped who he was, and so they became the titles of various parts of the book.

The book itself is a reflection of Shock's creative spirit: a blend of dead-on, detailed, accurate text woven together with a free-flow scrapbook of images and illustrations. It was very important to Shock that the book maintain a loose, nonlinear, dynamic flow. He would sometimes hand me a printed version of a story, while other times he would tell me the story and I would record it as audio. I merged these versions, combining the written with

RIGHT Original artwork (mockup) for the album *Fear of a Mixed Planet.*

FILE TOOLS EDIT
1. SELECT ANGLE (ADJUST VIEWPOINT)
2. CHOOSE PERCEPTION
BLEEP BLEEP
3. APPLY NEW VISION
4. DESIGN IMAGE
BLEEP!
PEER, SQUINT
INDENTIFY
DECIPHER,
ISTEN,
SCRUTINIZE
LOOK
FEEL
HMMM...
SUPER DORK CLOWN GEEK NERD FROM SPACE
OLD
AND
DS?
CANCEL
UP!
CLICK
CLICK
ROLLIN GFDS
BLEEP
SYSTEM RE-WRITE IN PROGRESS (50% COMPLETE)
BLURG GLIK!
DMOOF

the recorded to fully capture the essence of each. This is why at times the text feels like polished writing, and at others it flows like a conversation. This mix was intentional—it's how Shock lived, how he created, and how he wanted his story to be told. Some conversations are pieced together from different places and times. We wanted to establish the rhythm we felt while creating. The date stamps take us on a journey. Though not always precise, I worked to stay true to the spirit of the actual dates of our conversations (as well as my interviews with those he was close to), giving the book a sense of real-time storytelling.

These stories depict a distinct era in time, especially within hip hop. The stories and images are a product of their time, and the writing is born from the creative mind of artists who explored expression without inhibition. It is important to note that some of the stories may appear crude or edgy when viewed through the lens of today's social standards. The artists' uninhibited and unapologetic spirit allowed them to tell narratives that dove into the raw essence of their era. Hip hop as an art form has always been a reflection of the culture, society, and emotions of the moment. Shock's freedom of thought and expression is something I admire to this day, even when it challenges the sensibilities of a different era.

As you move through this book, I encourage you to surround yourself with auditory experiences. Shock's stories often involved more than just his words. As he relayed them to me, his stories were accompanied by piano riffs, drumming, reciting lyrics, or playing the music of others. View the artwork within the book, but keep a device nearby so you can play the music or look up videos that follow the story. This book has a soundtrack. When a track is mentioned, play it. When an artist is mentioned or interviewed, look them up and hear their sound. Miles Davis, Parliament Funkadelic, Public Enemy, N.W.A., Fiona Apple, Tupac, Ray Luv, Raw Fusion, Gold Money, Mystic, Murs, the Luniz, digital underground. The book is meant to be experienced in an interactive way and filled with the dynamic vibrancy that Shock saw in his world.

"You know, if this book ever becomes a movie, or if you ever make a movie out of all of this, it would have to have some fantasy in it. Mixed with reality. MC Blowfish and all . . . Tell a whole story with it . . ." —Shock G

"SAME SONG"

I came for the party, to get naughty, get my rocks on
Eat popcorn, watch you move your body to the pop song
that I'm singin', ding-a-lingin', funky beats ringin'
Everybody's swingin' in the place
as I kick up the J-A-Z-Z-Y style
R&B mixin' it with the hip hop swing beat
champagne in my hand, it won't be long 'til I'm gone
It's just the same old song.

—digital underground, 1990

Print File
ARCHIVAL PRESERVERS
WWW.PRINTFILE.COM
STYLE NO. 120-3HB
INSERT EMULSION SIDE DOWN
FILE NO:
ASSIGNMENT:
DATE:
25989

INTRODUCTION

Topanga Canyon, California

Greg Jacobs's Home
August 10, 2011

I first met Shock G at a digital underground show in the fall of 2001 at the Catwalk in Seattle. I was a college student—just beginning to form my career in photography. I was there to photograph some of the local headliners on that crisp late-autumn night. I pushed past the velvety curtains to backstage, toting my media essentials and camera gear, and nodded to the usual suspects. Before I found a place to hole up and organize, my eyes were drawn to a mysterious figure sitting by the corner, writing quietly. I assumed he was a spoken word artist, a bit shy and deep in his thoughts. Everyone else was drinking, loud and bumping into each other with that before-show energy. The room was filled with members of digital underground (Money B, Too Fly Eli, Esinchill Campbell, Nu-Stylez, Metaphysical) as well as local hip hop artists I knew and their mini entourages. Even a couple of moms were in the group all mingled together. It felt like a family reunion of sorts.

A long, dark, heavy wooden table stretched through the center of the dimly lit room, etched with evidence of concerts past and its beautifully rough and unrefined history. Along one side of the room was a bar, where that lone figure sat, leaning up against the corner wall. I went over to talk to him because he looked so peaceful amid all the activity. I was more curious than anything. As I approached, he welcomed the company and we began to chat about art and the importance of color choice. I hadn't realized who he was. Then I looked down to see that he was not writing at all, but in fact shading Humpty's nose with a Sharpie. This was Shock G!

When he got up to join the group, he looked taller than I had imagined and had a larger-than-life presence. He was smooth yet had a hard look to him at the same time. He playfully tousled my hair as if I were his baby sister, bummed a cigarette from someone, and started entertaining the group with a Humpty voice and a Tupac story. I could see that Shock was a true entertainer. After the show he came out with a group of us . . . me and some of the local hip hop artists who opened for him that night: Kas, Sonny Bonoho, Rebel. Everything closed at about 1 in the morning, and it was already past that time, so we drove around into the still Seattle night, following each other in cars and stopping in parking lots to figure out the best spot to go next. There was a sense of excitement in the air and conversations about somebody's new project or cover art. Everyone was feeding off Shock's presence, and I could see they felt potential in their own artistry more than ever.

I was right there with them. He exuded a natural creative energy that was energizing and contagious. It made everything we were working for seem within reach. Shock was genuinely curious about the art we were putting out. He wanted to hear more of the music and learn more about our projects. I showed him a mock-up of a book I was working on. He looked through it and agreed right then and there to write the foreword for it. He bumped us all up by showing he believed in us. We all talked until the early morning hours, first at Kas's house in South Seattle, then we all piled into Shock's hotel room. He left Seattle with armfuls of demo CDs, phone

FUMA
nchu
YEARS
OF

TOP: Humpty Hump performing for fans at the Catwalk, Seattle, WA, 2001. **BOTTOM LEFT:** Alexis with Too Fly Ely, the Catwalk, Seattle, WA, 2001. Photo by Esinchill Campbell. **BOTTOM RIGHT:** Shock G—just after chatting by the bar, first time meeting. **OPPOSITE:** Humpty, backstage at the Catwalk, Seattle, WA, 2001.

Metaphysical performs with Shock G. Catwalk, Seattle, WA, 2001.

numbers, and a draft of my book. I left with a Humpty jacket and a new trusted friend.

Ten years later, I find myself sitting in my rental car on my way to Greg's home just outside L.A., ready to start work on his book. I always feel a sense of excitement driving out of LAX. It's almost like the feeling I get back home in New York, like there's an energy here, things are happening, people are making moves—only in L.A. it's not as grimy. The rental agency gave me an upgrade on my car this time, so I feel extra baller-ish in my silver Cadillac with the windows all the way down, music loud, seat back, and that warm California breeze coming through. As I pull off the Pacific Coast Highway onto the winding, deep-orange, death-wish road to Topanga Canyon, I am reminded of why Shock chose this place, reminded of him saying what mattered to him was to feel connected to the universe, to nature. He'd say things like, "It's just me and the crickets out here. I can dance naked with the curtains open." I give Greg a quick call to tell him I'm on the way. "Hey Lex! Your flight good?" he says. "I'm gonna make you something to eat when you get here."

I didn't get to fully know Greg right away; that took some time. I met two of his well-known alter egos first: Shock G and Humpty Hump. Greg is much more complicated than those two. I see his alter egos as real separate people. At times it seems like he becomes more Shock G, Humpty Hump, Rackadelic, the Piano Man, Peanut Hakeem, or Icey-Michael Boston. Mostly, now, I see him as either Shock or Greg. Sometimes he's "regular dude," practical joker, and deep thinker Greg; other times he's bigger-than-life smooth pimp and superstar Shock G.

Shock G and Seattle artist Sonny Bonoho exchanging contact info backstage. Catwalk, Seattle, WA, 2001.

Rackadelic or the Piano Man will show up when he's contemplating art, music, and in his creative mind. I try not to work with Humpty. Humpty is too loud and showy and obnoxious.

As I turn onto the long, steep, dusty driveway leading up to his place, I pull this big shiny lug of a car into some sort of a spot, resting on the edge of a drop-off. I suddenly realize that it will be near-impossible to ever get out. A couple years ago, I brought my teeny grandmother here, to meet Shock and look at the sunset from his balcony. She was so terrified we might roll down the cliffside that she yelled at me, "Do you know how many sunsets I've seen in my life?!" Greg walked up to us and immediately charmed her. The two of them sang old songs together that day and kept in touch with handwritten notes for years to come.

Whenever I work with Greg, I too find myself in my grandmother's shoes, letting go of things that normally freak me out. Like my car, here, perched on a cliff. Greg lives in a different dimension. "He thinks in cartoons," as Saafir would say. It's easier to go with it than try to fight it with too much thought. So I think, Whatever, I'll figure it out. *I lean in to grab my bag from the passenger seat and look out into Topanga Canyon. I can just make out the City of Angels in the distance. I breathe in the fresh air and hear, "Lex! Come check this out!" He is standing at the top of a large red boulder just west of his front door. This is so like Shock. Who knows what he is about to show me. But I'm ready.*

Greg at home, Topanga Canyon, CA, 2004.

TOPA
CANY

ANGA
YON

Greg at home, Topanga Canyon, CA, 2004.

CHAPTER 1: TALES OF THE FUNKY

August 10, 2011

Knowing Shock and Humpty, I had originally visualized Greg living in something that might be featured on MTV Cribs, or the mansion from his video with Murs for the song "Risky Business." I pictured winding white marble staircases, multiple grand pianos, half a dozen Lamborghinis or Ferraris out front. But this place, Greg's real home, is different. This place is very Greg. It's a creative escape, tucked away from all the L.A. noise. At night, the only sound is a nearby owl, or the crickets doing their thing, and the only light comes from the moon, the stars, or the blue glow from a laptop working overtime. The place isn't big, but it is always open: huge windows, wraparound porches, and doors wide to let in the summer breeze. The place feels like a cabin. Beautiful cedar on all the walls and pine floors. Sheer cobalt blue curtains floating between some rooms.

Downstairs are a couple of keyboards, layered, an old upright piano painted rustic white, an easel with art supplies everywhere. You can look over the wall from the upstairs kitchen area into the lower level because it's open in that way. On the walls hang a letter from Afeni Shakur to Shock along with framed letters from people thanking him for his mentorship in some way. Images of George Clinton, Jerry Garcia, Scarface, Fiona Apple, Erykah Badu. There's a framed poster of the Monsters Inc. crew from the Pixar movie with a note underneath saying, "Meet digital underground?" A ton of layered Post-its and scrap paper is pasted above his desk with various quotes about art or peaceful living, photographs of family, and random bits of information or phone numbers. At times a lizard peeks its head in or troops of ants march past, but it's all part of living with nature. The place is full of history too. Many artists have come through to work with Shock, and creativity oozes through the walls. This was Marvin Gaye's old place, a creative escape for him as well. Greg likes to picture what it was like during that time. I tell Greg how much I love it up here.

Whenever I try to tell people what it's really like in Topanga, they have no real idea. But when they see all this, they are like, "Oooh . . ." As soon as someone walks into this place, they are immediately at ease. You might have been worrying if it was gonna be sketchy or if girls are gonna come home with us from Hollywood or something, but I think when you are here, you know it's not some excessive egomaniac who lives here. Or a violent person. There is no way you can live here and be violent. I mean, there's a piano and an easel.

I joke with him that he kinda could be violent and still have a piano.

Okay. Yeah, yeah. Hey, you want to see the bodies? Let me show you the other, *other* shed. Mwah-ha-ha-ha! You thought you were going back to New York?

We laugh at this idea a bit. I settle into my room and then come back out to the kitchen. Shock pours us both a cup of green tea and plops down on a barstool. I've known him for over a decade, yet I'm feeling nervous suddenly. I've been given this mission to capture a piece of history. Here is this person sitting in front of me who matters to so many people, and I'm the one who's

View of Los Angeles just steps from Greg's front door, Topanga Canyon, CA, 2011.

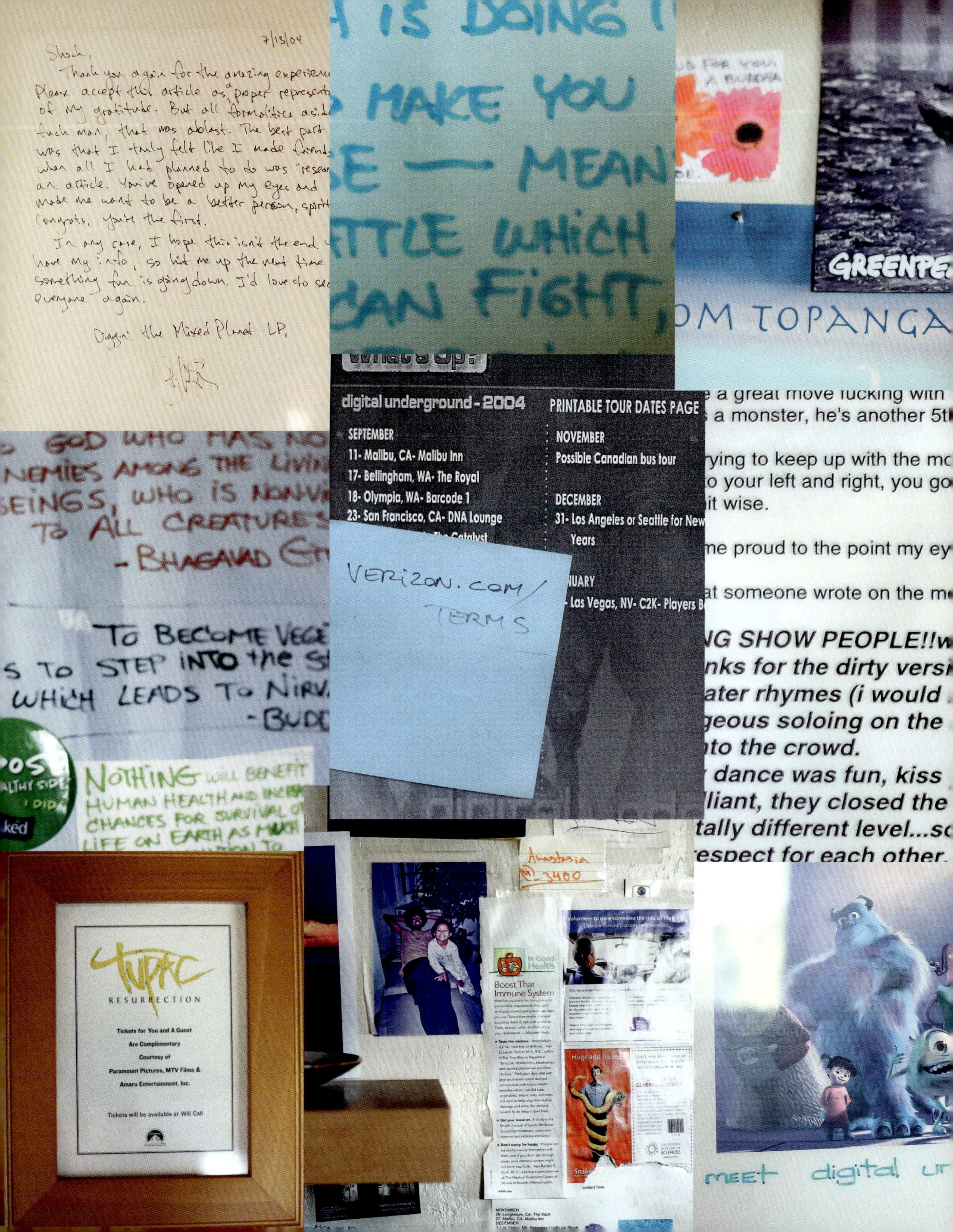

7/13/04
Shock,
Thank you again for the amazing experience
Please accept this article as a proper representation
of my gratitude. But all formalities aside
fuck man, that was a blast. The best part
was that I truly felt like I made friends
when all I had planned to do was "research"
an article. You've opened up my eyes and
made me want to be a better person, spirit
Congrats, you're the first.
In any case, I hope this isn't the end.
have my info, so hit me up the next time
something fun is going down. I'd love to see
everyone again.
Diggin' the Mixed Planet LP,
IS DOING
MAKE YOU
E — MEAN
TTLE WHICH
CAN FIGHT,
GREENPE
OM TOPANGA
digital underground - 2004
PRINTABLE TOUR DATES PAGE
SEPTEMBER
11- Malibu, CA- Malibu Inn
17- Bellingham, WA- The Royal
18- Olympia, WA- Barcode 1
23- San Francisco, CA- DNA Lounge
NOVEMBER
Possible Canadian bus tour
DECEMBER
31- Los Angeles or Seattle for New Years
- Las Vegas, NV- C2K- Players B
VERIZON.COM/
TERMS
e a great move fucking with
a monster, he's another 5t
rying to keep up with the m
o your left and right, you go
it wise.
me proud to the point my ey
at someone wrote on the m
NG SHOW PEOPLE!!w
nks for the dirty vers
ater rhymes (i would
geous soloing on the
nto the crowd.
dance was fun, kiss
lliant, they closed the
tally different level...s
espect for each other.
GOD WHO HAS NO
NEMIES AMONG THE LIVIN
BEINGS, WHO IS NONVI
TO ALL CREATURES
- BHAGAVAD GI
TO BECOME VEGE
S TO STEP INTO THE S
WHICH LEADS TO NIRV
- BUDD
NOTHING WILL BENEFIT
HUMAN HEALTH AND INCR
CHANCES FOR SURVIVAL OF
LIFE ON EARTH AS MUCH
TUPAC
RESURRECTION
Tickets for You and A Guest
Are Complimentary
Courtesy of
Paramount Pictures, MTV Films &
Amaru Entertainment, Inc.
Tickets will be available at Will Call
Anastasia
In Good Health
Boost That Immune System
Hugs and hisses
meet digital ur

Painted upright piano, easel, and paints. Inside the main room of Greg's place. Topanga Canyon, CA, 2011.
OPPOSITE: Pieces of Greg's wall above and near his desk—filled with Post-its, numbers, quotes, and handwritten letters, including a snapshot with his little sister, Liz.

supposed to catch his story. How do I even do that? I haven't done any formal interviewing before. I realize that I feel differently around Shock than I do with Greg. Greg feels like an old friend from when we were kids. He's like family in a way, a cousin. Shock is someone I look up to. He's grander than human. Right now, I'm sitting with Shock.

Soon he says, "Okay, let's go." And so the work begins. I'm a little stumbly, but I grab my recorder and ask him first to talk a bit about his various selves—Greg, Shock G, and Humpty. (Seems like a good place to start since I'm thinking about all of his personas.) I look up. He gives me this sideways smile. I'm sure he senses how I'm feeling. He's in my mind. I remember the moment backstage when I first met him and he tousled my hair. He's messing with me and comforting me at the same time. I'm trying to ask questions, but he keeps interrupting and goofing off. He knows I'm nervous and not in the flow yet. He's trying to pull me out of that. This is how he begins, grabbing the recorder from the ledge between us.

Hello. I'm sitting here . . . It's August 10, 2011, I'm sitting here with Alexis Wolfe. My name is Eddie Humphry, aka Greg Jacobs . . . Peanut Hakeem Anafu Washington, my nigga! . . . So one of the most interesting things about me is that after I was a child, I became a teenager, and I eventually moved on to be an adult. So what holds in the future for Shock G, you say? I'm kind of contemplating becoming a senior citizen.

I let out an awkward chuckle, grab the recorder, and end up turning it off. This is ridiculous. He's just playing with me.

No. I'm a heckler. I like to heckle. It makes you stronger. If a comedian's up there and struggling, trying to get through it, right after his punch line, I'll yell out, "Yo! Tell a joke, motherfucker!"

Somehow this snaps me out of it. It reminds me that he can just be Greg and I can just be Lex. He is trying to help me relax. With that on my mind,

I ask my first clear question: "Do you ever feel like you have to be somebody for others? When you leave Topanga, do you feel like you have to become Shock G or put on a bit of extra?"

No, not at all. If I do it, it's because I want to do it. It's because of how I'm feeling. Like, "I'm feeling Shock G today." But yeah, I guess there are times when I have to turn it on and I'm not in the mood. If it's showtime, or I'm at an event and people are expecting that person. If I'm not in the mood, I just psych myself up and do it. Just like people who smile at work to be polite. I just slap myself out of it, put that mask on. Then about an hour or so into it, you forget that you had to do that at all and you're just in the mood now.

We are all just regular people. I never felt more important than the person sitting next to me on the bus or on the plane. When I walk onstage, that's when I turn it on. Or when I interview with the cameras on MTV and all that, I'll try to be this superstar: SHOCK G! WHOOOO! I'M HUMPTY HUMP, NIGGA, I'M BIGGER THAN LIFE! But I don't actually feel that way inside. I'm just Greg. I felt like, "Yo, that's kinda cool how we put that together." I'd look at it from the outside. I always try to let people see that they can do it too. It's putting in a little extra effort. Stay home a few weekends instead of going out and work on your thing, whatever it is. That's how you get ahead.

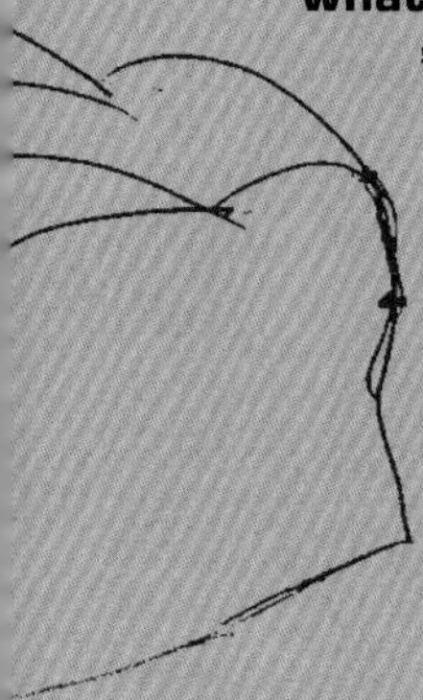

'Cause most people won't. Most people won't save money. Most people won't take the time to write a script. Most people won't take the time to plot out a video. I feel like, if I was doing anything special, it's that I was aware that effort actually can turn into something. But I never felt more talented than the next person.

Hey, you hungry? I'm gonna make us veggie burgers. You never had a veggie burger this good!

Shock's been vegetarian for years now, and he's proud of his recipe. He starts planning to make us veggie burgers for a late lunch/early dinner.

There are studies that say there is no such thing as geniuses. Nobody is born into it. It's ten thousand hours of practice that creates experts. Some people get it in four years, some people get it in twenty years. But once you get ten thousand hours of practicing dance, or practicing music, or shooting jump shots—whatever it is—any human being becomes an expert. I was always aware of that. My mother was the one who really showed me that. She always said to me that stars are just regular people. They put their shoes on one foot at a time, like anybody else. It's the lights and the makeup that make them seem extra special, "And don't ever forget that, Gregory!"

Shock pulls a green jar from his tiny fridge tucked under the kitchen counter. Pesto! This is the secret. *He begins to chop the onions.*

I know what I look like on an album cover. I also know that when I walk into a room full of women, and I'm not announced as Shock G, I'm just like any other dude. Out of one hundred girls, there's always those three to ten that will like me, and those other ninety that won't. Just like everybody else. But if I walked into that same room, and they announced, *"Ladies and gentlemen, digital underground!!!"* The girls would go, *"Oh girl, he cute!! Oh girl, he fine!"* Oh suddenly I'm fine? Last night I wasn't fine when I was anonymous. Now I'm fine? So I can't let it go to my head to think that I'm so fine. I know I ain't *that* fine. It was my wallet making me fine, or being onstage.

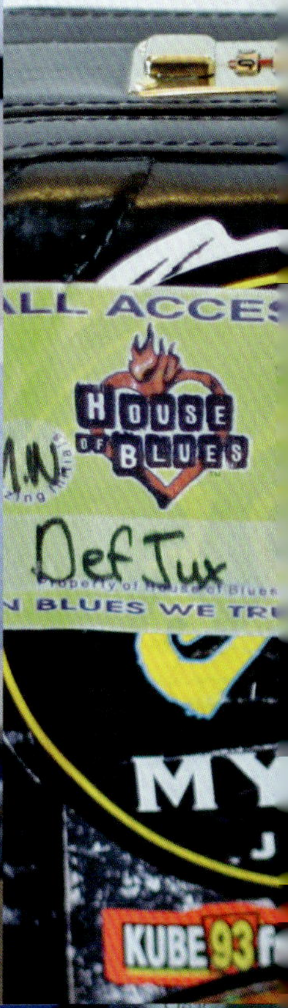
ALL ACCES
HOUSE OF BLUES
Def Jux
KUBE 93

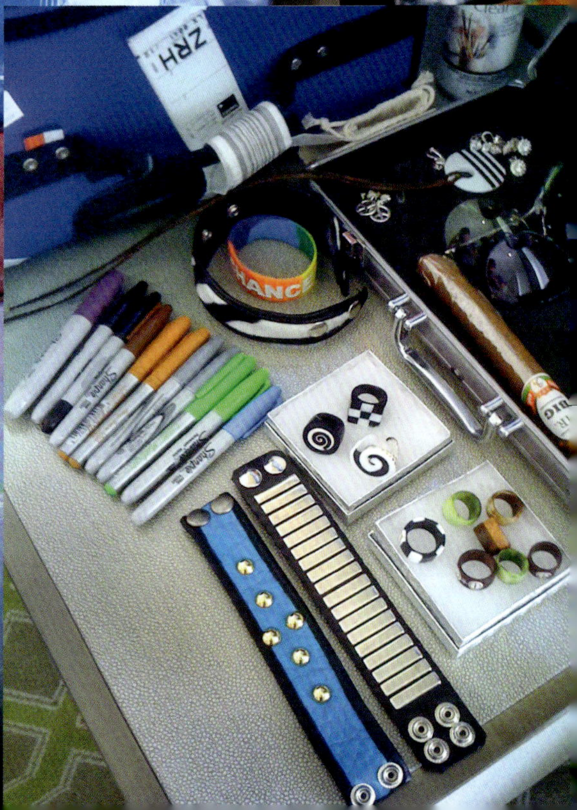

Shock's tour suitcase—filled with various accessories, Humpty Noses, colorful sharpies, and everything meticulously displayed. **LEFT:** A stack of original artwork packaged in preparation to be shipped out to friends and family.

Shock at home, Topanga Canyon, CA, 2011.

The onions are caramelizing, and smoke swirls around us. Greg's place doesn't have air-conditioning, but with all the windows and doors wide open, the breeze moves straight through the two-floor cabin. It feels more like we're outside than in.

I feel lucky that I grew up in a household that enabled me to have the freedom to focus on music and art. A lot of people don't have that freedom. That part is lucky. That part is blessed too, sure. But it's also lucky. It's not that you're chosen. If you think like that, you're gonna end up like Tupac or ODB. You've got to realize that all we're doing is channeling the light, and if you end up being lucky enough to be one of the head conductors to channel a lot of that light through, do it carefully. If you mishandle that light, it will get taken from you. Those are the people who get one quick career and they can't handle it. It's over right away. Or people who get in over their head. Fame can kill you as easily as being an outcast. Being rich is worse than being broke if you can't handle it.

I ask Shock, "Did it ever go to your head?"

It's unavoidable, unless you were some kind of . . . unless you were raised by Buddhist parents or something. There's no way that you can't get a little big-headed when you're this young and you're writing music and it's actually working, you know? I was wearing a lot of hats. We were the only West Coast group getting love on the East Coast. That lasted for a few years. It's not that my head got big, I think I stayed pretty humble. People always said I was polite and approachable, but I did get a distorted view of my own work. I got a distorted view of how random and lucky things are and that things happen to go your way sometimes for no clear reason . . . I was like, "Yo, I threw that album together. Imagine when I *really* work on something. I'm the Dr. Dre of my label, TNT Records. Atron won't even sign nobody without asking me if I think it's dope or not."

I had all these people fussing over me. People used to tell us there's no reason for us not to last. They said, "You guys are musicians and make your own music, there's no reason for y'all to fall off too fast. You have too much content. Nobody else does what you do." And for a little year and a half or so, that was true. So I was like, "We're an empire. We're an all-city grand imperial dance music and hip hop dynasty! This is just scratching the surface." I did that first album in two weeks sleeping on a girl's couch, working on Jimi's [Jimi Dright, Chopmaster J, original d.u. member] equipment and rushing through it. Wait until I get my own lab and all the equipment I really want. That's how I felt. Wait until we *really* do it. I haven't even collaborated with some of the people I want to collaborate with yet. But I wasn't just blind like that on my own self. I was blind about everyone around me. I thought we were all dope as fuck.

I said, "If they think I'm the shit, wait until they hear PeeWee." PeeWee plays guitar, drums, and keyboards. PeeWee is tight, better than anyone I know. He had flavor on the drums. We all just thought PeeWee was a genius. I was like, "If y'all like Humpty and Shock G, I'm goofy, I'm barely a rapper. I'm a piano player really, in my mind. If y'all like me, wait until you hear PeeWee!" He sounds like Eazy-E when he rhymes, except he's doper than Eazy-E, 'cause he plays instruments and can sing and writes his own raps. It wasn't just me, we all felt like that.

I thought we just needed to get played. I thought we're going to do it better and better each time. We thought *Sons of*

the P was going to sell even more than *Sex Packets* because *Sex Packets* was an experimental album. This one's going to connect it, all the good, and woo-woo, and we got Pac over here. We got Raw Fusion over here and Gold Money over here, and we're going to come out with a sister group, the digital underground Black Label. So we can do underground stuff and more political stuff, and we're still going to do this and this . . . we had it all coming. And then, little by little, came N.W.A., the Geto Boys, Dr. Dre, Snoop, Ice Cube . . . plus the underground records, they were all changing the game. Then came Scarface's solo records—Brad Jordan, one of the Geto Boys—then came a couple of dudes out of New York, Tim Dog, he had those songs, "DJ Quick Beat Down," "Michel'le," "Dog's Gonna Getcha."

Everything that was coming out then was a little more violent and thuggy. If it was outlaw, it was the business. So, I thought, *as long as that whole P-Funk thing is different, that will still help us*. But then other producers caught what we were doing and grabbed it too. Dre grabbed the P-Funk catalog after that, and Jermaine Dupree out of Atlanta started mixing live tracks, piano, bass, with samples. So I didn't have the patent on that no more either. We were expanding digital underground faster than we could capitalize on our charm. Whatever they liked about the last record, we were too busy adding new people to the group to get back to that sound. So it just started to confuse people. People were like, "What is it?" By the time we figured out what our roles were, the slip had already happened. The sales started dipping, then it was just like, "Okay, fuck it. digital's gone. Gold Money didn't happen. Raw Fusion didn't happen. Dungeon Squad didn't happen. Tupac and Luniz, okay—let's go!"

That's what it was. Fuze went on tour with the Luniz, he became their DJ. I started making sure my best beats were on the tapes that I sent Tupac. My thought was, *Then they'll get a chance. More people are going to hear them than us.* If something real special, something weird and fun came out of my drum machine, I'd save it. But if something sounded like a smash hit, I would offer that to Tupac first, because Tupac was the rising star. I thought he will take it to his highest potential. It felt like how many more sex songs and Humpty songs can we make anyway? We had our moment.

I felt good about it. It reminded me of Bootsy Collins's role in P-Funk. He had his moment where he was the front man. It lasted about two or three albums, but George was really the one with the philosophies and the special wordplay and the one who would get in the trenches and work with the thuggiest of thugs. Bootsy still supplied key music to the organization after it went on, and that's how I felt. I was able to have my little playground. There's digital underground over here, but we are changing the world through Tupac. He came up through our group. So far, his biggest hit was by me. It's time for me to keep working with him. After "So Many Tears," it was on! I was like, "Am I dreaming this? That's the third car that just went by bumping Tupac. Boom!" Now I can do whatever I want. That's the cool thing. Either you're hitting and you got to run with that, or you're not. And if you're not, that's when you can do whatever you want in the studio. So now I could still be a goofy artist. I could create. I could make songs like "Jerky Circus."

This is about when I realized that I didn't have that much control over it. I realized, "Oh, it's not us, it's just that the planets

TOP LEFT: Greg in his kitchen, Topanga Canyon, CA, 2011. **BOTTOM RIGHT:** Greg and Alexis at Alexis's grandma's place, Pasadena, CA, 2008.

KEEP IT BEAUTIFUL"
RAMA INN
HERE'S YOU
ERE'S YOUR
FARING "HALL
WHO'S CLEAN"
FEAR OF A MI
GOTCHOO
RIME IN TH

were aligned at that moment. Don't get carried away. Don't think it's *you*." When I listen to the interviews I did, the first *Rolling Stone* interview especially, I listen to it now and it turns my stomach. It's so arrogant. It's so . . . what's the word for it? It's just so *conceited*. So blindly conceited. I was saying stuff like, "Yeah, and then after we take over the hip hop charts, we're going to take over the dance charts. And then we're going to introduce our R&B and we're going to take over the R&B charts too." We just wouldn't give up. Monica [Monica Lynch, first employee and president of Tommy Boy Records] tried to tell us. She said, "I hope it doesn't go to your head." Well. I guess it did. It was hard not to think that we were embarking on a much crazier journey than we really were. I didn't even really love the sounds that I used on the first album because it was made using the cheap equipment we had. But, it turns out, that cheap equipment is what gave us an edge; nobody was using that. They were using the big, nice keyboards. The ones I was ready to go run out and get as soon as I got some dough.

At that same time they were also trying to turn us into a Humpty group. Every album they'd say, "Not enough Humpty." We were like, "Well, Humpty's not our lead singer." They looked at us like Public Enemy and Humpty was Chuck D. We looked at it like we're Wu-Tang Clan and Humpty's ODB, he's just one of many. We're giving everybody a shot. Because look at "Same Song." "Same Song" wound up being Shock G, Humpty, Money B, and Tupac. All four of us. But Monica Lynch said, "I've seen it happen to so many artists. They start making demands and they get exactly what they want. They stop listening to suggestions and they don't let the record company help or get involved in any way. That's when they start to fall." We thought we were different. Although, around "No Nose Job," I did have a feeling that this could be it for us when "Same Song" sold half as much as "The Humpty Dance," even with the big movie and everything. I was like, "This could be the last hurrah." So instead of making another song about chicks and self-indulgence, I thought, *I'm going to say something that means something, as Humpty.* So, just in case this is the last hurrah, at least I had got my little two cents in. Use the platform for something, you know? I wanted to make a statement, so I worked Humpty's look with his nose into a statement about anti-plastic surgery. I started writing the rhymes to "No Nose Job."

At that time Ice Cube was the hot new rapper. *America's Most Wanted* produced by Public Enemy was the top album. A lot of what was out was making fun of people who were selling out or hiding their Blackness. Meanwhile, Tupac is getting his album *2pacalypse Now* together and it is going to be political. So I'm hearing things like, "Humpty is a bubblegum gimmick, we'll see if it lasts." A lot of writers were saying that. One article said, "Hmm, big nose, little dick perhaps?" I was cracking up on that one. Shit was crazy. *Kiss You Back,* I felt, was the best music-forward album we had. But at that time I started to see that Humpty was on the cover of everything. Tommy Boy would use *only* the Humpty nose to show a picture of digital underground. They didn't use a picture of us. It wasn't me, Humpty, Money B on the cover of an album. Tom wasn't bad to us at all, but the worst thing he ever did was use a picture of a dime-store Groucho nose on our page for the year-end *Billboard* magazine. It wasn't even a picture of Humpty's glasses. It was a regular white Groucho nose that you could buy anywhere. They didn't even take the time to make it brown.

Fuck you for that shit, Tom. I love Tom Silverman now, I have a lot of respect for him, as much as I have for Rick Rubin, Russell Simmons, all of the people who recognized this art form before it was an art form. But at the time I was like, "Fuck that!" I guess he thought it was cool that people could look at the nose and immediately think digital underground. Oh yeah? But it ain't cool. Imagine if they did that for other groups. Imagine if they put a picture of a Kangol hat for LL. Not even one of LL's Kangols, just a hat that was kinda shaped like a Kangol. Or, instead of a picture of Flavor Flav, you put a clock. Not even the kind that he wears, just any old clock. An old lady's dresser clock and it says "Public Enemy" underneath. Yeah right. I felt like Shock G is getting sucked away by all of this. So, I thought, *I'm going to do a nice Shock G song*. That's what *Kiss You Back* was. It was to let Shock G shine.

They really wanted Humpty on that track too. They said, "If it's going to be the first single, then put Humpty on it." I tried to say Humpty doesn't belong on this track! But I ended up finding a place for it, and I was able to take a stand at the same time. It was a way to have Humpty on it, but also show that he really shouldn't be on it. I wanted to make it clear: he's too nasty for this one. "If you hold my nuts I'll . . . No, no Hump. Come on, man. Let's just keep it cool." That was actually me pumping Shock on that track. God. That was fun. That was probably the start of when I realized I could make Humpty work for me.

Shock has the pride of an accomplished chef as he sets down two ceramic plates with the burgers piled high with fixings. "Now tell me this is not the best veggie burger you ever had!" He has really embraced vegetarianism and is passionate about it. I've had to stop him from alienating people because he was pushing vegetarianism too hard. He feels the world would be a better place if we were all vegetarian, and he thinks it could save individual lives. At one point he even wanted to make a book that was like a big cupcake with a little pill in the middle that everyone had to "swallow" about vegetarianism. We finish up our burgers and Shock is cleaning up the dishes, looking out at the long dusty road through his kitchen windows.

I was not always vegetarian, you know. I was known for eating a Nation's cheeseburger in three bites total, no lie. I could do it with a Big Mac too and a Whopper. Three bites! Ask Sleuth or Schmoovy Schmoov, my ex-roommates. All I ate was burgers, chicken, and pizza, period. If someone had told me I was gonna be a vegetarian later in life, I would have laughed so hard I'd pass out.

"Word?" I say as I stand up and match his gaze down that long road. This makes me wonder about his childhood, the early, early days.

Overton Loyd for digital underground: "Doowutchyalike / Packet Man" single. Original artwork.

THE DAYS BEFORE DIGITAL UNDERGROUND

I don't know if you knew this already, but I was actually born in Brooklyn and we lived in New York for a while 'til we eventually moved to Tampa in 1969. We lived in an all-white neighborhood and I went to an all-white school. That lasted about a year of me coming home from school getting teased and picked on by all the kids every day. All the Black jokes. My mother demanded that we move. She said, "We cannot live in this neighborhood!" So we moved out of the house that the job at IBM had picked out for us. My dad worked for IBM. We found our own house in one of the first integrated neighborhoods. There were about ten of them around the United States, and Tampa had one of them. They offered families half the price of the house if you move in, to entice different races to live there. So we moved to Norwood, where it was a quarter Black, a quarter white, a quarter Hispanic, and a quarter other. Living there is really what started shaping me at a young age with this "red, white, Black, tan, yellow and brown, we can all get down" mentality.

That was also when I had my first band too. I was playing bass in the Norwood Specials. I wanted to play drums, but my family didn't take me seriously. My dad bought me toy-ass drums from a toy department, not from a music store. So I stayed playing bass. The bass I bought off somebody at my school or something. We used to play around the community when someone had a barbecue or whatever. We would let people hire us for their birthday parties. We never really played outside of the ten-block radius of our house.

When I was twelve years old, in 1978, two major things happened: My mom and pops divorced, and "Flash Light" came out. That was my first notice of Parliament. That haunting but seductive gospelish-sounding song with the aggressive pounding unison rhythm. It scared me and seduced me at the same time. "Flash Light" was the final piece of a puzzle that had been forming in my mental understanding of music, enlightenment, and freedom of expression for years right as I was beginning to dabble on the piano, discovering deeper rhythms and harmonies. From then on Parliament was officially my favorite music group, and they began consuming my illustrative subject matter as well. My interest in comic superheroes was replaced by P-Funk

"My first encounter with Greg was driving through Hollywood and randomly glimpsing him in his humptified haberdashery walking into a club. I thought, wait is that the same guy I'm starting to hear on the radio? . . . So seeing Shock G not only sampling George's Funk, but also his audacity, intrigued me enough to pull me out of my car and into the club. It never occurred to me that he was geeked out about meeting me as well. After that, we frequently kicked it with each other through the years."

—Overton Loyd

superheroes: Star Child (the Long Haired Sucka), Sir Nose D'Voidoffunk, Bootzilla, Uncle Jam, and Dr. Funkenstein. Their primary illustrator, Overton Loyd, became my absolute favorite artist in the world. He did lots of album covers, animated videos, and TV commercials for Parliament, Funkadelic, and Bootsy's Rubber Band back then.

This is about when we moved to New York again. Well, my mom basically left my dad and took the kids. That's what happened. We went to live in Far Rockaway, New York, with my grandmother and my aunt, Kim. Kim played the drums and for my birthday she gave me her drum set. So I got my first real drums. They were hand-me-downs, but they were a serious set. At that point I'm *really* playing the drums. Mom noticed my fascination with music and took me to meet Musique, her friends who sang "Push Push in the Bush," which was a famous disco song at the time.

I think music was always the more dominant love over visual art because anywhere that music was allowed, music took over as the agenda. For instance, in places where music wasn't allowed—classrooms, trains, buses—this is when visual art would emerge, to overcome my boredom usually. But when we were all at home around turntables or instruments, it was hard to sit still and draw; the urge to get involved with the music would overpower me.

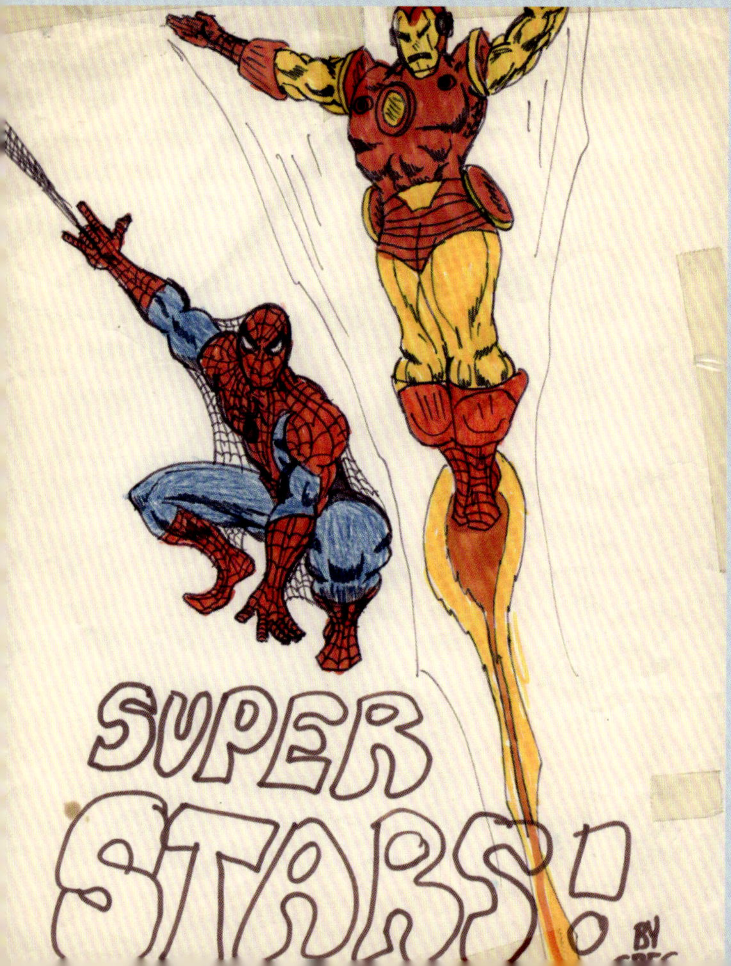

LEFT: Early sketches of superheroes circa 1976.

RIGHT AND OPPOSITE: Sketch and final front page of Greg's twenty-plus-page comic *Eightball* from 1979.

GREG RACKER
PRESENTS
EIGHT BALL!
ISSUE ONE
Racker

P-FUNK, THE MOTOR BOOTY AFFAIR, AND THE UNREACHABLE REACHES OF GRAFFITI ART

A while later, I was living in New York City, going to PS 180, and hip hop was just starting to bud. There wasn't a lot of rhyming yet, but there was a lot of DJing and breaking. The rapping was just starting to come on. I abandoned playing drums in bands and instead began DJing in rap crews. Instead of superheroes, me and all my friends from school became obsessed with graffiti and tagging. Suddenly, finding more creative ways to write my graffiti tag "Rackadelic" or my emcee name "Shock G" took over my focus. Shock G was my northern tag. It depended on who I was with—Shock G for my NY hip hop homies, Rackadelic for my Florida P-Funk homies. I was born Gregory Racker, not Greg Jacobs. I used to excitedly tell my classmates at school about the P-Funk concerts, and everyone would crowd around as I acted it all out and imitated the sounds. Someone said, "Damn Rack, all you talk about is Funkadelic! You're Rackadelic!" and that was it. I began using that as my pen name.

The Overton Loyd P-Funk stuff, as well as the NYC graffiti artists, helped me abandon the tendency to automatically and unconsciously give Caucasian features to characters as I drew them. From all the *Mad* magazine, Warner Bros. cartoons, and Superman stuff, as kids we didn't even realize that we often started with a basic Euro character design before we even thought about it. But when P-Funk and hip hop came along, we suddenly were freed to not think in those terms anymore and stopped making our characters imitate the white mainstream so much.

It wasn't so much a sudden epiphany, more like a gradual hindsight discovery. It was like, "Hey, we've been surviving for years, enjoying this P-Funk, celebrating this hip hop and not one skinny blond queen has been prematurely crowned yet, not one privileged and advantaged Euro-hero has existed the whole time, or not one person has been deemed 'too Black' for the sound or the look (like what was going on with commercial radio and television at the time). Wow, that's different. Oh well, let's keep on rockin'." Big lips, big hips, curvy bodies, cool leans, and phat sneakers all became the new flav. It wasn't something that we consciously set out to do either, we weren't deliberately avoiding any type of people or ideology. We were just so busy dancing, creating, and appreciating that we forgot to follow the usual standards and stereotypes.

Hip hop made b-girls more sexy, and it made them the preferred type of woman. While the American mass media was force-feeding us Farrah Fawcett and *Charlie's Angels* all day, hip hop catered to b-girls, street girls, breakdancers, and girls who recognized and preferred b-boys themselves. Meanwhile P-Funk was releasing albums with titles like *The Motor Booty Affair* with pics of thick curvy sistas all throughout the packaging. It didn't diss Euro-styled women, it was just oblivious to them. Even the famous Ohio Players girl-laden album covers still favored the Euro-styled sista, light-skinned, thin, etc.

Street scene from Greg Racker comic, 1979.

Not P-Funk. George and his army spoke to us like nobody else did, made us feel good about the simple pleasures in life. One day, about six months after "Flash Light" hit, "One Nation Under a Groove" came on the radio, and my cousin Cush, who was also a singer in our band and a backup DJ in the Master Blasters, pulled me aside and said, "You know those are your boys, that's Parliament," and pointed out to me that they, Bootsy's Rubber Band, and Funkadelic were all the same group. That was it, I was blown away. All three had been separately becoming my favorites anyways, and then to learn it was all the same act? I've been a representer ever since and still consider myself a Funkadelic first, everything else second.

Around that same time, about the late seventies, I began having favorite graff artists too. Lee was one of them because he bombed the Brooklyn Bridge in an area that everyone thought was unreachable. Way beyond the roadway level, hanging out in space over the East River, was a huge block-letter LEE that every boat and car that passed couldn't help but see. It was awesome. It was a banner to all that hip hop was alive and flourishing. Plus it was in such a difficult area that it lasted for years before they finally cleaned it off. We used to wonder, "How the fuck did he get out there?" We imagined him hanging from hi-tech *Mission Impossible* cables like Tom Cruise. He was ahead of his time, this was in 1978. Another hero of mine was Sonic,

from Far Rockaway, Queens. He used to make his "O" smiling, smoking a spliff, and with a gangsta brim on it. It was so fly to me that I had to bite it sometimes when I did the "O" in Shock G. It didn't matter though because by the time I started writing, Sonic had already stopped, so it was more like paying homage. He used to do seven-foot-high solid black-and-white pieces that covered the entire train car. So big that his was the only piece legible when the express train came blasting through the station without stopping. To this day, when I write "Shock G," I still make my "O" smile, though I've upgraded the thin white spliff to a phat chocolate Swisha.

I went to seventh and eighth grade in New York. Then my dad got custody again, so my brother Kent and I moved back to Tampa with him. But by now, hip hop was in me. I had already sold my drums and got turntables. When I lived in New York, my dad was trying to stay on our good side, so he would buy Kent and me stuff. I was like, "Well, I need two turntables and a mixer now," and he bought me fresh turntables and a mixer. I was a DJ for Beach 47 Street Crew in New York, older dudes. They were sixteen and seventeen and I was thirteen, but I was the one with the equipment so they let me be in the crew. So I'm in the crew, but I don't really get to touch the mic yet. I'm going by MC Starchild. My older cousins were like, "That's corny! You should be Shah G. Because you're Greg." Everyone was Shah-something at that time. But I heard Shock when they said it. So I became Shock G. That was it. From then on.

So, back in Tampa, that's when I ended up going to Greco Middle School. This is my second time moving to Tampa. "Rapper's Delight" wasn't out yet. I was really into Funkadelic, so I was with another group, called Parliament II, named after Parliament Funkadelic, and I played drums in that group. We won the talent show. And I got a trophy for being most talented in 1979 at Greco Middle School. Man, that was fun.

Greg interrupts himself:

There's a great story of Parliament II playing that talent show, but you have got to hear Cush tell his version of this story. Cush is hilarious! He tells it better. He shoulda been a stand-up comedian.

We decide to make a point of going to see Cush. I've got to hear that story.

MASTER BLASTERS

I dropped out of high school in the eleventh grade, and by then I had the Master Blasters, a DJ crew of five members: MC K Bar, MC Ronnie Ron, DJ Cush, DJ Flame, and DJ Shock G. All of us were transplants from NYC whose families had moved to Florida recently after we had gotten into hip hop. We were known for DJing around the Central Florida area throughout my high school days, 1979 through 1981. Every time an emcee moved to Tampa from New York, they would find us. Because we'd be DJing at the parties and all the New York cats would come up to the DJ booth and be like, "Y'all from New York?" That's where I met Omar and DJ Flame. Cush, I already knew, even when I moved to New York. He would visit us. My family had taken Cush in like he was a third brother, or a cousin, like another son. His family was messed up and all alcoholics. They used to fight and have shootouts all the time, so he couldn't go to Disney World. He grew up with my dad kinda being his dad.

I moved out from New York to Tampa. We had just settled in and everything and I was outside on my bike. I see Greg and Kent roll by on their bicycles. Kent stops and talks with me and everything, I'm asking where he's from. Well, Greg rolled by on his bicycle and didn't say anything. He rolled by a couple of times and said nothing. It turned out the reason why was not that he was unfriendly. It was because of the fact that his mother was sending him to the store for the same item like three or four times and he was kinda angry about that. But once that was all over, he did stop and talk. We were pretty young then, but we were about six houses down and we became like a kind of a large family. Down the street this old group called 5th Dimension, an old R&B group, used to practice. Guitars and drums and everything. So when you're like ten or eleven years old, that is exciting to see. That is really what got Greg into music from a young age. He knew from a little kid what he wanted to do in life. For the rest of us, it was trial and error on many things, but he always knew it was music. —Cush

Back then Kent, my blood brother, was breakin'. Kent's crew was the Bay City Breakers. They were serious breakers. Cardboard in the trunk. Box in the back seat, so fresh, always extra batteries in the glove compartment so they were always ready for a battle. Anywhere. "Pull the car over, get the cardboard out!" If we saw anyone else breaking while I was riding with him, we'd have to go and get out and show them up. Put our music on *LOUD*.

LEFT: Greg at his middle school, holding a Tommy Boy bag. He felt it was ridiculous, but he humored me. Tampa, FL, 2012.
ABOVE: Shock G's smoking signature/tag.

But in Tampa at the time there weren't a lot of other people doing any of that. Rappers weren't really around. We were the only crew that I knew of. There were little spots where you would hear someone rhyme or someone was visiting from New York, but we were the only ones lighting it up in Tampa.

But Tampa wasn't ready for us. We would put certain classic break beats on and niggas would run from the floor like rats when you turn the light on, because they just didn't understand. And we were like, "Man these bean-pickers just don't know." But we would still do it. And then one day "Rapper's Delight" came out on the radio. First rap song on a radio station. I was going to Chamberlain High School at the time and everybody in the school ran up to us like, "You made a record! We heard it on the radio!" And we were like, "Aw man, that's not us. This is what we have been trying to tell you! That's the new thing! Everybody does it." Everybody in Florida thought we were the only rappers in the world. They thought it was our own style. So when "Rapper's Delight" came out, they were like, "Hey, that's Greg 'n' 'em! That's the Master Blasters! Why you keep saying Sugar Hill Gang?" Then we heard it on the radio. They played a whole ten-minute version. It was dope.

I was also a radio DJ briefly for WTMP when I was fifteen years old and was billed as the youngest on-air DJ in the state of Florida. My show was only twice a week, three hours each, on Friday and Saturday afternoon. Or maybe evenings, I forget the time slot, but it was prime, not four a.m. or nothing. I went by Gregory Racker. ("It's Gregory Racker on your dial!") I pursued that job as half part of my "appear busy until I figure out what to do with my life" campaign and half part of a rebellious war with my dad in which he was forcing me to find a job. So with the radio station I felt like I won because technically it was "a job," but it drove my dad nuts because it was something I loved and something I did for recreation anyway. He wanted something in which I struggled and sweated more, to "teach me some discipline." He always tried to steer my brother and me into administrative-type stuff, not music and arts. Pops usually preached against any freestyle arts like mural painting, comic strips, cartooning, music. Once my dad told me I should study architecture because of my art talent. That's as far as it went. My mom, on the other hand, Shirley Ann Jacobs Kraft, totally supported anything I showed an interest in. She believed it was much more important that I loved whatever I did rather than chase any particular career because it paid a lot.

WTMP hired me based on a normal interview, plus my popularity as the main dude in the Master Blasters DJ crew. We were already known for crankin' it around the Tampa Bay area. Our cassette tapes were so popular at Chamberlain High, King High, and Hillsborough High schools. That's why the day "Rapper's Delight" came out, everyone thought it was us. The station gig only lasted about seven months. I got fired for playing "Not Just Knee Deep" by Funkadelic over a time slot in which I was supposed to have played three mandatory playlist songs, give commercials in between, give a brief weather and traffic update, and announce the station identification at the top of the hour. Instead, from about ten to five minutes after the hour, I blasted the fifteen-minute full album version of "Knee Deep." *Mmmm,* that was so worth getting fired over. Radio stations never play the fifteen-minute anything, but I rocked the entire "Knee Deep" with the guitar solo and everything. A music victory.

I left Tampa *again* at the age of sixteen. But this time I was just hustling. I ran away from home in a way. This is how I did it: I knew if I just ran away from home, my dad would come chasing after me and I couldn't really get away. So I got a job with a traveling sales company where I sold vacuums door-to-door and cleaning products and shit—and this was an official job. I worked in Tampa first, and when the job moved on to the next city, he let me leave. The next city was Miami. This is what I would do: If people were home, I'd sell them a vacuum cleaner. If they weren't home, I'd try the door. If the door was open, I'd get in the house and I'd go straight to the bedroom and I'd only take jewelry, guns, and money. I'd put it in my vacuum cleaner bag and bring it to the main office when they came to pick us up in the van. After about three weeks of that, I had about ten or fifteen thousand dollars' worth of stuff, so I quit and went downtown and found a little pool hall that was kinda sketchy. I sold all the guns and jewelry. After that, I got me a little hotel room and got myself some new clothes.

I walked down to the main avenue in Miami and just stood there like, "*Whoa. I'm free.*" You don't know what that feeling was like. I was seventeen years old. No parents. No adults. No job yet. Not sure yet what I was gonna do. But I had on brand-new sneakers, three hundred in my pocket, and a hotel room for two weeks. That was the beginning of my whole journey backpacking through the United States, in and out of small crimes and hustles, stealing cars, pimping hoes, being a gigolo, playing three-card monte, being a mural artist, and producing people for hire. I already had the studio game down, you know. I was doing all this other stuff to keep me alive until I was twenty-one.

That whole first year, whatever city I was in, I would call home and go, "Yeah, we're in, uh . . . in Ohio now." But I wouldn't really be in Ohio, 'cause I wasn't with that sales job anymore. And anytime they'd go, "Well, uh . . . where's . . . uh, let me talk to your boss," I'd go, "Oh man, I gotta go now, bye." *Click*. I'd always get off the phone if they started questioning me about if I still officially worked with this place. For about two years my family could sense that I was up to something, but they couldn't prove that I wasn't with that company anymore. I'd send them gifts at Christmas, and I'd even come to town and visit from time to time. They would ask, "What's going on with the company?" and I would make stuff up like, "Oh yeah, we're gonna be in Vegas next." I would just make shit up. Really, I was living somewhere for a while until I got into too much trouble, then I would not go to court, bail out, and live somewhere else. I would move and start over with a new name. "Now I live in Pittsburgh, or now I live in Chicago."

In Florida they had a loophole that if you had a birth certificate and a Social Security card, they would give you the ID card that same day. They would take a picture of you and you would walk away with it right then. Mistake. They should mail it to you. Because I was good with doctoring stuff up. I'd go to Kinko's, and make a Social Security card with a different name. I'd change up my birth certificate, and I actually had five or six fresh, unused driver's licenses at any given time, with all different names all from Florida. So if I ever got caught with anything, it would show up as my first offense. They'd give me an OR: You can be released on Own Recognizance because it's your first offense. When you have only one offense ever, they release you. They never keep you in jail; they just give you a court date. I would skip town before that date, cut up that license, and never use that name again. I actually left Tampa with a bunch of them. That's how I stayed out of jail. I'd get arrested sometimes, but once I got out, I would move on to the next city and start over fresh with a different name.

I loved it. I was having fun! It was a party. It was a party everywhere I went.

DUMO, GIGOLO, SAN DIEGO, AND TWO HOOKERS IN A STOLEN CAMARO

I wound up being an assistant to a professional burglar named Dumo. Dumo had witnessed me trying to fence stolen guns in a pool hall, said he knew someone who'd buy them and that he needed a new partner himself. He invited me to work with him, just like that, over a pool game. He was a short but muscular cat who looked like Mike Tyson with a big round afro. My funniest memory of Dumo is how he'd simply snatch the burglar alarms off the wall mid-ring to stop the noise. Those big, square old-school alarm boxes that used to be bolted onto the outside wall of places; he'd just stand on an upside-down garbage can and wrestle them off the wall. Such a funny sight that was.

Once we were drilling a hole through the brick wall of a downtown electronics store from the alley. We'd noticed that the alarm system only covered the storefront doors and glass windows but not the actual building walls. We started on Thursday after hours, worked all night, then came back Friday and Saturday night to continue. We hid the area with a big dumpster in between nights. We picked Saturday night as the completion night as this place was closed on Sunday. We figured we'd have until Monday morning before the burglary was discovered—more time to get further outta town and fence the items. Around 3 A.M. on Sunday morning we started breaking through the final layer of concrete and could see inside the store. The hole was almost big enough to crawl through. Just as we were clearing away the final pieces, we heard a huge explosion on the street around the corner, so big that it shook the wall we were working on.

We ran around front and to our disappointing surprise, a van full of desperate Cubans had drove right through the front glass. They all jumped out and started filling the van with whatever they could, all while the alarm was echoing loudly through the humid downtown Miami night. Dumo and I watched in amazement and disbelief as they filled up the van and smashed off, all in a few seconds, leaving us standing there on the sidewalk in shock with our drilling equipment still in hand. We couldn't believe it. Two weeks' worth of planning and three nights' worth of drilling down the drain in a matter of seconds.

I used to do some of this shit with other friends too. The way we would do it, we would be at Macy's during the day. Back then, like, let's say this is the female shoe department. Here's all the stuff that you could choose from. They also have these cabinets with all the overstock in them. We would climb in the cabinets and hide until the store was closed, then we would come out and spray our spray to see the trip lights, step over those. They didn't have them like they do now all over the place. It would be like one here, then about another thirty feet another one. Thinking burglars wouldn't see them. We'd see them, step over them, fill our bag up. We'd put cameras, anything expensive, and the last thing we'd do is get a chair, throw it through the door, and run and jump in our truck and be out. That's crazy, huh? That's how we used to rob Macy's. We'd rent a pickup truck. We always needed speakers. We'd blow the speakers all the time and need new ones. I built some pretty big speakers once. Huge.

I tell Shock this is funny because I spoke to Cush on the phone, and Cush told me that he actually built the speakers. Shock laughs.

Cush said he built 'em? Well, I designed them, and I know I could draw you the design right now . . . Look, I'm gonna draw it.

Greg finds a napkin and takes the next ten minutes or so describing the speakers to me, while he sketches them out in great detail.

Ask Cush to draw you that, he couldn't do it! 'Cause he didn't do it! Maybe he built some of it, I don't know, but I designed 'em.

CROSS-COUNTRY

A year or so into this period of travel and discovery, I got stuck without any money while hitchhiking between New Orleans and San Diego. My last good distance ride was in Texas somewhere with a trucker who suddenly said, "This is my turn" at a desolate side road off the highway. Before he made the turn, he dropped me off in the middle of nowhere. After spending a long, lonely, and desperate six hours or so on the side of the freeway, with no cars stopping, finally a bite. A nice Benz stops with an older couple in it. Actually, only the husband was old, the wife was thirty-something and reminded me of Cher. After a few minutes of quiet travel, the gray-haired man in the driver seat said, "Do you think my wife's pretty?" I said, "Yeah, sure, she's beautiful. Congratulations." I went right back into my private mental meeting with myself to finish plotting out my journey. Then he said, "Do you think you would like to have sex with her?" I paused, not sure what was going on. "You see," he continued, "I'm a lot older than she is, and she has much more of an appetite than a man my age can satisfy. We can pay you." I said, "Um, okay, how much?" He said, "Would seventy dollars be okay?" I calmly said, "Yeah, that sounds pretty good," but in my mind I was like *Yes! I got a bus ticket to San Diego now!*

We pull over, she gets out and climbs in the back seat with me, and we pull back onto the freeway. Facing forward she lifted up her dress, pulled her panties down, and sat in my lap. As we fucked for a few minutes, my eyes drifted off, and I notice the old man staring at us in the rearview mirror with a tranced-out look in his eyes, like he was getting off watching his wife fuck a stranger. I don't remember much more; it was too long ago, almost thirty years. All I remember is the jacked-up way that it ended. They were anxious to get rid of me the second she climbed off me. We pulled over, both of us got out, she got back in the front seat, I leaned in and took the envelope he handed me, and right as I was taking the cash outta the envelope, they sped off. Forty bucks. *Damn, oh well, at least I got some cash now,* I thought. It got me a bus ticket to Phoenix, from which I hitchhiked the rest of the way. This was my first gigolo experience, and my first lesson in getting paid upfront too.

SAN DIEGO

I had a great hot-car operation going on in San Diego with a good fence in Mexico later that same year. It was easy. I'd steal the cars in L.A., drive them down to the border, park them on the U.S. side, walk across into Mexico, cab it to the Chicago Club (a dance-bar in downtown Tijuana), and sell the keys to my contact, along with the directions to where the car was parked. I used to steal cars like it wasn't *shit*. Camaros, Corvettes, five hundred dollars. A brand-new Corvette, five hundred dollars. Just so I could get rid of it quickly. Give me five hundred dollars and it's yours. What? They give me the five hundred dollars, I give them the keys. I don't know what they would do with it, probably tear it up and sell the parts, maybe use the cars to take Mexicans who had snuck across the border on foot deeper into California, I don't know. But that wasn't my concern. I didn't have the prices high because I wanted to keep it where they could get the money right now. That was my main illegal hustle, stealing cars.

On my fifth car in two months, I made a bad mistake and offered to drive two hookers back to their hotel. The three of us met at a breakfast diner I had stopped at on Broadway in downtown San Diego, about two-thirds of the way to the border from L.A. Little did I know, they were being followed by undercover agents who were part of a street team designed to clean up San Diego's then-rampant hoe stroll. After making plans to come back and see them—"You're cute, you wanna come upstairs?" "I can't, I gotta be in Mexico before the sun comes up. I'll come back later today." "Okay, sugar, you cute little thang you"—right as I pulled away from their hotel, two unmarked vans came screeching in on both sides with doors flying open and cops jumping out with guns drawn all around me. "FREEZE!! TAKE YOUR HANDS OFF THE WHEEL NOW!!! GET OUT OF THE VEHICLE!!" yada yada. Turns out they suspected I was the girls' pimp, ran the plates (which came back stolen), and arrested me for grand theft auto and pimping and pandering. At my arraignment, the pimping and pandering was dropped and the GTA was reduced to joyriding—I'd convinced them I was just a kid who found a car with the keys in it and simply went cruising.

Here's the bad luck part: I was arrested on a Monday, waited all week to go to court (San Diego jails were dysfunctionally overcrowded back then), was finally arraigned on Thursday, and my OR ("Own Recognizance") was ordered that Friday. I was to be released the next business day but, since it was Friday, my release went on hold until Monday. Turns out, that Saturday, after the owner had been given back their car, they found my briefcase in the trunk and called it in to the sheriffs. The sheriffs discovered my professional car thief tools inside the case, and called in just in time to stop my release on Monday morning. This resulted in me being charged again with grand theft auto. This time it stuck. I got sentenced to six months at a mini-prison facility up in the hills outside of San Diego.

Having a thousand bucks in your pocket when you're eighteen years old feels like you're king of the world, especially when you earned it in such an exciting way. I guess I got too comfy, and made that fatal stop at that diner, instead of continuing straight to the border like I should have. The car's owner must have just called it in around the time I was enjoying breakfast and flirting with those two prostitutes. Damn stupid move. Once on lockdown in the mini-prison, art became a means of survival; I drew portraits for sale of inmates who would send the art to their loved ones at home. A full portrait went for two packs of cigarettes.

PITTSBURGH

Another time, while doing weeks in Pittsburgh County for three-card monte, hustling, I did large murals on inmates' cell walls, two total I believe, for five packs of cigarettes per mural. They usually wanted life-sized portraits of naked women. As long as it was in pencil or washable ink, the guards tolerated it. It began with one I did in my own cell. I drew a pimp and hoe scene with a pimp, a Cadillac at the curb, and two hookers flashing sexy skin on the sidewalk with a neon-sign strip bar in the background. When people saw it, they wanted their own, so I charged smokes. Pittsburgh County (Allegheny County Jail) was a large brick-walled hardcore old-fashioned penitentiary-styled jail facility. It was like a redbrick and brownstone version of Alcatraz. There were only two times a day—"morning rec" and "afternoon rec"—when the cells were open to cross-mingle. During recreation time the cell doors and tier hallway doors were left open. You could stay in your cell if you wished, or visit other cells, but most took advantage of that time to use the yard or the library or the TV room. It was in these rec times that I would get the murals done.

These were rough times until I got back on my feet, including a few freezing nights of sleeping on passenger trains in the train yard. My daily survival routine was: Panhandle all day until I had enough for a fresh outfit. Hit the dance clubs at night to try and find a chick to go home with. If no luck, crash out in the back seats of the porno theaters till 3:30 or 4 A.M., when the last movie let out. Then babysit a cup of coffee at either Denny's or the bus station until sunrise, when the train lines opened for business again. Then get four or five hours of sleep riding back and forth to the end of the line until around noon or so, and then hit the streets and start all over again the next day. This was the bottom-of-the-barrel routine, when there were no art supplies, no car-theft tools, when there was absolutely nothing to work with. If I was able to purchase a decent upscale-looking outfit, and accessorize it with a few decent costume jewelry pieces, I could work the more professionally patronized happy hour bars in addition to the late-night dance clubs when looking for a new chick to adopt me.

It was at one of these happy hour lounges where I met Barbara, the lady who became my sugar mama/gigolo "client" for a few months. She used to pay me to see her twice a week, in addition to paying my rent, for a brief few months when I lived in Pittsburgh along this three-year adventure stretch. Of course, once I got on my feet again, I disappeared on her, in a grand finale, and took her for as much money as I could.

MIAMI

I did a week in Miami County under Roberto Negron once for paper hanging (check fraud) while awaiting trial but then skipped town on an OR and never went back to court. To this day. My paper-hanging hustle was even easier than my carjack hustle. Basically I would take three hundred bucks and buy ten thirty-dollar money orders made payable to one of my aliases. I would carefully draw an additional zero onto the money order where it said "30 dollars & 00 cents" to make it "300 dollars" instead. I was really good at making it look identical to the officially printed numerals. I would quickly go from check-cashing spot to check-cashing spot and cash all ten money orders within an hour, before the fraud circulated the banks.

Another really easy paper game in the eighties was this: You go to any bumble-fuck city around the United States, somewhere you have no intention of ever living in real life, and you open a bank account in a fictitious name with, say, three hundred bucks. Then for the next two months you make regular withdrawals and deposits, being sure to talk it up socially with the tellers until they get to know you by sight. Also being sure to hit up all nine or ten branches over this period, making two or three transactions per week at every branch. All I'm doing is putting the same money in and out of the account, to appear normal and active.

On the big day I get a map and plan the quickest most-connected route from branch to branch and do a connected run of all the banks in that city. I repeatedly withdrew my same three hundred bucks at every branch to make a quick three thousand, after which I would split town and start over again in another city far across the United States somewhere. Back then, every teller wasn't equipped with a computer as they are today. Instead, they took breaks every hour to file all their latest transactions into the main bank computer, every hour at the quickest. So there was an hour lag in confirmation of what anyone's last transaction was, and you could actually withdraw the same money over and over until the bank caught up.

The crucial factor was to know when that hour began, so that you didn't go past the hour mark and get caught in the next accounting hour. That's how I got busted in Miami. I pushed my luck and got greedy and tried to hit those last few branches for those extra three-huns when I knew I was close to the hour time limit. They popped me at the last branch with the $2,700 in cash on me from the last nine branches. UGHHHH! When I got busted, all I kept saying over and over in my head was *Why couldn't you just quit with the twenty-seven-hun?!!*

L.A. TO SAN FRANCISCO

I got spooked one day, when my mom lived in California. I was in a bank and I did the scam and my mom walked in. "Gregory? What are you doing here?" "Hey, Ma. Uh . . . I, I gotta go." And I just left. I ran. I couldn't look my mom in the eyes. Word got out to the family. "He's not in fucking Kentucky. He's in L.A.!" I had to pick up and move again to another city. I was this young kid thinking I could outsmart the adults. I was still doing crimes and pimpin' . . . and running. The most girls I ever had at a time was two. I had my bottom chick, Ebony, and then another girl, which I pulled together for about an eight-month stretch. I had two hoes. So I was like, *Yeah—*

I'm pimpin'. But at that time I was traveling with Booby and Salt Pretty and Texas Red. Niggas who had like seventeen hoes each or something like that. So I had pimp stories for days and that's why I was able to talk about it so easily. And that's why I made "Good Thing We're Rappin'."

To me, Too $hort wasn't no pimp. AMG wasn't a pimp. They were just talking about fucking. I was like, real pimps don't fuck 'em. You don't hit her with a pimp stick until she comes with that extra sting and then you bless her with that pimp D. It's like the reward for bringing in a lot of money, and then you keep her starving for another two weeks. That's really what the pimp game is. But these dudes were talking about how much they just get pussy. That wasn't pimp shit. Then one day it just frustrated me when I was deep into digital underground and I was like, I'm gonna make a pimp song and show these niggas what pimping really is. So actually all that shit is a true story in "Good Thing We're Rappin'." It didn't all happen in one story like that. But they are all pieces of true things that *did* happen. Like we did beat a dude down with a pool stick once. There were all those scenarios that all happened, but it happened spread out over a three-year period. It wasn't one day like I said in the song.

The whole time all of this is going on, I was doing music. I was always trying to get my demo off the ground. Even when I was a greasy-ass, long-painted fingernail, snakeskin knee-high Bally boot, Ralph and Eddie silk tweed Armani jacket—dressing creep! I still always had my four-track recorder and a keyboard and a drum machine or two at my little residency hotel. And all the pimps used to tease me like, "Yo, shit. Shocky Shock! You do that rap thing, huh? Ya, man, that's cute. Come on, nah, let's go get this bitch, man." You know, like they just thought it was cute. But I was really trying to get above that pimp shit. I was mostly remixing things that were already done at that time. I did "Atomic Dog." I had some originals too. Mostly I would mix stuff and then send it home to Cush or Kenny-K or someone like, "Yo, guess what I just made!" It wasn't really as much to get a record deal as it was to just make something dope. Send it out to Shah T and Stretch out in New York. Just to say I'm up on it. I'd write to them, like, "Yo, you heard that new one, by Grandmaster Flash called 'The Message'?" That was out while I was traveling around.

Then one day, I had an epiphany. I was in Frisco at the time, on Geary in the Pickwick Hotel, and I had a hoe out. I guess it was like '84, it was when I turned twenty-one. Now,

Shock at an Oakland, CA, recording studio, writing lyrics in the closet, 2011.

I knew I couldn't get tried as a young adult anymore. I would be tried as an adult. Some states it was eighteen and others it was twenty-one. But once I turned twenty-one, I knew that my fingerprints were going in the FBI central computer. And now all that other shit is gonna catch up with me if I keep crime-ing. I looked around and realized all my friends were hustlers. The only girls I knew were hoes. All these middle-aged cats had no teeth and were going in and out of jail. Everybody was hooked on crack and shit. And I was like, *I don't see any fruitful car thieves or anyone with benefits out here*. They weren't going to sit back with their grandkids like, "Yeah, I was a car thief and a pimp my whole life." There wasn't none. They all got burned out, shot, put in prison.

I was like, *This life ain't for me. What yous doin'? You have a dad, you don't have to be out here. You should go to school for music. This ain't working*. What I realized was no matter how much I hustled and no matter how much money I made, one day, two months later, I'm starting all over again. Broke. In a new city. I'm burning up the United States quickly. What you gonna do after that? You know? I had a whole 'nother run of checks I was about to do. I only had about two, three hundred dollars on me, and I was about to do another three thousand dollars' worth of checks. But I know every time I do it there's a risk involved. I remember cutting all the checks up and looking out the window of the hotel and then just throwing them out. I watched them rain down all over Frisco. I was like, *I'm done with this shit*. I pawned my clothes, left whatever girl I was with at that time, and got enough to get a bus ticket home.

TAMPA

I moved back to Tampa for the third time. That's when I said, "Dad, I want to move back in and go back to school and study music." I could see you don't get old with no pension doing all this other shit I was up to. My dad met me at a restaurant, and I thought he was gonna be like, "Yeh, yeah alright, come on home." But he just heard me out and said, *"Hmmm."* Then he said, "That's interesting and you sound pretty serious, but I'm gonna have to say no." He was like, "I don't know if I want you around your little brother right now. He's doing good in school, and I don't know. Because how many times have you said that you're gonna clean up and stop and you keep going back to jail." He had already bailed me out for stealing cars or getting caught shoplifting. Some of those Macy's things would go awry and he'd have to bail me out. So he actually didn't believe me.

I knew I was SERIOUS. But he just said no. So I took the little bit of whatever I had and got a $150 a month fuckin' terrible one-room roach-infested place where you gotta use a key to go outside to use the bathroom and everybody there uses that same bathroom. Ray's Residency Motel or some shit. I signed up at Buffalo High, the adult high school in Florida. I started fuckin' studying to get my GED. Now, I'm twenty-one and I'm studying at the high school. It's like the flunkies and failures. I'd be sitting there at the class and at lunchtime in the yard and people drive by—"Greg? Is that you? Come here, man, is that you?" I'd walk over to the fence. "What you doin' in there?" "Trying to get my GED, man." "Man, we thought you was gonna be the first one in college. We thought you was gonna be the *main* one. You should be in Hollywood by now."

I had to eat that fuckin' shame. "I know. I was doing stupid shit, you know." We used to drive by the school and tease those people. Look at all those dumbasses! Look at all those grown people left back and now they gotta get they GED. And now I was one of 'em. But even though the class was supposed to be a year, at about two months into it I decided, "Ima try to take the test." If you take the test and fail, you're not allowed to come back for another six months. So I was like, *Ooof. Oh well. Let's see.* I took it and passed it the first time. Quit, got my GED. Went back to my dad's house and knocked on the door again. I was like, "Dad. I got my GED on my own. I mean it. I'm serious. I've been working at Church's Chicken." It was the only job I could find in Tampa. I got a minimum-wage job. "You already know where I've been living," because word got around. "I got my GED. I'm serious." He sighed. "Come on in," he said, and opened the door and let me walk by. He kinda looked at me like . . . *ugh*. It was just like in the movies. It was tense for a few weeks. But a little while went by and now I'm just back at home again.

Then, suddenly, I'm in a couple of bands. I joined The Four Horsemen, an emcee crew with DJ Kenny-K, the MC Dazzlin Doc-P, myself, and MC Scoobie. I was also moonlighting as a jazz pianist here and there, and playing keys in Warren Brooks's R&B band. I was going to Hillsborough Community College in 1983 for a two-year Associate of Arts degree, which required a person to take a little art history, a little music theory, and one direct craft study such as painting, dancing, or a musical instrument. I took piano for the easy credit. I already played by ear and had two regular nighttime piano bar gigs in the area—one at Rough Riders (a bar in the Spaghetti Warehouse complex, right near campus) and one nearby at Carmines on Broadway and 21st.

I studied music theory under Jim Burge. When school let out, I would stay in the piano rooms until it closed up. Be the same thing every time. Dude would lock the whole school up and come get me last. He would open the door and I would be in there. *Dunannana da . . . dunanana du*, trying to get it right. "You ready to go, youngblood?" I'd go, "Oh shit!" I didn't even notice he was in the room. "Damn, it's 11 o'clock already?" He used to say, "You sound better and better every time, man. You stick with it, you gonna wind up playing your thing, man. You gonna do something, boy. Well, it's 11 o'clock, we gotta go." I'd be like, "Oh man, I almost got it. Can't you lock up something else first? Go lock up the phys ed room." He would lock the whole school up before the piano room just so I could get that last minute. "I already did the gym. I already know you want every second you can get. Look, I'm gon' lock up the gate, last thing when we walk out, and get in my car."

That's how we used to learn shit. We'd lock ourselves in the closet with an

(ASSHOLE-PHONEBOOKS)

instrument over the course of a summer. By the time Christmas came around, I'd be hot on turntables or hot on piano or whatever. You know, the hours go by you gotta git it. I was constantly trying to learn jazz and blues because all the older musicians used to say, "You learn blues, you can play anything. That's the root. That's what funk came from. That's what rock comes from. That's what hip hop and all that came from, the blues. You gotta 'learn them scales.' There's twelve keys so you gotta learn every scale. The blues scale up and down in C, in C sharp, in B, in B minor, in B sharp . . . all twelve of 'em. And then you gotta learn the jazz scale, all twelve of 'em, then the classical scale, all twelve of 'em. It takes years to get good on the keyboards."

So I was trying to learn it. I knew they meant it, because everybody who didn't know sounded kinda toy. But everybody that could play the blues when they played funk or hip hop, you could hear the richness in it. It was like the difference when I played that solo in "Same Song," or when someone else is playing around with the keyboard on a Too $hort record. It's all screechy. They're not doing the bluesy bit. Throwing the cords, highlighting the notes and shit. That depth, I knew something was missing from my playing. So I was back to being a dork again and just making music. Now I'm studying piano and jazz theory. I was only listening to jazz and blues, and I have this thirst for music history. I wanted to know, who was the first one to use this chord? I gotta know, was it Ray Charles?

Me and my brother both, we were just discovering blues and jazz and how it had fueled hip hop and rock and funk. We could hear it and so we had traced it record to record. Wow, that's what made Grandmaster Flash and them do that, and that's what made James Brown do what he did, and that's what made Chuck Berry do this, and that's what made BB King and Ray Charles do that. This record is what made them do it. We found every record that started the trend that made the vine grow, and we were just digging in the crates. We went through a period like that for about three years where we were just hungry for it—learning all the jazz chords, all the blues chords, seeing how music arrived here from slavery. When Africans first met the Europeans and touched the European instruments, the saxophone, the piano with the African rhythms and sounds, that's what started jazz and blues. When the slaves were allowed to start recording. We traced it all the way back, and that's what we were into. I wouldn't even date a girl at that time if she didn't have a piano.

Honestly, I attended college for two reasons: to get my dad off my back and to be able to live at home until I figured something out. I had been living on my own, raggedly, since age seventeen and I was now twenty-two. I wanted to appear busy until I figured something out. But I had absolutely no faith that college would deliver me into a great job or grand career, I just couldn't see it. At least not for what I had in mind—freedom, creativity, unlimited travel, all that. It was during that time at Highline Community College that I met Davita. She was drop-dead gorgeous! Golden-brown skin. Rich green eyes. She wanted to be an actress, and I wound up being her piano player for her auditions at Disney World in Orlando. She was in some of the first Showtime and Cinemax movies. But they always cast her as the hoe. They would always cast the white girl as the lead, so she used to get pissed about that. But she was doing her thing and while I was her piano player, and while we rehearsed, that's when we started falling in love.

Next thing you know, me and her started a business together called the Demo Engineers. We would record you, make your demo, give you a list of record companies, photograph you, give you an 8 × 10, do your bio, give you two songs, and give you what we called packets. So we give you the packet with all that stuff and the list of record companies, good luck. That was three hundred dollars. And the business card said "Make your own rap record" because rap was so new that everybody wanted a part of the craze. We were hooking that shit up for people. However, nobody that I know of actually got a deal from it. We snuck away to L.A. eventually. We picked L.A. over New York because we were broke. We figured if we wound up sleeping in our car, at least it wouldn't be snowing. After a year of struggle in L.A., including many failed auditions on her part and many battle of the band losses on mine, we decided New York was a better idea: more hip hop, less racism.

My thinking back then was I gotta do something that's cool in life. Musical work or making an invention, owning my own business. If the Demo Engineers became this big thing, I would still be doing that to this day. Open an office in New York. Anything but a regular nine-to-five. I always knew I would do music in some aspect though, because it just came to me naturally. I could hear it. I could see it. I just felt like it was something I could figure out.

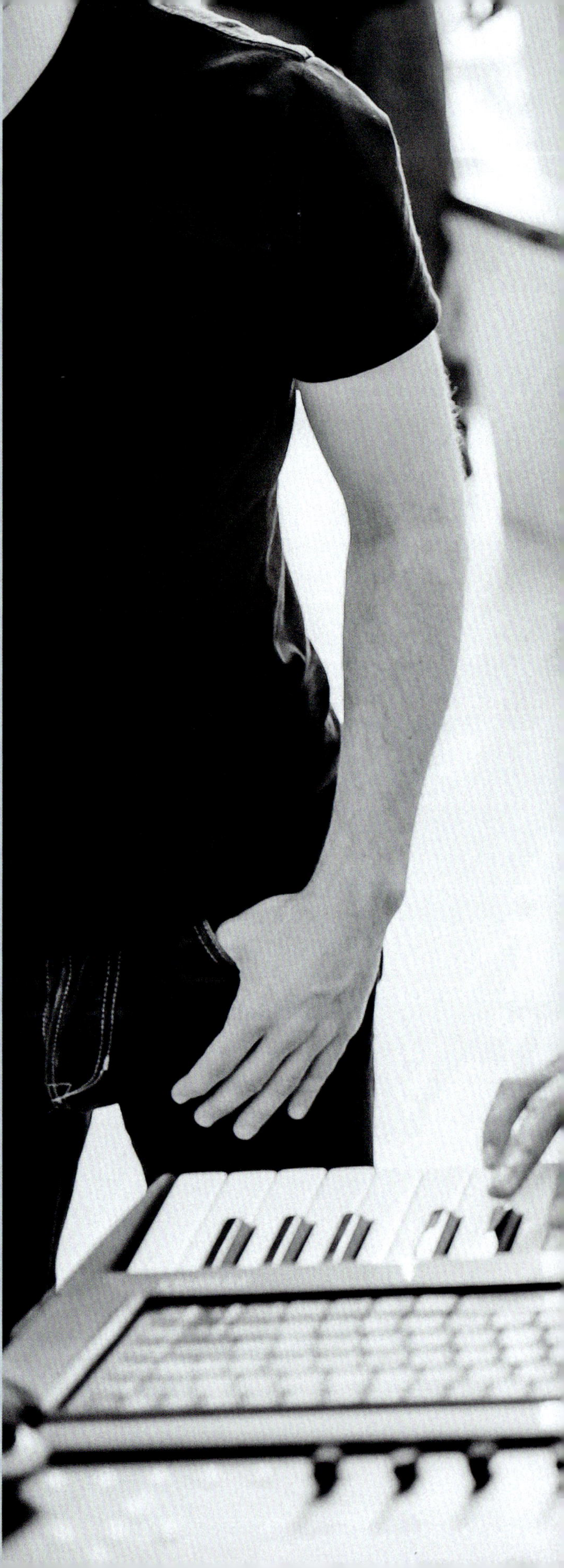

Shock G in the studio with Ski Beatz, Murs, McKenzie Eddy, and Greg Spero. Brooklyn, NY, 2011.

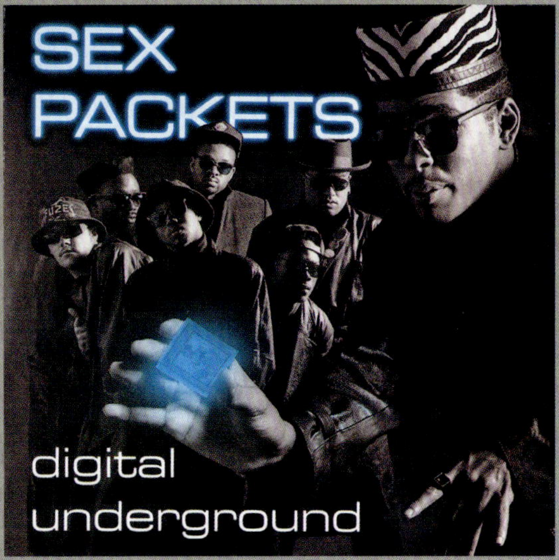

Sex Packets (1990)

Sons of the P (1991)

Future Rhythm (1996)

The Body-Hat Syndrome (1993)

Who Got the Gravy? (1998)

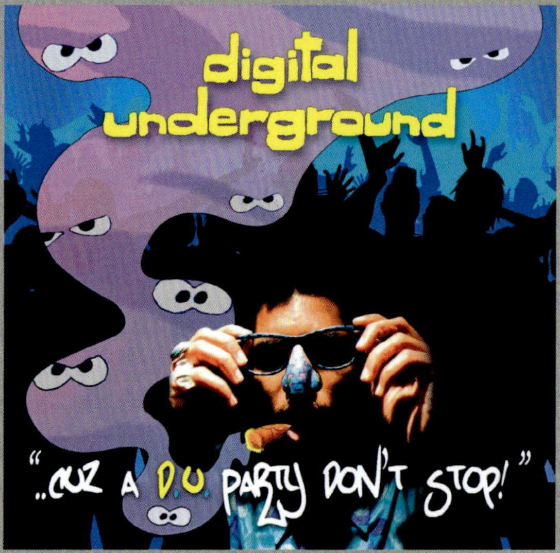

..Cuz a D.U. Party Don't Stop! (2008)

This Is an EP Release (1991)

The Greenlight EP (2010)

Fear of a Mixed Planet (2004)

Playwutchyalike: The Best of Digital Underground (2003)

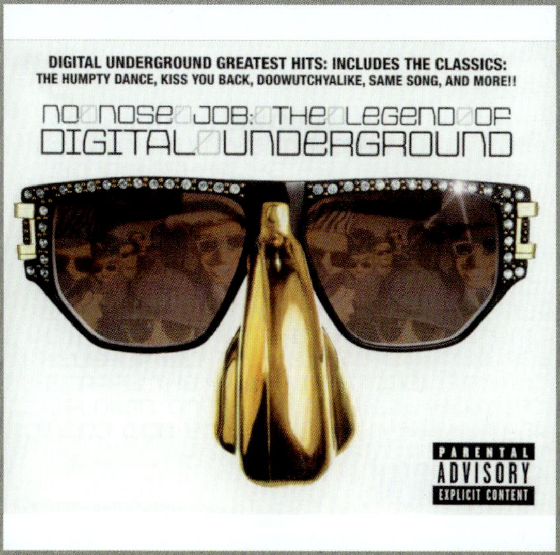

No Nose Job: The Legend of Digital Underground (2001)

Shockwaves: Best of the Shock Tracks (1989–2004)

CHAPTER DOOWUTCH

2:

YALIKE

August 12, 2011

It's a nice, cool morning. An owl, or maybe it's a dove, hoots in the distance. I'm outside on Greg's porch, drinking instant coffee and getting ready to begin the next recorded interview session. Shock had left a stack of digital underground photos from the early nineties out for me. I'm stuck on some pictures of Greg asleep on the tour bus, and young Tupac walking the streets of Japan, all smiles. Looking at these images makes everything real for me. It must have been wild to be part of all that!

I walk inside and plop the photos on the kitchen counter. When Greg comes upstairs, I ask him to tell me about the beginnings of digital underground. He grabs a coconut water and says, "Alright, listen, let me make us some breakfast first." After looking through some of the old pics together, he is ready to tell the story.

Shock G and Jaybeatz Jackson hold up a collage of images from tour, Oakland, CA, 2011.

The start of digital underground was by chance. I knew I had to get out of L.A. But my original plan was head to New York with my girlfriend. That's also when I abandoned my pop's last name, Racker, and began to use Jacobs, my mom's maiden name. I needed a change. Our plan was to take I-5 north up through the Bay Area, then catch 80 East to New York. But our food and gas money ran out in Oakland. I had to make a new plan and get a job in the Bay Area. So I sold keyboards and drum machines at Music Unlimited in San Leandro. Too $hort, Sheila E's band (which later became Tony Toni Toné), Tech & Sway (formally Flynamic Force, who later became "The Wake-Up Show" and MTV hosts) all used to be my regular customers and to this day know me as "Greg Jacobs, keyboards, can I help you?"

Jimi [Dright] was just one of my customers. He came in and bought thousands of dollars' worth of stuff. Really, what happened was his mother-in-law was sick of him not having a job. She asked him what he needed to get his music off the ground. They were just trying to get him to bring some money into the household. He had two kids and then there was their own daughter. So they all came into my store with the credit card and approved him for four, five grand. I sold him my dream system. I put it together perfectly. I said, "You need this sampler, this drum machine, these speakers, this four-track machine." My thing was, if I had five grand, this is how I would do it. He believed that I knew what I was doing because I was also showing him songs and shit. He asked me to show him how to use it. I said, "I'll make you a deal. I'll come over and record a demo and while I'm doing that, I'll show you all the steps and teach you." So, while I was teaching him how to do it, I recorded "Your Life's a Cartoon" and "Underwater Rimes."

I mixed it down and left with my tape going, "Oooh, I can't wait to show this to Kenny! Kenny gonna love this!" I was back to just doing it for my friends. I wasn't really thinking bigger than that anymore. But I had left the multitrack at Jimi's, and behind my back he mixed it down and sent it to his friend in L.A., who used to produce Barry White. Then Jimi called me one day, while I was at work, and said, "Yo, Greg. Uh, my friend Darryl wants to put you in the studio." Who? "Darryl Ross." I was like, "How he know me?" Jimi had sent him a tape. "'Underwater Rimes.' They like that shit, man! They like it. But you gotta put me in the mix too, whatever we do from now on, it's fifty-fifty." Meanwhile, I'm still at work at the music store hearing "Keyboards, line one." So, I say to Jimi, "Yeah, okay, I gotta go. Whatever, yeah, okay, sure." *Click*. I was like, *Make a deal*, pshh, *whatever*. For me, after ten years of trying, getting a record deal was just a fantasy. I wasn't looking for a record deal anymore. I was still excited to make music, but I never thought I'd record an album. So now Jimi thinks he has a hookup, big deal.

But it turned out that his friend Darryl actually did send for us, recorded us, and signed us to Tabu Records that same year, 1987. The deal didn't go anywhere, though, and they never put the record out. I had to go back to Music Unlimited and beg for my job back. Then, in 1988, Darryl introduced us to Atron Gregory, who was road-managing for N.W.A. and J.J. Fad at the time. Atron signed us to Macola Records, who *did* put out the single, even sold a few thousand copies, but we didn't make any real money. I had to go back and beg for my job again, a second time, and they hired me again for the third time. Finally, in 1989, Atron and I started our own label, TNT Records, and re-released "Underwater Rimes" but with different cover art that I drew this time. It charted in Cali and a few places around the world, even went to number one in Amsterdam.

Shock G's original release with digital underground (1988): A-side, "Underwater Rimes"; B-side, "Your Life's a Cartoon."

I was a road manager for N.W.A. and actually all of Ruthless Records. I was technically the artist representative for the company. There was a friend of mine named Rodney Franklin who I had worked with before. A jazz keyboardist, jazz pianist from Berkeley, California. He had a relationship with one of Jimi Dright's siblings. So he called me and said, "You know, these guys are pretty good," and asked me if I wanted to meet them. Of course, I said sure. They came down to L.A. and we met at a Thai restaurant. I just loved Shock. I knew I wanted to work with Shock. Jimi was animated, and they were both just over-the-top looking at them together. Great guys. Those two particular songs were very unique sounding, at that time and even to this day. So I said, "Let's do this." I had always wanted to start my own company. I also had a relationship with Macola Records. What we were able to do with Macola was put our records out ourselves for the most part. They would press them for us, distribute them for us, and they would do some minimal promotion. Then we would have to pay the promotion pricing either by giving them some records, some boxes of records to sell, or we'd pay some money.

I was on the road at that time and that's partially how I funded the project. I was able to go out on the road, take that money we made, and put it in the little marketing and promotion that we did. I saved $1,500, and I paid for KSOL to play the record. Up here in the Bay Area, the Bay market. That was a top radio station at the time. We were selling records. But Macola had a habit of selling a thousand records out the front door and then a thousand out the back door. So we never felt like we got a real count of what we actually sold.

Daria Kelly was the buyer for Leopold's Records at the time. Leopold's no longer exists, but it was a big record store for years in Berkeley, California. So Daria had sent the record over to Ed Strickland at Tommy Boy Records, and they offered us $50,000 to do the record. I think it was $50,000, but it was a whole lot more than five [thousand], which was what Priority had offered. Really, in the grand scheme of things, it still isn't much money, even back then. But it was the best we had. They offered us $50,000, ten cents an album basically, or 10 percent an album, which isn't even ten cents. If an album's ten bucks, it's a buck an album. But then with packaging and all that, we would basically get fifty cents a record profit. I really liked the guys, I really liked Shock and I wanted to help them move on and so that was the best I could do.

Right around that time, Reggie Jackson's brother called me. He said, "You can't put these guys' records out because I have a contract with them." And he's all, "I'm going to sue you. I'm going to take all of your shit motherfucker this, motherfucker that, you can't do this shit. What the fuck's wrong with you?" So I was like, "Okay, listen, let me come up and meet with you." I came up to the Bay Area (I lived in L.A. at the time), met with him, and he said, "Hey, I've spent all this money on these guys and I'm the one who paid for that demo." I'm like, "I don't know what you're talking about." We kind of got into it, but nothing physical.

I called Shock. I'm like, "Man, I spent all my money on this and now I don't think we can do it." He goes, "Don't drop us. Please, please don't drop us. It wasn't a serious thing we had with them." I don't really know what went on, but what I do know is that we may have given them some money. Definitely not royalties. Maybe Jimi gave him some money. I may have just ignored him, but I pretty much just took Shock's plea, because I liked the music, and I liked him, I liked his creativity. So we just moved on in whatever way we could. I shouldn't say we moved on, but we just kept it moving. Just kept moving.

—Atron Gregory

Humpty, Dr. Dre, Eazy-E, Atron Gregory, and Tupac at the "Same Song" video shoot in Burbank, CA, 1991.

MONEY #2
YAMAHA JAPAN
#1
DJ FUZE
@THE FENIX UNDERGROUND,
SEATTLE 1997

We were not always digital underground. Our first name was Spice Regime. As things began to materialize with Jimi, I insisted we use a name that was vague and left room for more members down the road, in hopes to eventually replenish the group with my original crew members back East. I had a pact with my earlier groups, the Four Horsemen and the Master Blasters, that if anyone made it, we would bring on everyone else. But by the time digital underground formed, only two of the original members could actually make it out to California and onto the digital underground records: Kenny-K (RIP, who appears on "Hip Hop Doll," "Danger Zone," and "The Way We Swing" as a vocalist, plus he did the scratches on "Hip Hop Doll") and the MC Dazzlin Doc-P (who rapped on "Tribute to the Old Skool" from the *Sex Packets* LP bonus cassette version). Oh yeah, and I guess MC Ronnie Ron rapped on "Family of the Underground" from *Sons of the P* album, but he had long since quit rapping by then and had become a family man, as had the rest of the original crew. All of them got locked down with a wife and kids before digital underground began, and they were unavailable to tour by then.

So with Spice Regime . . . at the time hip hop was using references to food in a lot of names. Everything was "fresh" or "flavor." So we thought that "spice" had something to do with all that. We decided on Spice Regime for the original name of our group. We were with Macola Records then and they liked our stuff, but they did not like Spice Regime. So Jimi and I spent a day going over what could be the new name. I thought we needed something modern, like "Disc Drive" or "Digital City." Naw . . . we just kept throwing shit out, "Electric Underground." We went through a lot of names. And at some

HUMPTY WAS HERE
HUMPTY WAS HERE

OPPOSITE from top to bottom: At Giovanni's restaurant in Berkeley, CA, 1990, just after touring. Muns wearing Fuze's jacket with the Michael Jordan autograph; Food fight on tour—Halloween night; wearing wigs—front of stage. Tokyo, Japan, 1989. Image captured by DJ Fuze; Fans, Tokyo, Japan, 1989; Queen Latifah backstage, with Monica Lynch on the far left and Shock G in the background.

THIS PAGE: *Sex Packets* local release party at "Das Klub," 1990.

point we said, "digital underground." I forget if Jimi said "digital" and I said "underground" or the other way around, but that was it. We went, digital underground! That's dope. We just kept saying it over and over. I liked it because it was modern and high-tech. It was how the records were made. We thought the logo should look digital too. But it was also "underground." At the time hip hop was still underground. People thought it was a fad and it wasn't gonna last. Even in the late eighties they still thought it was just a fad. Most of the hip hop artists were still not played. I liked "underground" for that reason. I liked "digital" because all the equipment was digital. I thought it should be written all lowercase to look more "digital." So digital underground summed up hip hop at the time: It was *digital* and it was *underground*. It also had a lot to do with the Macola people at the time, because they liked it. If they had said no, we would be something else. The record label liked it. So we kept it.

When digital underground started in '88, '89, being an emcee was such a different thing, and R&B guys didn't get it. Jazz people didn't get it. People liked hip hop much more if it wasn't connected in any way to R&B: if it was just turntables, an emcee, a drum machine, and no instruments. A rapper was more legit if he didn't play an instrument. For me, I didn't want to come off like I was trying to be Prince, saying I play this instrument and I do this. I dumbed myself down. You had to dumb yourself down if you wanted to be a rapper at that time. So I played up that I used to be a pimp and a car thief, when actually those were only three small years of my entire existence. I played up the streets because that's what they wanted a rapper to be: a convict, coming from nothing. Then people would say to us, who's the piano man on the records? And we would just tell them, "Well, he doesn't want to be associated with hip hop. He's a serious R&B musician from Detroit," so that people would buy that the piano man was legit and so that people would buy that Shock G was legit.

I felt that I had to keep those two parts of myself separate. If you came into the business talking like, "I'm an instrumentalist," people would start questioning the validity of your emcee-ism. An emcee is supposed to be a thug. So I let Shock G remain a little bit thuggy, and I acted like I didn't know nothing about the music aspect. For the piano parts we just put "piano man, anonymous"—we didn't even let the label know that it was really me. Only Tom Silverman knew that it was me on the piano. Everybody

ABOVE: Shock G in his signature zebra print performing on the first digital underground US tour.
OPPOSITE: Public Enemy tour, 1990.

Humpty Hump and Kent (as Shock G) at the 1989 MTV Video Music Awards. Photograph by Jeff Kravitz.

11/26/89
IN FLIGHT SIPPING BLOODY MARYS

Alex,

I don't know why it took me so long to write. I'm sorry I've been so lazy, but seems we never get a chance to relax (If we're not on a bus, we're loading equipment, or rushing to an airport, or checking in to a hotel, or doing an interview, or unloading at the show, or getting up at X@@!!X$☆? in the !!X$&XX morning to catch another plane, etc. etc. etc. etc.

Sometimes in order to truly relax and enjoy this tour I must not think about the states or who I should write or call, but just _experience_ Europe. I must admitt however, despite a few problems here and there, it's been really Kool. I have so much to write about and to tell you that I don't even know where to begin! First of all, if my writing is messy, it's because I'm on a plane right now between Sweden and Finland. By the way, I'm _freezing_!! I caught a cold in Denmark but it seems to be going →

...away now. (2)

Alex, You must forgive me for not writing sooner. Do you miss me? I miss you sometimes, especially your suttle sense of humor. You and Deisty seemed to be having alot of fun that night you called. That's really great. I know that Sometimes you can get the scoop from Deisty as to where we are or whatever. Tell Deisty Shock says wussup! and that she's the shit!! and Merry Christmas!

You know what?

Jimmy fell off a four and ½ foot stage in Amsterdam. It was completely hilarious!! (He was O.K.) Oh! I saw the girls you told me about there, too! it was unbeleiveable!!

Alex, I put various post cards in this package of some of the nicer cities we hit. By the time you get this letter I'll probably be in Tampa Bay with my Dad & Brother. The People here in Europe love us so much, →

(3.) ...that I'm thinking about moving over here. The Ladies in Sweden are consistantly beautiful, unlike any country I've ever been to. (at least for white girls.)

I'm not making the kind of money people expect me to, so please do _not_ buy me anything really nice for christmas 'cause I'm gonna' have a hard enough time handling my relatives, much less good friends and lovers! (n-um-sayin'!)

Yes, you can probably tell from my conversation that I've had a couple of Drinks by now. I _had_ to Alex. There is _sooo_ much fucking turbelance right now as I write this, that I'm scared to DEATH!!! Not only that, but we're running about 3 hours late right now because the landing gear didn't work on our intentional plane so we had to all get off and change to a new plane before we [illegible] →

...Maybe, we'll be late enough to miss the Show tonight in Finland and have a nite off for the first time in about 2 weeks. We _just_ landed, (that's why my writing has gotten _very_ sloppy) and I have to fold-up this little table now so bye bye!!

Listen, I'll call you from Florida.

See Ya.

Shock G

OOPS! I FORGOT YOU DON'T LIKE THAT.

Gregory

XXX

OPPOSITE: A letter to Alex (friend) from Greg while on the first Europe tour, 1990.
THIS PAGE: Fuze took a bunch of these images on buses and planes. Greg was always falling asleep en route.

TOP: The Piano Man—Shock G's posthumous jazz record, produced by Atron Gregory. TNT Records/Solo Piano Group, 2022.
BOTTOM: Greg and Kent perform as Shock G and Humpty Hump. Image courtesy of Saafir.

else at Tommy Boy thought we had this mystery piano man who would sneak in and do sessions for us, but he didn't want to be selling out by doing rap and funk stuff so he would rather be listed as anonymous. The story was he didn't want to be associated with a rap group, but he liked us and he would play on our records exclusively. We had people saying, "I betchu that's Bernie Worrell from P-Funk!" and "No, I betchu that's Herbie Hancock!" We had 'em guessing. Piano Man was kept separate for a reason. Humpty was different. Humpty was just a joke to keep separate. But for Piano Man it was more serious.

I was also drawing the artwork for the records under the name Rackadelic. That was my tag name. I thought it was more powerful to use a different name for the visual art and to act as a separate person. I was just doing it until I could find someone else who could really draw. My thought was, I'll do the piano parts and the artwork to get it going until we find someone to really do it. PeeWee did end up being the Piano Man for a little while. I really just wanted to be Shock G. I never intended to keep all of that going forever, like it did. I grew up on Grandmaster Flash and the Furious Five, with seven members in the group: EZ Mike, Flash, and five emcees. Then there was Parliament Funkadelic, which was a supergroup. With digital underground we wanted it to look thick like that too. We thought the input of a lot of people would make it richer. That was the reason why we kept adding a lot of emcees through the years. That's also the reason why I split up a lot of my own characters, to give it the vision that I wanted of a big organization, even though most of them were me. I didn't want it to look like only one man in a room with a bunch of equipment, like Prince. That was corny to me. I love Prince, don't get me wrong! But in a hip hop sense, in the late eighties, it was corny to be that way. Teddy Riley had done that. Prince had done that. A lot of musicians had done that already. But nobody had a bunch of musicians all contributing to one rap group, so that was a selling point to me.

I wasn't paying attention to the fact that I was actually pulling it off by doing so many parts myself. In hindsight, maybe I would have gotten more respect if I had said that I was doing everything. But after a while, it just became cool to hide it. The Humpty shit was obvious. I know that worked! But I guess I thought I was more of a rapper if I wasn't also a producer, a musician, and doing the artwork. "Produced by the Underground Mixhowulike Squad" or "D-Flow Production Squad" I always put on our albums. But now, looking back, I would take all my credit! I would put "Produced by Shock G" on it. In hindsight, Tommy Boy could have marketed me like that: "We got this wonder artist who can play all the instruments and produce and also rap!" I was always second-guessing myself. My thought was if people knew it was me playing the piano, they wouldn't listen to it the same. But if they thought it's this serious Detroit dude, who might have been on Parliament or Highland Players, they would listen differently. By the same token, if they knew that's me playing the piano, I thought they wouldn't take my rap seriously. "How could he be this b-boy from New York, if he's that much of a musician?" I wanted to be taken seriously in each thing that I did. I thought if they knew it was me on each thing, they'd go, "Aw man, naw, that's just Greg." I always felt like if you look right at me, I'm nothing special. I'm just a skinny nigga with big teeth, big deal.

Most people think we were an overnight

MACK FOR LIFE
THERE WILL BE NO NOSE JOB DID YOU CATCH IT? THERE WILL BE NO NOSE JOB.
HUMPTY HAS REACHED THAT POINT OF INNER ACCEPTANCE OF HIS-SELF AND IS NO LONGER ASHAMED OF HAVING A BIG BROWN NOSE. THEY SAY THAT HE CAN SELL MORE RECORDS IF HE HAD A NICE NEET PIN NOSE.
MD
WAIT A MINUTE... WHY IS HUMPTY MAKING SUCH A B
STINK ABOUT ALL
NOSE BUSINESS
DOESN'T HE REALIZE
CARES ABOUT HIS
DOESN'T HE KNOW THA
ONLY AN IDIOT WOULD
LIEVE THAT HE IS
EGYPTIAN KINGS?
NO NOSE JOB
I GUESS HUMPTY JUST DOESN'T GIVE A F--K. HOW CAN HE FACE HIMSELF EACH MORN -ING IN THE MIRROR?
HAS HE LOST HIS FUNKY MIND? DOESN'T HE KNOW THAT PEOP WITH BROWN NOSES ARE NOT FROM EGYPT BUT FROM THE GHETTOS OF AMERICA AND B-4 THAT THEY CAME FROM... , UH... FROM A PLACE IN AFRICA CALLED CLEVELAND.
WAIT A MINUTE ...THA CAN TR
SONS OF THE P
SONS OF THE P
SONS OF THE P
SONS OF THE
SONS OF THE P
D FLOW
THE ORIGINAL DOLIO FLOW STARTED HERE WITH DFLO MOVING TOWARDS COMPLETE HARM
MAYBE HE ON TO SOME HERE.
NO
ALL BLACK PEOPLE ARE
CLEVELAND
IN HUMP WE TRUST
RACKADELIC 1991

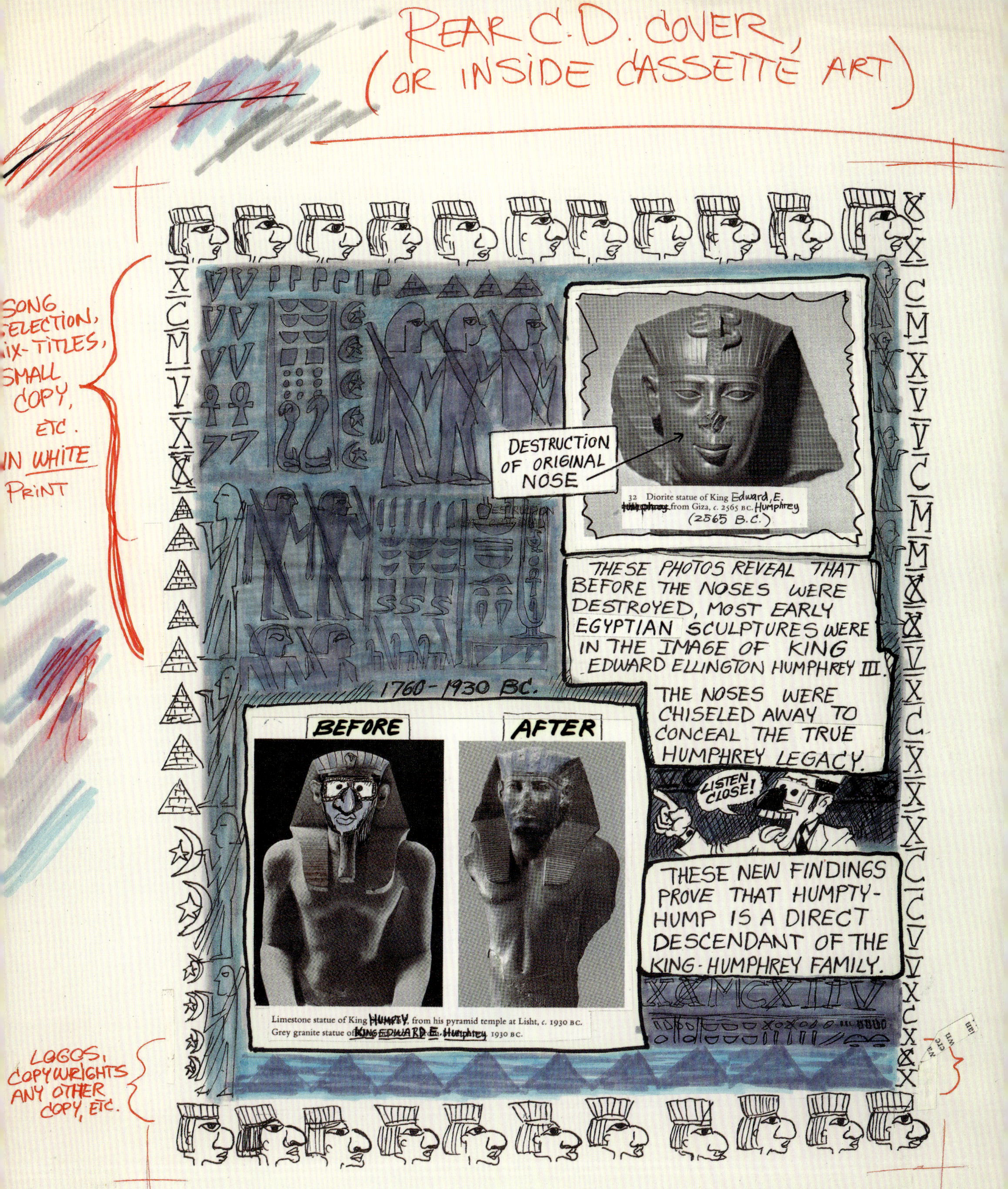

ABOVE AND OPPOSITE: Designs for *No Nose Job* inserts, courtesy of Tommy Boy Records / Reservoir Media.

success. Just because the world heard of us overnight doesn't mean that's how it was. It's not like one day I'm a fry cook. Day two, I'm rapping on TV. Day three, I'm on tour with Public Enemy. There were so many intervals along the way that if I didn't have my earlier experiences, if I hadn't been working at it for so long, I may not have made that hurdle. Some niggas act like it's going to knock at a door. Just show up. Knock knock. Who is it? Job. By the time we went on tour, I was already experienced enough to make it work.

When people came to see our show, they'd be laughing so hard! They were like, "Shock be rocking. He got that thing." They used to say I had a little thing I would do. I used to show up with SHOCK G tagged all down the side of my white gym pants with tassels, like Muhammad Ali tassels on my big high-top Pumas. I looked pretty crazy. I didn't fit the regular. They always said, "Shock never looked right, but he didn't look ancient. At least he isn't ancient and he's not wack." But they didn't know what kind of nigga I was. That's what people were saying. They knew I wasn't an Oakland nigga, and they couldn't tell if I was from New York because they were already on Adidas and

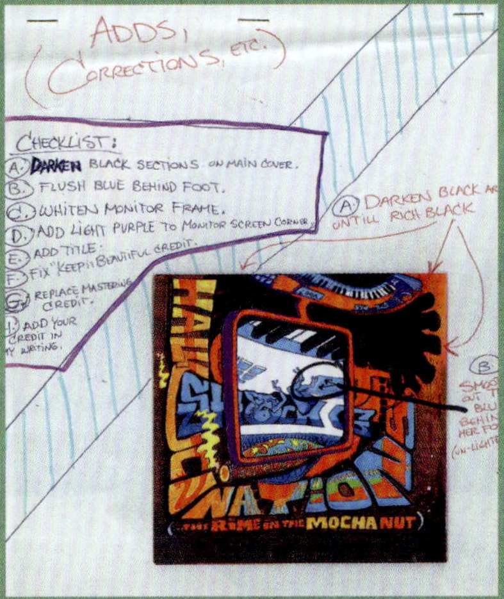

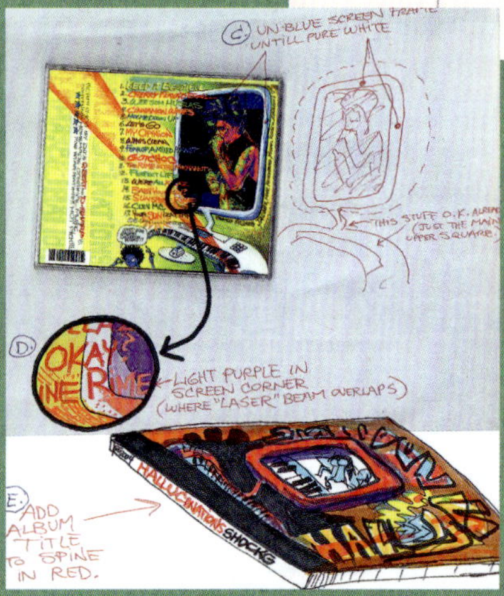

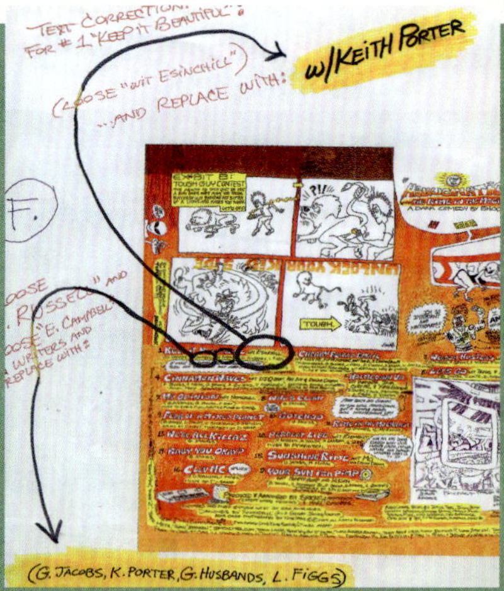

OPPOSITE AND RIGHT: Original artwork for *The Return of the Crazy One* and *The Body-Hat Syndrome*. **OPPOSITE, BOTTOM:** Designs and instructions for *Fear of a Mixed Planet* CD artwork.

I was wearing Pumas. I liked Pumas. I had the black. I liked the cat—I used to draw it. Mine didn't look exactly like Pumas either. They had big fat laces, tassels. I'd put them in a bushel and take the time to tie the last string so they would hang right off to the side. They were like *this* thick. If you had too many, it would look like a pom-pom, so it had to be just right. Look like a bell on each side. When they started fraying at the bottom, they looked so dope. Shit was hip hop. I didn't want the tongue sticking out. I didn't want to do anything I saw anyone else doing.

"THE RETURN OF THE CRAZY ONE!"
B/W CARRY THE W
BY... digital unders
PRODUCED BY THE D-FLO P
FOR STAYIN' BUSY PRODUCTIO
HELLO KNUCKAS AND SHNUCKAS, AND WELCOME TO...
Humptyville
NITE SPOT
FREE! NO I.D. REQUIRED
OUR HOST
EDDIE HUMPHREY
ABSOLUTELY NO RATIONAL THINKING ALLOWED
ILL-SIGNS EVERYW
EIGHT DRINK MINIMUM
DRESS CODE ENFORCED!
DJ ROOM
LIVE SHOW
STRICTLY ENFORCED
NINE DRINK MINIMUM
NO SHOES
NO FUNNY-STYLE CLOTHES!
BOOTS SNEAKERS HOODIES AND CAPS ONLY!
LADIES NO OVER-DRESSING
SEVENTY PERCENT OF BODY MUST SHOW
MEN
LADIES
DRAG QUEENS
VODKA
GIN
GALLO FRENCH RED

Original artwork for The Return of the Crazy One.

When we met with Shock G, he met all our expectations. But we got a bonus. When Tommy Boy signed digital underground we didn't just sign Greg Jacobs, we signed all his multiple personalities: Shock G, Edward Ellington Humphrey III, The Piano Man, MC Blowfish, The Computer Woman. And even the visual artist Rackadelic.

Shock not only is a musical genius, but he is also a visual genius. A true visionary, he once shared with me his vision for a funk and hip hop amusement park and Rackadelic even sketched out ideas for the rides.

He is like the Nikola Tesla of hip hop. Except that he has a great sense of humor. You were never sure when he was serious or when he was joking. Because he is so smart and such an excellent musician, sometimes he is very serious, but you might never know it.

His vision of the world always rejects the status quo. He has a keen eye for what might really be going on under the thin veneer that we call "reality."

—Tom Silverman
(Tommy Boy Records)

"UNDERWATER RIMES"

Tommy Boy Records caught wind of us after an employee at Leopold's Records in Berkeley gave a copy of our "Underwater Rimes" single to their rep one day as he was in town making his rounds at their store. After digging the single, and after we broke twenty thousand copies on our own, Tommy Boy surprised us by contacting Atron and offering us a single/video/album deal. Here I was with Tommy Boy knocking at our door and nobody to DJ for us. This is what led me to ask around if anyone knew a DJ we could use temporarily until my DJ Kenny-K made it out. DJ Fuze, a friend of a friend of Jimi's, came and met us at Starlight Sound in Richmond, California, where I was recording new songs for Tommy Boy. He said he had heard "Your Life's a Cartoon" on the radio and liked my rapping style. Fuze was originally only supposed to do one show with us, the Tommy Boy showcase when we opened for Tone Loc at the Omni, at which time they would make the decision to sign us or not.

But four months later, when it was time to go on tour, Kenny-K still wasn't ready. Little did either of us know, he was x-ing himself out of digital underground with that decision. As a result, I had to ask Fuze to DJ the tour, who in turn insisted I bring his music partner Money B so that their work together wasn't interrupted. They had Raw Fusion at that time. During the course of rehearsing and preparing for this tour, we recorded more songs and shot videos for "Doowutchyalike" and "The Humpty Dance," and by the time we returned from that first extensive two-month overseas tour, we had jelled into a group. People recognized Fuze and Mun as the people in the videos. The publicity department at Tommy Boy started including their names in all the bios, press releases, and liner notes. Magazine articles started pouring in, mentioning their names as set band members. It all happened so fast that before I really planned out the personnel, Mun, Fuze, Tupac, PeeWee, and Big Money Odis all wound up getting added to the roster and became staples of digital underground, each either by default or coincidence. Ha-ha, blessings in disguise. Pac, PeeWee, and Odis were all TNT labelmates who I started using in the studio just because they were around. And DJ Jay-Z [producer/DJ/live drummer] was Pee's cousin, so he would occasionally play me and Pac new beats that we snatched up and made songs out of ("Crooked Ass Niggaz," "Flowin on the D-Line," "Return of the Crazy One," etc.).

The Bay Area fatefully turned out to be the perfect launch pad for

my sound because there was so much P-Funk awareness there in the late eighties. Needless to say, they ate up digital underground, they used to even play our four-track cassette demos on the air at KPFA, the UC Berkeley station. This was all way before Dr. Dre got on the P-Funk bandwagon. He didn't go there until after the third N.W.A. album, like '92 or so with *The Chronic*. But X Clan, EPMD, and digital underground especially—we were sampling George heavily back in '88. There was still no rap section in most record stores, they crammed it in among the R&B records. And the "rap" chart was new and tiny in *Billboard* magazine, only ten songs at first. Television only featured a small rap hour once a week at first, and then once a day, with *Yo! MTV Raps*.

The emergence of *Yo!* didn't have artists suddenly thinking in terms of video, we already were. Many of our favorites of the early eighties did have videos (Sugarhill Gang, Furious Five, Kurtis Blow, Dougie Fresh & the Get Fresh Crew, Whodini, Fat Boys, Run DMC, etc.). By '81, MTV and other local stations were already playing a handful of rap videos from the gate, mixed in with all the pop stuff. The late eighties were a time when both album art and video were kinda running neck and neck; they both were given equal consideration from new and aspiring rap artists. From inside the industry we felt that quality art was still necessary because the majority of releases still didn't have videos yet. Videos were a privilege of the larger budgeted groups, which was about a fifth of the total hip hop record-making community. And even among the 20 percent that did shoot videos, fewer still made it onto the *Yo!* show.

digital
TRAPPED
ABSOLUTELY NO NOSE JOB!!

APOLLO NIGHT

The Apollo
Harlem, New York City

It was '91 and digital underground was booked to perform on *Showtime at the Apollo*. A week prior, at our rehearsal studio in Oakland, we were brainstorming a way we could make our performance special and unforgettable.

At the time there was this show called the *Gong Show* and there was this guy called the Unknown Comic. That's what gave me the idea. I already knew how the crowd was at the Apollo, so I was like let's put bags on our heads and come out. Then when we get booed, we change the song and take them off. They thought it was crazy at first. We all went back and forth a bit. Shock looked at Money B, Money B looked back at him. But to me, I knew it would work. It just made sense.

—PeeWee

Pee was like: "Naw, wait y'all, what if we really did that shit?" We looked at him, confused, thinking he was still stuck in the same joke. Realizing he was serious, we all silently gazed up with our heads tilted sideways, looking at nothing and trying to visualize it.

"Hmm . . . if we did do it," said Fuze, "we'd have to make sure the audience really didn't know who we were, or else it wouldn't work."

"And the timing would have to be perfect," added Money B.

"And the beat would have to be as wack as possible, to make absolutely sure we get booed," I said. "'Cause it doesn't work unless they boo us."

"Let's say we're from Beaumont, Texas!" At that time the Geto Boys weren't out yet, there was no Houston Revolution. In 1991, saying "Beaumont, Texas" and talkin' about you're a rapper? Not cool.

We convinced ourselves we could make it work. We had these big question marks on fuckin' bags with the eyeballs cut out, it was just stupid! I remember we spent about a half-hour pondering it before we finally decided we were for sure gonna do it. We knew there were many small details that could make it or break it, so we spent the remainder of that week figuring it out, planning and practicing.

The resulting performance went down in Apollo history as the greatest audience sneak attack ever executed. We tricked the entire house, staff, and TV-viewing audience. The only people who knew were the owner, the president of the network, whoever was in control of the TV show, and the person who pulled the cord for the curtain. I don't remember if we told the host Mark Curry or not. "Where you all from?" he asked Mun first. But Mun wasn't allowed to talk because his voice would have given him away, so he was just quiet. PeeWee could talk because people didn't know his voice, and I could talk because I could throw my voice. "Where you from?" he asked again.

"From Beaumont, Texas."

"They're from Beaumont, Texas, everybody, give it up . . ."

"BOO!" They were booing already! When we were planning, we were like, what if they don't boo? That'll ruin it. We knew we needed the siren to go off; we had to get booted offstage by the Sandman. But they were booing us soon as we walked out! I heard one lady say, "Take them bags back to Key Food!"

We go, "We're from Beaumont, Texas," and we had this Hammer beat going with these loud annoying bells in it. "We're the Noname Rappers, yes we are. The Noname Rappers go real far. Say Texas in the house, you say it!"

"BOO!!" They were booing so hard! We spun out of the bags and capes at the very last second, showing our digital underground jackets and revealing our true identity—Shock G, Money B, and PeeWee—just as the curtain opened revealing Tupac, DJ Fuze, and the rest of digital underground behind us. At that very moment "Kiss You Back" burst out of the speakers. BOOM!!

The room erupted into complete chaos as the audience leaped from their seats and bum-rushed the edge of the stage. All the girls ran down and flooded the stage. I forgot the lyrics and everything! I couldn't believe how good it went. We had the beginning beat repeating four times so they would have time to open the curtain, and I was just standing there going "Wow . . ." And then, oh right, right! "Shimmy, shimmy cocoa pop . . ."

Something in the beginning was off because for a few seconds we were all just going, "Damn!" We worked through every detail and every possible option except for the one where it's gonna kill 'em! It went too well. Epic experience; the sense of accomplishment afterward was massive. It was mission impossible hip hop style. We were one of the groups that had the nerve or the confidence, or maybe we were just goofy enough to try some shit like that. Great call, Pee! Thanks for makin' us break and really imagine it.

THIS PAGE AND OVERLEAF:
Original artwork / comic insert for The Body-Hat Syndrome. Courtesy of Tommy Boy / Reservoir Media.

WHEEE! WHEEE! YEAH! FUN! YAY! WHEEE! FUN! YAY! FUN!
GAMEBOY
Yo MONEY-B, CHECK IT. ME & CLEE GOT THIS FAT IDEA FOR THE CHORUS-PART OF DOPE-A-DELIC! ...Yo MON, ... MON!! MONEY-B!!!
D-FLO SONG BOOK TOP SECRET
CAN'T YOU SEE I'M PLAYIN' WIT MY NEW GAME-BOY?!!
(GIANT SIZE)
GAMEBOY
$!!x ?? #x!!
READ THIS WAY READ THIS WAY THAT WAY
LAY IT IN YOUR POCKET
INTERMISSION
FEMALE SWINGERS LEARN TO USE A FINGER AT THE....
...WE INTERUPT OUR REGULAR PROGRAM, TO BRING YOU THIS CIRCUS UPDATE.
OVER ON THE RICHMOND SCENE...
I COULDN'T MAKE IT BY THE STUDIO THIS WEEK, I HAD TO GET MY CAR WASHED. AND THEN WAXED AND POLISHED. AND THEN OF COURSE I HAD TO GET THE WHOLE INSIDE SOAKED IN $50 AN OUNCE ARMANI PIMP COLOGNE & FRAGRANCE. I HAD MY RIMS DIPPED IN FRENCH BATH-OIL. MY LICENSE PLATE IS HAND MADE BY WOMEN IN PRISON. MY GLOVE-LEATHER RAG-TOP IS TREATED WITH BILL-BLASS LEATHER SOAK. MY BLAH-BLAH-BLAH, IS BLAH BLAH BLAH. MY OTHER BLAH BLAH BLAH IS BLAH BLAH BLAH.
BEEP BEEP BEEP
BIGG
WELCOME TO THE FREAKS JERKIT CIRCUS CIRCUS
I'M YOUR HOST "SCHMOOVY SCHMOOV" HERE AT THE D-FLO CIRCUS TODAY, AND I'LL BE INTRODUCING OUR FREAKY-DEAK LINE-UP.
FLY GIRL KINKYS WORK THOSE PINKIES!
TIP... DON'T GET CAUGHT WIT YO' DICK IN YOUR HAND! ALWAYS TRAVEL ALONE WHILE AT THE CIRCUS!
...WE'LL HAVE FULL DETAILS TO-NIGHT AT ELEVEN
"AINT EASY BEIN' A DIGI" PAGE THREE (3)
STILL MORE

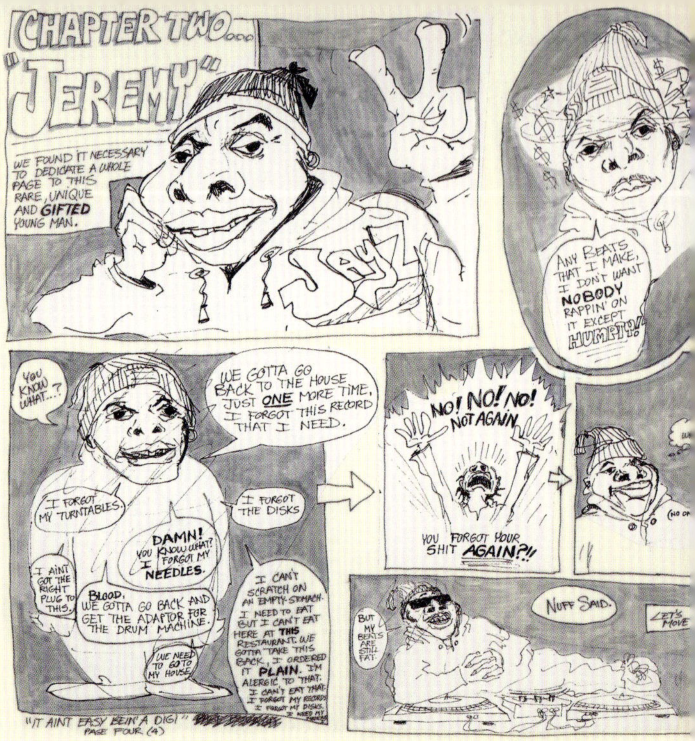
CHAPTER TWO...
"JEREMY"
WE FOUND IT NECESSARY TO DEDICATE A WHOLE PAGE TO THIS RARE, UNIQUE AND GIFTED YOUNG MAN.
ANY BEATS THAT I MAKE, I DON'T WANT NOBODY RAPPIN' ON IT EXCEPT HUMPTY!!
YOU KNOW WHAT...?
WE GOTTA GO BACK TO THE HOUSE JUST ONE MORE TIME, I FORGOT THIS RECORD THAT I NEED.
I FORGOT MY TURNTABLES.
I FORGOT THE DISKS
DAMN! YOU KNOW WHAT? I FORGOT MY NEEDLES.
I AINT GOT THE RIGHT PLUG TO THIS.
BLOOD, WE GOTTA GO BACK AND GET THE ADAPTOR FOR THE DRUM MACHINE.
WE NEED TO GO TO MY HOUSE.
I CAN'T SCRATCH ON AN EMPTY STOMACH. I NEED TO EAT BUT I CAN'T EAT HERE AT THIS RESTAURANT. WE GOTTA TAKE THIS BACK, I ORDERED IT PLAIN. I'M ALERGIC TO THAT. I CAN'T EAT THAT. I FORGOT MY RECORDS. I FORGOT MY DISKS.
NO! NO! NO! NOT AGAIN
YOU FORGOT YOUR SHIT AGAIN?!!
NUFF SAID.
BUT MY BEATS ARE STILL FAT.
LET'S MOVE
"IT AINT EASY BEIN' A DIGI" PAGE FOUR (4)

LET'S DROP IN AT THE underground TURNTABLE LAB...
HOW'S THE TURNTABLE SOLO COMIN' ALONG, FUZE?
STRAIN STRAIN SUFFER STRAIN CONCENTRATE SWEAT STRAIN
digital lover
GRUNT RRR..
FOOT ACTION
..AND NOW, LIKE MANY ARTISTS, DJ FUZE FINDS HIS-SELF FACING THE IN-ESCAPABLE QUESTION: CAN HE TOP HIS LAST MATERIAL? WILL HE RIVAL THE 'NOSE-JOB' SCRATCH?
HEY, WUSSUP PEE WEE! WHERE YOU GOIN?
WUSSUP HUMP. I GOTTA DO SOMETHIN IN MINNESOTA
WIT' GEORGE CLINTON. THEN I GOTTA MEET TOO $HORT DOWN IN TEXAS AND CATCH UP WIT THAT DJ-QUIK TOUR.
...THEN, I'M SUPPOSED TO GO IN THE STUDIO WIT STRETCH AND PLAY KEYBOARDS ON A LIVE SQUAD TRACK. THEN I'M ...
D-FLO AIR
WELL DON'T FORGET ME AND SHOCK WANT YOU TO DO SOMETHIN ON THE NEW DU THANG.
O.K. WELL I SHOULD BE BACK BY JANUARY... OH! WAIT A MINUTE, IN JANUARY I'M SUPPOSED TO DO A DRUM TRACK ON SPICE-1'S NEW ALBUM, AND THEN I GOTTA GO TO.... CLEVELAND AND PUT SOME HORNS ON THAT NU-BUBBLE-NIGGA'S ALBUM, OH YEAH THEN.. I GOTTA... BLAH BLAH BLAH BLAH BLAH BLAH BLAH ETC.
NEVERMIND NIGGA' PEACE!
DADDY NEVER LEFT 'YA
RICH NIGGA BUM
...AND FINALLY, THRU SOME MIRACLE OF NATURE, THE underground MANAGES TO GET 10 OR 12 ACTUAL SONGS DONE, AND HAVE GOT SOMETHIN' THAT CAN PASS FOR AN ALBUM!
(SONGS? LET'S SAY EXPERIMENTS)
YOUR TYPICAL D-FLO CONGREGATIONAL MEETING.
...BUT YOU NOT HEARIN' ME, BRAN NU SWETTA IS THE BOMB!
DIGITAL LOVER.
D-FLO
EVERYBODY I KNOW SAYS MY PART ON DOPE-A-DELIC IS THE FATTEST SHIT IN HIP-HOP!
PROTECT YOURSELF AGAINST FALSELY AQUIRED DILUTED EDUCATION SYNDROME
I'M NOT ON MY OWN DICK! I'M NOT ON MY OWN DICK! I'M NOT ON MY OWN DICK! I'M
MON'S STANG
...TO BE CONTINUED! (THAT'S THE SAD PART ABOUT IT.)
THAT'S IT
DON'T MISS! NEXT MONTH: GERMAN HIP-HOP BUNGY JUMPERS, MC BLOW-FISH AND SPECIAL BASS-LINE SPOTLIGHT!
RACKADELIC '93
"IT AINT EASY BEIN A DIGI" (7) PAGE SEVEN THE FINAL FRONTIER. THE LAST STRAW. THE KIT AND KABOODLE. ETC.

...MEANWHILE IN L.A...
CILEDAEPOD
7294FD7283LMZF28FDB
GREAT! ANOTHER FAT PUBLISHING DEAL! (FOR WHO KNOWS WHO!) NOW, IF I COULD JUST GET digital underground TO TURN IN THE NEW ALBUM!!
OOPS, THAT'S RIGHT, I GOTTA CALL PAC...
PHONE
adidas
DEMO
THIS IS ATRON, I THINK THE DRUMS WERE MIXED TOO LOW!
MEANWHILE ... ON THE
HOLLER IF YA HEAR ME!!
DIAL -BOX SELECTION NUMBER... FD47038253
REAL NUBIAN
MIX THE FUNKIN' DRUMS LOUDER!!!
SWEAT! SWEAT! SWEAT! STRESS SWEAT
JUST FOR THE RECORD, PAC AND DEON ARE GONNA KILL ME WHEN THEY SEE THIS!
"IT AIN'T EASY BEIN' A digi" PAGE FIVE (5)

PLATINUM

Platinum means one million copies sold. At fourteen bucks per album, four bucks are retail store markup, two bucks are for distribution cost, three bucks are the manufacturer cost, four more bucks are record company recoup. Then one buck or less is left to split between the writers and performers in the group. Of that buck, for us, twenty cents went to sampled writers, fifteen cents went to management. That left the rest of us with sixty-five cents per CD sold. One million times sixty-five cents is $650,000, out of which the government taxes about a third. The remaining $400,000 was split between myself, Money B, DJ Fuze, and Chopmaster J [Jimi Dright], depending on who wrote or did what. After another album or two of that kinda money plus touring, yes, we were all able to buy decent middle-priced homes either for ourselves or for our parents. Then it's simply back to work baby, gotta pay the mortgage now and keep the taxes current—not an easy task when you sell a little less each year as the popularity wears off.

Financially rich? Not, hardly. There have been some nice little checks here and there from sales and publishing royalties, but the music industry is not what most people think it is. Unless you're one of the top-name super-mogul product-endorsing entrepreneurs, or you own your own product top to bottom. The thing about digital underground was that we *didn't* own our own labels. We recorded for TNT/Tommy Boy/Warner Bros., and with TNT/Death Row/Interscope. This meant just a few cents per record. More profitable endeavors? For me personally it was about an even fifty-fifty between record sales and touring profits. I didn't get approached for too many product endorsements or outside business opportunities. I did turn down a slew of movie roles and TV offers in the early nineties, because touring was so good for us. If it required me to move to L.A. or to not tour for a while, I always chose to tour with digital underground. Touring was an unbelievably fun experience to witness and be a part of. We weren't the average everyday rap crew. The vibe was always so festive and positive. It would've been hard to walk away from that to sit in a trailer all day waiting for makeup.

So where did the money go? Well, I can't speak for the other group members and various managers and agents, but my personal share? Okay, let's see: I spent $30,000 on a fun car to drive (a '74 De Tomaso Pantera—a Ferrari-styled muscle car with a big-block Ford V8). I bought my dad a new SUV for his birthday. I maintained my brother's auto insurance and my parents' yard care service for a while. I flew all my high school best friends and cousins out from the East Coast to all the major digital underground release parties and video shoots and covered their hotels and expenses. Up until the Oakland fire in 1991, I lived in a regular apartment. But after that I spent $170,000 on a condo in Emeryville. Three years later, I got married to Melissa (Mel), sold the condo, and spent $150,000 on a house up in the Poconos, Pennsylvania. I bought a brand-new Toyota Forerunner as my second more practical car for $25,000 (this was the only new car I ever owned until 2010, when I bought a Camaro, RS 6-speed manual).

In 1991, I gave $10,000 to a bone marrow drive in an effort to save the life of Mr. Richard Navies (a Berkeley High teacher and human rights activist). He was the person responsible for introducing African Studies to the U.S. school system in the 1970s. We didn't find a match for him, but the drive did produce a match and saved the life of a young kid in Texas. Later that year I spent $15,000 building a special nine-screen video-wall DJ booth for DJ Fuze, which I designed myself. It featured a twelve-foot riser and a hanging mirror angled over him so the crowd could see his hands on the platters. Another $3,000 went to two sets of giant prop hands that our dancers used onstage to animate the handclap sounds in our songs (later we donated these to the Luniz when they performed "I Got 5 On It" worldwide). We used the props all that year: on the Budweiser Superfest tour with LL Cool J and Bell Biv DeVoe, at the Monsters of Rap pay-per-view show with Naughty by Nature, Queen Latifah, Tupac, and Gold Money at the Warfield Theatre in Frisco, then again at the KMEL Summer Jam at the Shoreline Amphitheatre. Every two years or so, I would spend about $34,000 to have a nice new backdrop/stage banner made with a cool design, so that we looked halfway professional up there. Usually it would have the current album art and digital underground logo on it. (This used to be enuff! These dayz ya need those programmable LED light-panel-laser-effect walls 'n sheeiot!)

(YOUR BASIC ASSHOLE)

In 1992, I lent our good friend and head of security Nzazi Muhammed $40,000 to start his Wellness Center, a yoga/healing/martial arts shop in Santa Monica, California. In 1993, I gave the rapper Saafir $7,000 so he could buy a motorcycle as a thank-you gift for him contributing so much to *The Body Hat Syndrome* album. At the "Return of the Crazy One" party/video shoot in 1993, I spent $2,000 in liquor and $1,500 in popcorn. There was a 12 × 15-foot popcorn bowl in the middle of the dance floor with orders to keep it heaping all night. In 1994, I spent $50,000 on my wedding to Melissa and the huge reception/party for which Mind Motion was the DJ and Human Flavor and Raphael Saadiq performed with a live band in a different room. On the roof of that party we had a saxophonist and harp player performing love songs all night, and in the main room we featured an open bar and all the shrimp you could eat for five hundred guests.

In January of 2005, I gave $20,000 in airline tickets and supply money to California friends who lost family in the [December 2004 Indian Ocean] tsunami and went home to search for surviving family members in Sri Lanka. In addition to all this, I spent an insane amount of money over the years in bar and grill tabs, street drugs (just the fun ones), bail money, and extra hotel rooms on tour for surprise overnight friends and guests. Let's see . . . oh yeah—taxis, trains, and last-minute plane tickets all around the world trying to keep up with the tour after waking up at new friends' houses the morning after a house party. Also, Christmas gifts, birthday gifts, and friends' loans were often in the thousands over the years. For instance, it was common for Tupac or myself to give each other or a close friend two or three grand out of our pocket—"guilt money" for those last-minute face-to-face birthday rememberings.

On top of all that, I probably give away at least $200 a month to random homeless people and storefront charities, supermarkets, gas stations all around the United States, all the time, and still today. I never had big respect for money, and if I see someone in real need, I'll easily give a stranger whatever's in my pocket. When I look back on this, I'm actually proud of how I treated my money. There's definitely a great feeling of fulfillment in giving, and a dignity in not being stingy. I think digital underground has been extremely lucky for being just the right amount of not too big/not too small.

WARNING
This gallery contains graphic images that some viewers may find disturbing

Pages from Greg's personal journal and various notes and sketches.

"EAT BOILED PEANUTZ"

It's late in the afternoon, and Greg and I are sitting around snacking on peanuts.

"You ever tried boiled peanuts? You gotta come with me to Tampa sometime to try the boiled peanuts! I can't believe you've never had them. They are all over the South. They're everywhere!"

This makes me think of Shock's alter ego, Peanut Hakeem and "Eat Boiled Peanutz." I wonder if that alter ego was created with these boiled peanuts in mind. It's just like Shock to have created an entire character from a food item. Peanut Hakeem, Humpty Hump, Sex Packets . . . Realism mixes with fantasy always. I ask if he still has a copy of the actual "Sex Packet Pamphlets" that they used to leave in bus stops and train stations.

UNDERGROUND AVE
101
GOT THEM PACKETS, PEOPLE
RACKADELIC

PACKET MAN

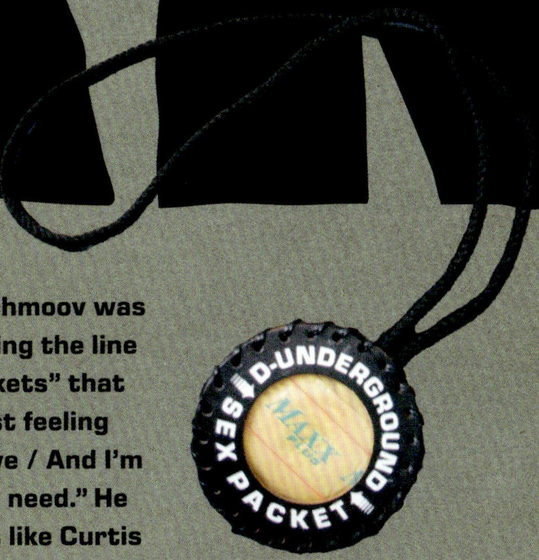

S*ex Packets* didn't feel like 100 percent hip hop. It felt like some psychedelic, space funk to me. It felt like we were doing what P-Funk or Prince would be doing had they used samplers. There are times where the intoxication of one type or another helped the creation of it a little bit. When we were writing "Sex Packets," me and Fuze, there were definitely some psychedelics involved. Little shrooms, little ecstasy. It helped the process. Other songs, we were completely sober for, but "Sex Packets" had that psychedelic feel to it. That's what people use Adderall for. College kids studying for tests. After the test they go back to their lives. They don't become dope fiends. This isn't my drug of choice anymore. It hasn't been for a while.

Schmoovy Schmoov, one of the singers in the group, was into P-Funk and Prince just like me. We both had around thirty to forty Parliament albums, so we would be on some P-Funk shit together. Schmoov was the cat singing the line on "Sex Packets" that goes "I'm just feeling what you love / And I'm givin' 'til you need." He kind of sings like Curtis Mayfield, but he was actually a suit-and-tie guy working at MCI making a lot of money. Schmoov would come to the studio because he liked us and was down to help us out, but he didn't really take us seriously because we were doing that rap fad he heard about. Meanwhile, in his briefcase he had an actual plan to create sex packets for astronauts. The nigga was nuts. Schmoov really believed he was going to get a grant from the United States government to develop this technology to help astronauts have simulated sex from a pill when they traveled. I thought it was a brilliant idea, but I didn't think technology had reached a point to where

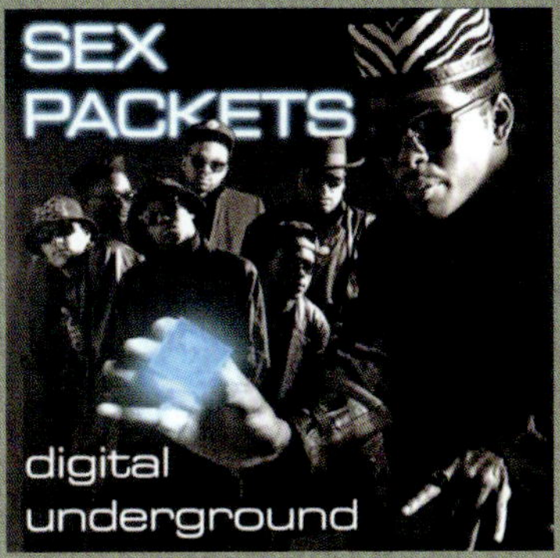

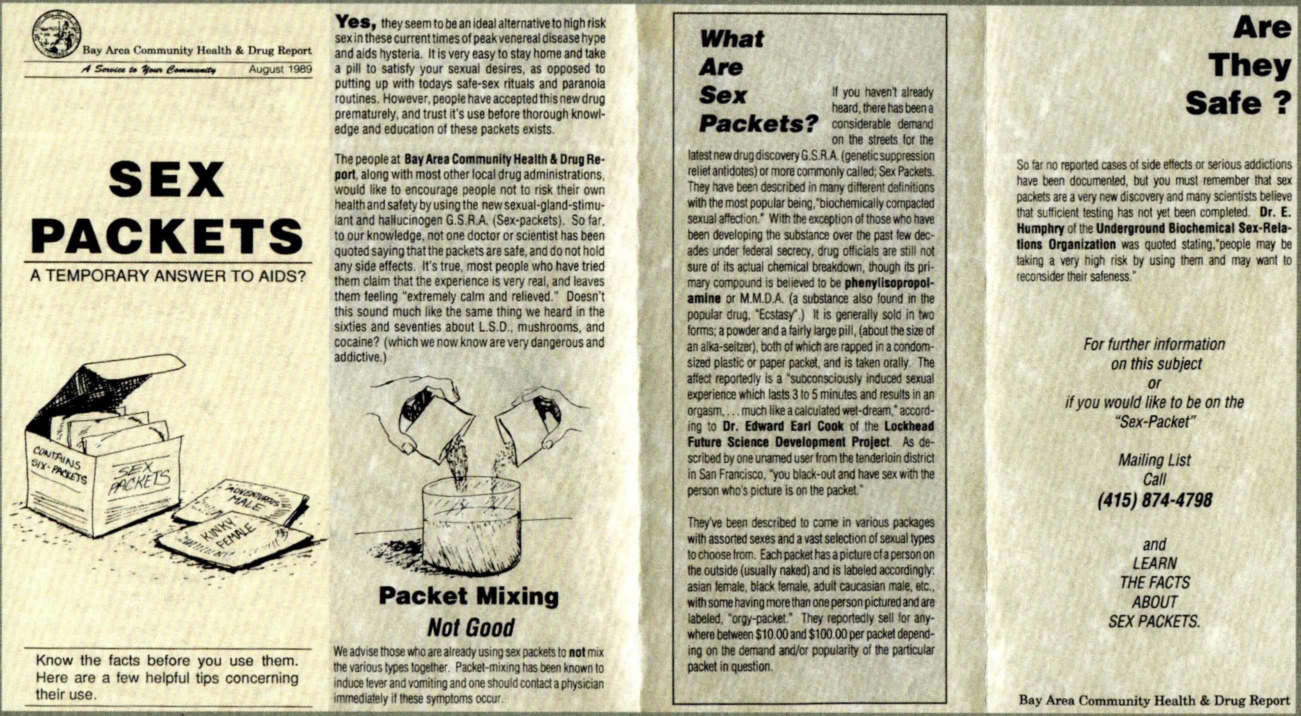

Bay Area Community Health & Drug Report

A Service to Your Community August 1989

SEX PACKETS

A TEMPORARY ANSWER TO AIDS?

Know the facts before you use them. Here are a few helpful tips concerning their use.

Yes, they seem to be an ideal alternative to high risk sex in these current times of peak venereal disease hype and aids hysteria. It is very easy to stay home and take a pill to satisfy your sexual desires, as opposed to putting up with todays safe-sex rituals and paranoia routines. However, people have accepted this new drug prematurely, and trust it's use before thorough knowledge and education of these packets exists.

The people at **Bay Area Community Health & Drug Report**, along with most other local drug administrations, would like to encourage people not to risk their own health and safety by using the new sexual-gland-stimulant and hallucinogen G.S.R.A. (Sex-packets). So far, to our knowledge, not one doctor or scientist has been quoted saying that the packets are safe, and do not hold any side effects. It's true, most people who have tried them claim that the experience is very real, and leaves them feeling "extremely calm and relieved." Doesn't this sound much like the same thing we heard in the sixties and seventies about L.S.D., mushrooms, and cocaine? (which we now know are very dangerous and addictive.)

Packet Mixing

Not Good

We advise those who are already using sex packets to **not** mix the various types together. Packet-mixing has been known to induce fever and vomiting and one should contact a physician immediately if these symptoms occur.

What Are Sex Packets?

If you haven't already heard, there has been a considerable demand on the streets for the latest new drug discovery G.S.R.A. (genetic suppression relief antidotes) or more commonly called; Sex Packets. They have been described in many different definitions with the most popular being, "biochemically compacted sexual affection." With the exception of those who have been developing the substance over the past few decades under federal secrecy, drug officials are still not sure of its actual chemical breakdown, though its primary compound is believed to be **phenylisopropolamine** or M.M.D.A. (a substance also found in the popular drug, "Ecstasy".) It is generally sold in two forms; a powder and a fairly large pill, (about the size of an alka-seltzer), both of which are rapped in a condom-sized plastic or paper packet, and is taken orally. The affect reportedly is a "subconsciously induced sexual experience which lasts 3 to 5 minutes and results in an orgasm, . . . much like a calculated wet-dream," according to **Dr. Edward Earl Cook** of the **Lockhead Future Science Development Project**. As described by one unamed user from the tenderloin district in San Francisco, "you black-out and have sex with the person who's picture is on the packet."

They've been described to come in various packages with assorted sexes and a vast selection of sexual types to choose from. Each packet has a picture of a person on the outside (usually naked) and is labeled accordingly: asian female, black female, adult caucasian male, etc., with some having more than one person pictured and are labeled, "orgy-packet." They reportedly sell for anywhere between \$10.00 and \$100.00 per packet depending on the demand and/or popularity of the particular packet in question.

Are They Safe ?

So far no reported cases of side effects or serious addictions have been documented, but you must remember that sex packets are a very new discovery and many scientists believe that sufficient testing has not yet been completed. **Dr. E. Humphry** of the **Underground Biochemical Sex-Relations Organization** was quoted stating,"people may be taking a very high risk by using them and may want to reconsider their safeness."

For further information
on this subject
or
if you would like to be on the
"Sex-Packet"
Mailing List
Call
(415) 874-4798
and
LEARN
THE FACTS
ABOUT
SEX PACKETS.

Bay Area Community Health & Drug Report

we could induce a dream and allow someone to see whoever they wanted and have sex with them. Acid and ecstasy were close, but it wasn't quite that. As we were putting together the concept of the album, I told him, "You know what though? 'Sex Packets' would make a cold concept for a song. Let me try to flip it."

At the time I was living on Schmoov's couch because my girl had thrown me out. We would sit there recording shit all day and night. He came home from work one day and I had it all figured out. I had him listen to what I put together, I had the hook all the way. He added a line or two to it. About five Long Island iced teas later, we had the song finished melody-wise. We started going over the sex packet concept to make sure people couldn't poke holes in it. We started studying the properties of ecstasy and LSD and what all the jargon was. We created a story where there was a professor at Stanford University who designed sex packets for astronauts' travel so they could be sexually satisfied. The name of it was GSRA, which stood for Genetic Suppression Release Antidote. We said that the powerful drug leaked onto the streets of San Francisco and people started calling it "sex packets" on the street. We didn't stop there, we went to Kinko's and made a serious-looking pamphlet on how to use sex packets because it was dangerous and fucking people up. We made thousands of those pamphlets and left them on the back of buses and at hospitals, all over the place. People started believing that it was a real thing and that our song came after the fact. In response to it. We even had a newspaper article printed up about the dangers of this drug.

After all that it was Tommy Boy's idea to name the entire album after the "Sex Packets" song. The label was all about numbers. They told us, "Statistics show that the word 'sex' attracts the eye ten times

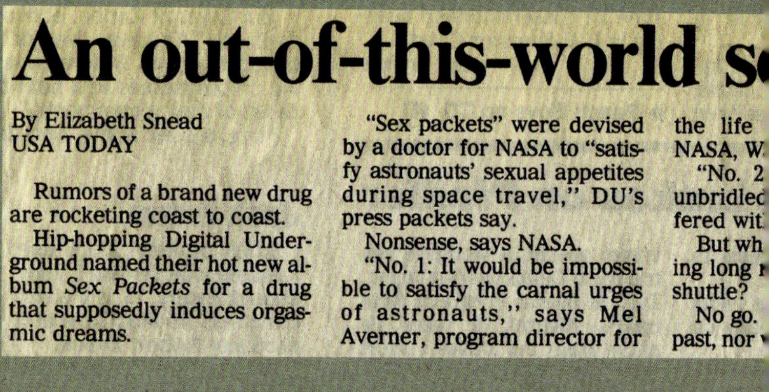

An out-of-this-world s

By Elizabeth Snead
USA TODAY

Rumors of a brand new drug are rocketing coast to coast.

Hip-hopping Digital Underground named their hot new album *Sex Packets* for a drug that supposedly induces orgasmic dreams.

"Sex packets" were devised by a doctor for NASA to "satisfy astronauts' sexual appetites during space travel," DU's press packets say.

Nonsense, says NASA.

"No. 1: It would be impossible to satisfy the carnal urges of astronauts," says Mel Averner, program director for the life
NASA, W

"No. 2
unbridled
fered wit

But wh
ing long
shuttle?

No go.
past, nor

more in record stores." To them, it was just about that shit, but to us it made a great concept to the album. That's what made me write another song called "Packet Man" to help explain the concept of sex packets to people so they wouldn't have to read so much into it. The moment when we knew *Sex Packets* was a hit was after we dropped "The Humpty Dance." We had just finished the album, and the final song was a remix of "Freaks of the Industry." What you hear is not how we originally recorded the song. The album kept getting knocked down because of sample clearances. Diana Ross did not want us using the original beat for "Love Hangover" because her people didn't want to associate their client with the lyrics on "Freaks of the Industry." The second-to-last song we finished was "The Humpty Dance," which was sent out and leaked to radio station DJs and TV channels.

We were still on tour in Europe not knowing that the song was blowing up in the States. We didn't even think it was going to be a hit. Some people in digital underground were like, "I don't know Shock, it's kind of funky sounding, but is that hip hop?" We left for Europe in October and came back in January and shit went crazy while we were out. Suddenly "The Humpty Dance" was all you heard when cars went by; the bass was just crazy. It was one of the biggest dance songs of that year. I remember when we performed "The Humpty Dance" onstage at the Coliseum while we were on tour with Public Enemy and LL Cool J, the whole dome would stand up and rap the entire song with us for all three verses! They knew all of the lyrics and everybody would do "The Humpty Dance." People actually thought Humpty was a real person. This was another time we fooled 'em! We had a Humpty double so that I could be onstage or walking around as Shock G with Humpty in the same room. That even fooled a lot of the people we were on tour with!

That thing with the sex packets. When people found out who I was, they would come up to me and go, "Can you get me the packets?" I was like, "What are you talking about?" I didn't know what that was, I had to go and look it up. I think they thought I was lying. They thought I could get actual sex packets for them, and they would look at me like, "Yeah you can get them, but you're his mom so you're not going to do it. Whatever." I told him, "You know little kids are listening to this too."

—Shirley (Greg's mom)

Actual newspaper article and pamphlet printed and distributed throughout the Bay Area continue the illusion of Sex Packets being a real thing.

drug? It's just a dream

vision of .C. nowledge, ver interssion." e upcomthe space not in the ne future, be working on such a pill," he says. And besides, "The astronauts wouldn't take it."

It seems likely that no one has *ever* taken it.

"I haven't heard anything about Sex Packets," says Joey Davidow, editor of *L.A. Style* magazine. "And with an item that good, someone would have come to me with the information."

Style music editor Robert Lloyd agrees: "If it was true, you'd know somebody by now who had some."

Says Digital Underground's New York spokesman Bill Adler: "You do know it's just a fantasy, don't you?"

OF COURSE the cartoon story was slightly stretched at times, but in fact, Sex Packets were invented back in 1986 by Dr. Edward Earl Cook. They were originally designed for astronauts during long periods of space travel. Tests show that men function better, think clearer, and are more productive when sexually satisfied. So Dr. Cook along with a few colleagues developed the packet so that the U.S. space projects would be superior to other countries. This research was done at a Northern California University.

However, the "packet theory" leaked out and started being manufactured for sale in the streets. At the present time (1989) in the San Francisco Bay Area Sex Packets are as common as prostitution and even becoming more popular as people learn that the packets are far safer than any other form of sex (including masturbation). "'We, The Underground,' actually know people who use them extensively as well as people who deal them. We've dedicated two songs on our current LP to educating the public about Sex Packets. These songs are an actual account of what we saw, researched, and even tried."

Peace,

Greg (Shock G) Jacobs
Edward E. (Humpty Hump) Humphry
Ron (Money B) Brooks
David (Fuse) Elliot
Richard (M.C. Blowfish) Bigman
Neil (Sleuth) Johnson
Jimi (Chopmaster J) Dright

PAGE-3

AMIDST MANY RUMOURS OF HOW IT ALL BEGAN, HERE IS THE REAL STORY BEHIND THE UNDERGROUNDS' DEBUT ALBUM....
SEX-PACKETS
RING
COULD YOU GET THAT FOR ME PLEASE, SUTURA?
JULY 6th 1989 CAIRO, EGYPT
....OR THIS COULD BE DEEP WITHIN THE REALM OF A HIGH-POWERED MULTI-GEOGRAPHICAL ORGY-PACKET.
SHOCK, IT'S MONEY-B CALLING FROM PHILLY. HE SAYS THE DOC WAS KIDNAPPED LAST NITE.
YOU MEAN D.O.C. THE RAPPER?
NO BABY, OF COURSE NOT. HE MEANS DR. COOK WHO DEVELOPS THE SEX PACKETS.
OH SHIT! GIMMIE THE PHONE.
MECCA, COULD'YA COOL IT WIT' THE GRAPES FOR A SECOND?
PHONE BOOTH AT 29th AND BROAD, NORTH PHILLY
YO MONEY, CALL SLEUTH AND TELL HIM TO GATHER-UP THE CREW AND THEN GET A PLANE INTO OAKLAND. I'LL MEET YOU ALL THERE IN THE MORNING.
THE NEXT MORNING IN OAKLAND...
SO WHAT ARE THEIR DEMANDS?
THEY WANT THE PACKET FORMULA WITHIN 24 HOURS OR ELSE THEY'RE GONNA KILL THE DOCTOR.
AIRPORT PARKING
TWA PAN-AM DELTA
DEPARTURE EASTERN GRANIFF
IF WE GIVE THOSE PUNKS THE FORMULA THEY'LL HAVE THE WHOLE COUNTRY STRUNG OUT IN SIX MONTHS.
WE'VE GOT TO THINK OF A WAY OUT!
LOT G
SLEUTH
MEANWHILE...
I'D RATHER DIE THEN TURN OVER SUCH AN IMPORTANT DISCOVERY TO YOU TWO CLOWNS!
OH YEAH? WELL WE JUST MIGHT BEABLE TO ARRANGE THAT, DOC.
LATER THAT NITE, AFTER A LONG ROUND-TABLE MEETING, THE UNDERGROUND DEVISES A PLAN TO RESCUE THE DOCTOR, AND TO WARN THE WORLD OF THE STRONG ADDICTIVENESS OF SEX-PACKETS.
THE UNDERGROUND GETTIN' BUSY
BOWEE!!

OKAY HERE'S THE FORMULA. WERE READY TO MAKE THE TRADE.
NO, DON'T DO IT! IT'S NOT WORTH IT!
WE HAVE NO CHOICE DOC.
OPEN THE BRIEFCASE.
FIRST, MY PARTER HERE IS GONNA TRY SOME OF IT TO MAKE SURE IT'S THE REAL THING.
GULP!
TEST PACKET
OH, YES! OH YES! OH YES BABY IT FEELS GOOD! PLEASE DONT STOP! OH, DON'T STOP BABY! OOOOOH!
LATER, IN THE STUDIO...
FUSE
HOW LONG DO YOU THINK IT WILL TAKE THOSE THUGS TO GET THOSE THINGS ALL OVER THE STREETS?
NOT AS FAST AS IT TAKES US TO LAY THE WHOLE STORY DOWN ON 24-TRACK
...AND WHEN OUR ALBUM HITS THE STREETS, IT WILL EXPOSE THE WHOLE SEX-PACKET OPERATION AND PUT ALL OF THE BOOTLEG PACKET-MEN OUT OF BUSINESS.
WORD. LET'S GET BUSY.
FUS
...SEX PACKETS A DOLLAR OR TWO JUST TELL ME HOW MANY FOR YOU THIS TIME...
IT'S REALLY TOO BAD WE HAD TO GIVE THE FORMULA AWAY TO THOSE TWO SUCKERS EARLIER. SUCH A WASTE!
OH, I ALMOST FORGOT TO TELL YOU GUYS, SHOCK AND I PUT TOGETHER A DUMMY-FORMULA JUST IN CASE SOMETHING LIKE THIS HAPPENED.
HELLA' UNDER
RECORDS
WHAT WE GAVE THEM WAS ONLY ONE-THIRD SEX-PACKET.
OH YEAH? WHAT WAS THE OTHER TWO THIRDS?
POWER LAXATIVE.
...AND IT SHOULD BE HITTIN' THOSE CLOWNS WHERE IT HURTS RIGHT ABOUT NOW!
HA! HA! HA! HA! HA! HA! HA! HA! HA!
FIN.

“The Humpty Dance” is so goofy. It wasn’t even a real dance, it came from a mix of things. Money B’s little brother, my uncle. All I added was the wobbly, “throw-your-hands-up-there’s-an-earthquake” part. When we saw people on *Arsenio Hall* and other rap groups doing “The Humpty Dance” from Scoob & Scrap Lover and Big Daddy Kane to Tone Loc’s dancers, we looked at it like, “Wow, people are treating this like it’s a real dance.”

We ended up going platinum with *Sex Packets*. That was the life. Queen Latifah would tell me that “Sex Packets” was one of her favorite songs and that she had it on her lovemaking R&B tape next to Al B. Sure. I couldn’t believe we had this reaction to an album we put together in two weeks. I was just joking with that shit. It was easy to get caught up with all the success. I thought that would never happen to me. But after *Sex Packets,* I started to go down the same path many artists do, which Monica Lynch warned me about. I was gassed into thinking that I was the sole reason for digital underground’s success.

Monica was hot, by the way. I used to date her best friend. She is the one who called me and said, “You know what, Shock? What if Humpty had his own song?” I was like . . . *Hmmm. I’ll try it!* That Friday the whole group went out as usual and I stayed back like, *No, no, I don’t want to go. I’m working on something.* I rarely said no to going out to the Frisco Palladium. This time I didn’t go and neither did Fuze. He was on headphones working on other equipment. Raw Fusion had their own equipment, so he was working on that. I had my headphones on, working on Jimi’s equipment, which was considered my equipment at that house. I walked around the kitchen and wrote the lyrics for the better part of the day. When I was recording it, there was nobody there but Fuze. I was like, “Fuze, Fuze!” He took the headphones off. “Do me a favor, I need you to say something. Are you ready? Right here, go: ‘The Humpty Dance is your chance to do the hump.’ ” So Fuze is the one who put the backgrounds on it.

I know this sounds like something artists say, but the four-track “The Humpty Dance” and the four-track “I Get Around” on the home cassette, they were brighter. They were more metallic in the cymbals. Something about once we got them in the studio that tape turned all the tin and aluminum-sounding “ting, ting, dings” into wood. It took all the metal out of it. But at first it had a lot of metallic ching. We just couldn’t get that same sound in the studio no matter how hard we tried. But “The Humpty Dance” actually picked up something in the studio and that was that bass drum pushing through the bass line. When you hear that *whoooom whoomp,* there were no drums. The bass overpowered the drums. It wasn’t until Steve Counter, the engineer, was like, “I want to try a few things on the drums” and he put compression limiters on it . . . that’s what makes it punchy. He got it so punchy that even when the bass was gone, suddenly it had drums. That part sounded better in the pro version. But the home version had more cymbal crashes and hi-hats, they were tinier and crisper. Couldn’t get that in the studio version.

So yeah, “The Humpty Dance” was an

afterthought, which explains why there's no picture of Humpty on the cover, right in the photo, because we had already done the photo shoot with Victor Hall. That was his concept. It was all Tommy Boy's idea to name the album after the song "Sex Packets," like I said. We were already starting to come up with some long pretentious names like, *And Then There Was digital underground* or *Allow Us to Introduce the Packet*. I don't know, we just wanted it grand. We had a big long name like that. They were like, nope. *Sex Packets*. We was like, "Okay." Everything was easy. Easy because it was Tommy Boy. We would have fought against it if it was Macola or Virgin or Warner, any company that had all that R&B. But because Tommy Boy had hip hop, it was an honor. We were just happy to have an album out. We thought, they know what they are doing. Somebody said, "Call it *Sex Packets,*" and we were like, "Okay." I think it was Monica Lynch. She used to always bring 'em.

There almost would be no me without Monica Lynch. There was another time, I came to New York and she stopped by the hotel and said, "Shock, I saw this downtown. I don't know if you'll like it, but it reminded me of you." It was that long zebra robe from these pictures, that long weird double-flap thing with the zebra all the way down. I had already taken that picture with the African Kufi with the zebra print, but that is as far as it went. I didn't have any clothes that way. She found that robe in a secondhand shop downtown and bought it thinking of me. I was like, "I love it!" First two tours or so, I was living in that. That became the Shock G robe. Thank you, Monica!

***Sex Packets* was my debut. For any artist your debut is the collection of all of your life experiences until you make that first album. The second album is that next six months of new experiences. There's a lot of people who say, "Man, the first album was really it!" Well, yeah it was. You've been working on your first album your whole life. The second album, there's nothing much new to say, except whatever happened in those few months between the albums.**

"I love that," I say. Jazz plays in the background at Shock's house as it often does. His last words hang in the air. He starts singing a bit, mixing with the background noise. He's making the sounds of the beats, tings, bass, piano. We don't say anything at all for a while. Suddenly I feel like I should be asking questions. I really like what he just said. He's talking about the Sex Packets; I mean is this an interview or not? He appears totally comfortable with the extremely long pause and absence of talk. Eventually he senses my unease.

What? Do you want no music? Different music? Well, I always said I wouldn't do another interview without Spanish guitar under it! C'mon, there's no rush, let's get in the car. I want to show you something.

We don't drive far. He takes me to the top of Topanga Overlook, a tiny park with a view of the entire San Fernando Valley. It's absolutely beautiful, a golden sunset is falling and we are above and away from the city. Rose gold sparkles on the faraway buildings, and the canyon is rich with a burnt-orange reddish hue. A stunning bird's-eye view. We park the car, but we stay in it. I'm wondering why he brought me here, aside from the view. I roll down my window and breathe in that fresh mountain air. I hear his words in my head, "There's no rush." I get it now. I remember something he told me long ago. "You can't push these things," he said. "You planted the seed, watered it, now you have to let it grow. If you keep trying to dig it up to see if it's growing, it will never happen." I reach my arm out the car window to feel the evening breeze. Yep. It will happen when it's supposed to. No rush.

ONE NIGHT, (MID JUNE) I WROTE THIS LETTER TO DEF JAM 4 A SAMPLE CLEARANCE...→ (CONT. NEXT P...)

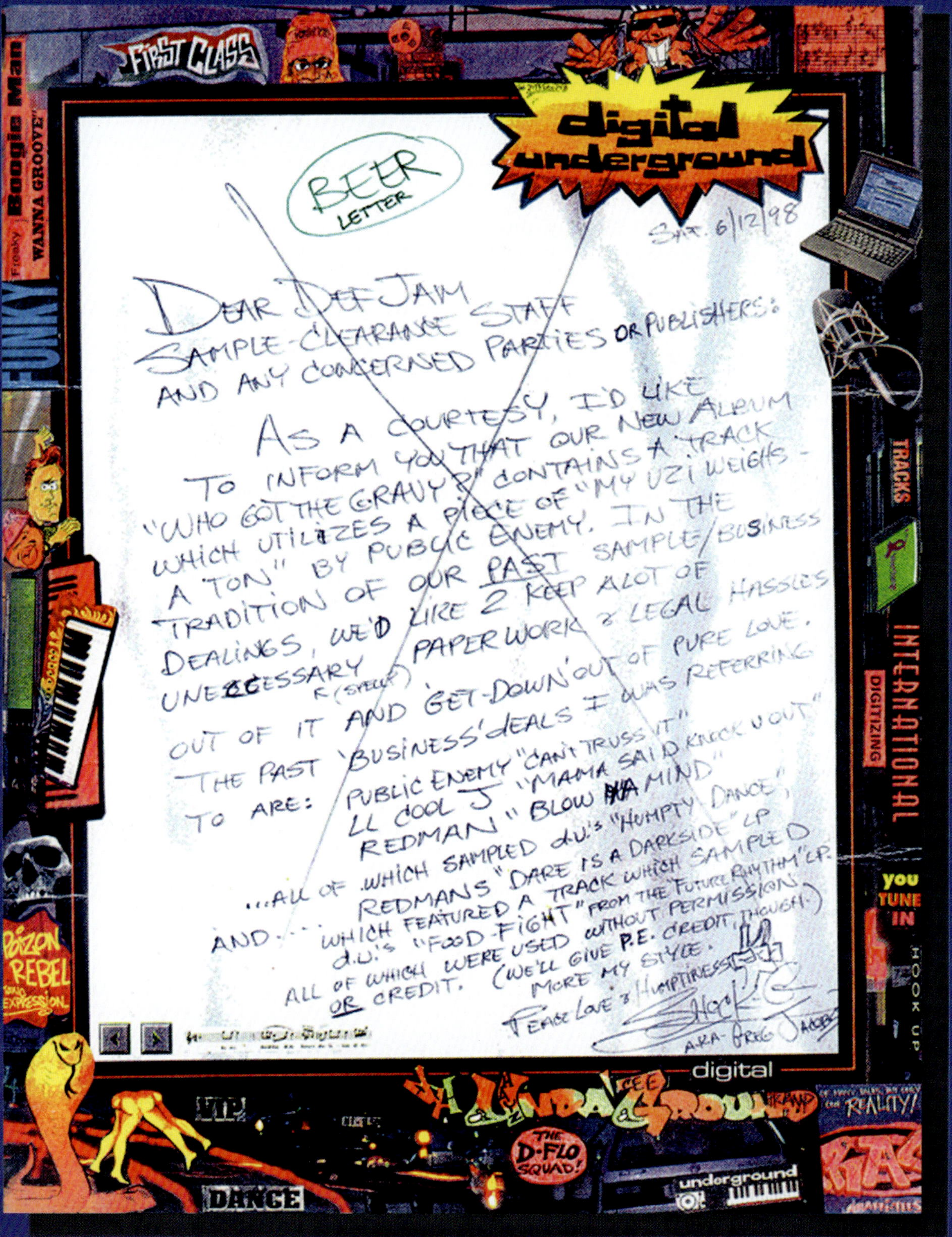

BEER LETTER

SAT. 6/12/98

DEAR DEF JAM
SAMPLE-CLEARANCE STAFF
AND ANY CONCERNED PARTIES OR PUBLISHERS:

AS A COURTESY, I'D LIKE
TO INFORM YOU THAT OUR NEW ALBUM
"WHO GOT THE GRAVY?" CONTAINS A TRACK
WHICH UTILIZES A PIECE OF "MY UZI WEIGHS
A TON" BY PUBLIC ENEMY. IN THE
TRADITION OF OUR PAST SAMPLE/BUSINESS
DEALINGS, WE'D LIKE 2 KEEP ALOT OF
UNECESSARY PAPER WORK & LEGAL HASSLES
(K (SPELL?))
OUT OF IT AND 'GET-DOWN' OUT OF PURE LOVE.

THE PAST 'BUSINESS' DEALS I WAS REFERRING
TO ARE: PUBLIC ENEMY "CAN'T TRUSS IT"
LL COOL J "MAMA SAID KNOCK U OUT"
REDMAN "BLOW YA MIND"
...ALL OF WHICH SAMPLED d.u.'s "HUMPTY DANCE",
AND... REDMAN'S "DARE IS A DARKSIDE" LP
WHICH FEATURED A TRACK WHICH SAMPLED
d.u.'s "FOOD-FIGHT" FROM THE "FUTURE RHYTHM" LP.
ALL OF WHICH WERE USED WITHOUT PERMISSION
OR CREDIT. (WE'LL GIVE P.E. CREDIT, THOUGH.)
MORE MY STYLE.

PEACE LOVE & HUMPTINESS
SHOCK-G
A.K.A. GREG JACOBS

...E NEXT NITE, I'M ROLLIN (X-IN) WIT ANDREA, AND WE READ IT BACK WHILE ...E PEAKIN, AND IT SOUNDS ALL-MEAN & ARROGANT TO US, SO I CROSS IT OUT, ...D RE-WRITE THIS "GENTLER MORE LOVING" WAY. ↓ NEXT DAY I THOUGHT THIS ONE WAS TOO PUSSY AND RE-WROTE IT AGAIN MORE IN THE MIDDLE OF BOTH. (YOU CAN HEAR A BIG DIFFERANCE IN THE ONE OFF "X") WHOLE DIFFERENT TONE!

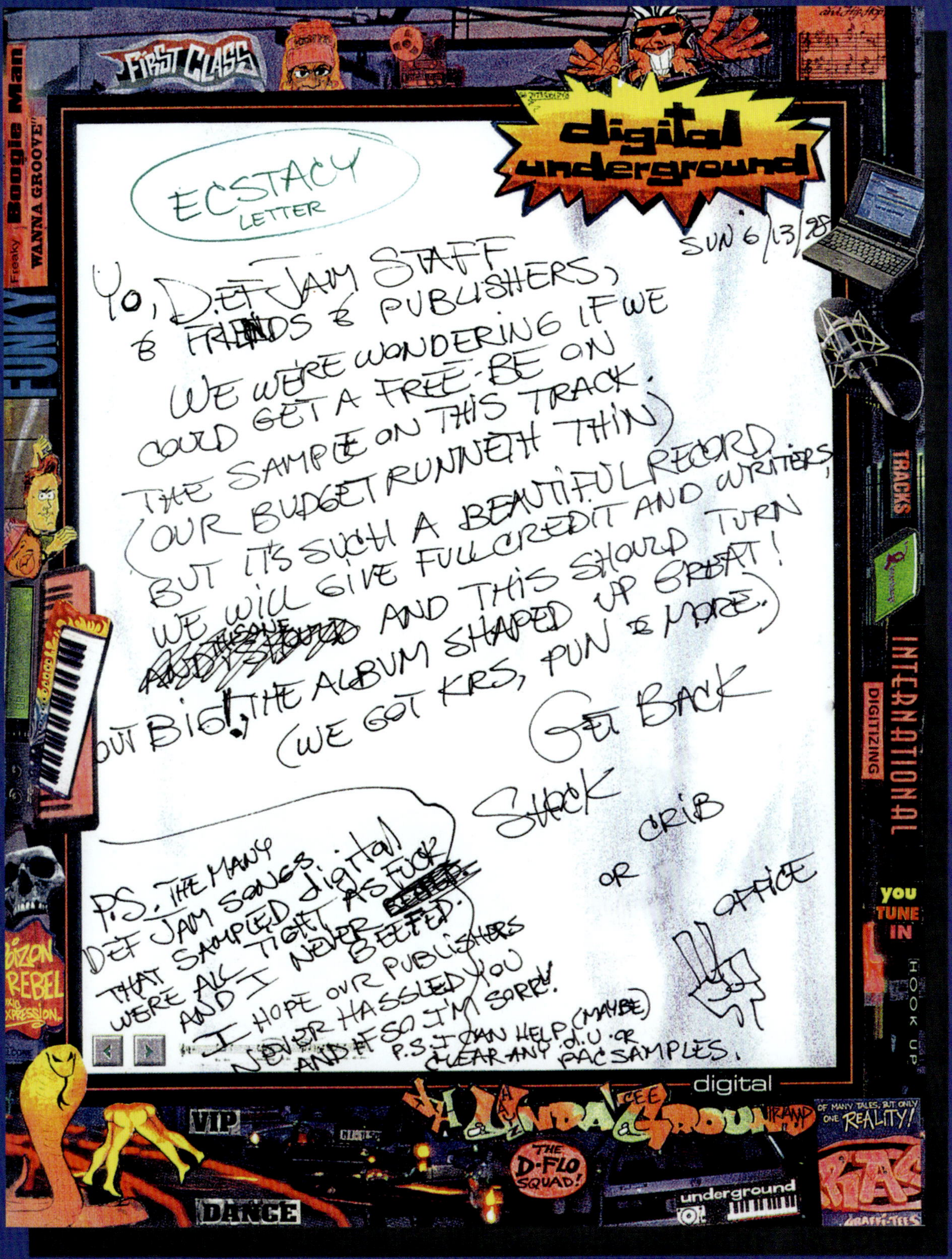

ECSTACY LETTER

SUN 6/13/28

Yo, DEF JAM STAFF
& FRIENDS & PUBLISHERS,

WE WERE WONDERING IF WE COULD GET A FREE-BE ON THE SAMPLE ON THIS TRACK (OUR BUDGET RUNNETH THIN) BUT IT'S SUCH A BEAUTIFUL RECORD WE WILL GIVE FULL CREDIT AND WRITERS, ~~AND THIS SHOULD~~ AND THIS SHOULD TURN OUT BIG!, THE ALBUM SHAPED UP GREAT! (WE GOT KRS, PUN & MORE.)

Get BACK

SHOCK

CRIB OR OFFICE

P.S. THE MANY DEF JAM SONGS THAT SAMPLED digital WERE ALL TIGHT AS FUCK AND I NEVER BEEFED.
I HOPE OUR PUBLISHERS NEVER HASSLED YOU AND IF SO I'M SORRY.
P.S. I CAN HELP (MAYBE) CLEAR ANY D.U. OR PAC SAMPLES.

Tupac and Shock G during an onstage interview at Summer Jam, Mountain View, CA, 1992.

CHAPTER 3: TU
THE REGULAR L

AC AND

FE

August 14, 2011

Maybe it's me with the East Coast time difference and my early morning steps around the house, rummaging through things that has us both up early. Greg's already on the computer, and I stand at the counter looking through memorabilia. He hands me a huge white folder filled at least an inch thick with typed pages. He had started a book in 2006 about Tupac, Walking With Pac, *and those words are printed on the cover. I flip through the folder and look at the writing. I appreciate the significance of Shock handing this work over to me. I set the book down, and ask, "What was Tupac like? In the beginning?"*

Back then he was just another rapper. Now he's not, but back then he was. Tupac, to everybody in digital underground, couldn't do nothing! He couldn't drive a car and wrecked every car he ever had within the first two weeks. In basketball his jumper was so fucked. "Give me the ball man, I'm on the team too!" That was Pac. We would never give him the ball! Whenever we did, he'd take some crazy-ass shot and now we gotta go down the street and try to get that ball. I'm telling you, he missed everything! His jump shot was just as fucked as his Humpty Dance. You should have seen him! He'd jump to the side with his legs up, looking all crazy.

Then there was the part about Pac, where he just wouldn't shut up. He was tough and fly on the mic, but he was always, always getting us into trouble! There were many times when I saw Pac get into a car, and I'd go, "Yeah, I'm going to get in this other car, 'cause I already know that car is going to jail!" I took Pac on because Atron Gregory, our manager at the time, asked me as a favor to take Tupac on tour. He said if we don't give him something, we're going to lose him altogether and he did not want to lose him. See, Pac was signed to our label, TNT Records, which I was a 10 percent owner of. I drew that "bomb" logo for TNT Records as Rackadelic, and I would oversee a little bit of who we signed or not. For that they gave me 10 percent of the label. So, not only did this trip make Tupac digital underground's labelmate, but he's now also on tour with us. When he came with us, we had already done all the songs for *2Pacalypse Now*. The album was done and we were shopping him. He didn't have an album name at the beginning.

TOP: Greg, Kent, and Pac just arrived in Japan, 1989. **BOTTOM:** Pac and Shock perform on tour in Japan: Tokyo and Osaka, 1989–1990.

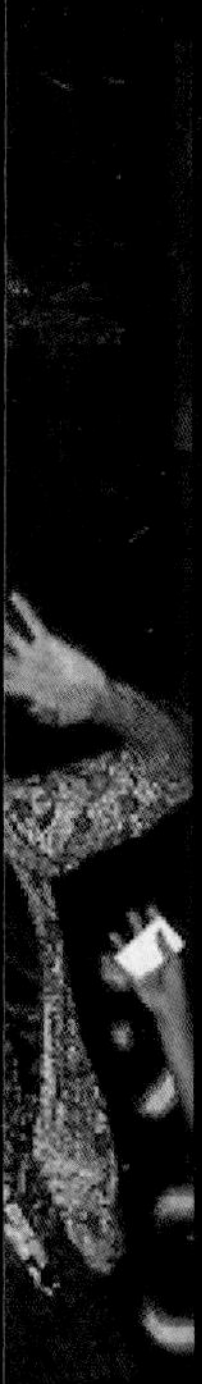

One day, midtour he was like, "Guess what I'm gonna call my album?" He already had all the songs recorded and we were in the last stages of mixing it. We had put together the best four solos on the album that we were giving to Tommy Boy. To me there're two Pacs: the brilliant, open-minded, optimistic Tupac who loved and trusted more than he feared and disgusted, and who set out to change the world for the better. And the psycho, paranoid Pac who cursed out his own heroes and who wrote songs about his gun being the only one he trusted. I didn't know that Tupac. I knew Pac the human being, not the tortured beast the world turned him into.

It took us a while to sign him actually. The record companies felt like politically conscious rap was on a decline. Meanwhile, N.W.A. and the Geto Boys were on the rise. That gangsta stuff was in. Pac wasn't gangsta enough. If you listen to it, his first album wasn't gangsta. It was revolutionary, but it wasn't thugged out. It was more political, so it took us a while to get him a deal. Meanwhile, a year slipped by and that's when, and also why, we took him on tour. I thought Pac was better than anyone else in Oakland. I liked him more than I liked Too $hort, and I liked him more than I liked Hammer. But, to be honest, I didn't like him more than LL, or EPMD, or Slick Rick, or X Clan. A lot of good shit was out right then. I thought Pac was decent, but *2Pacalypse Now,* that's what he sounded like. He had a Chuck D kinda air. That's who he really liked at the time. Then he started liking Ren from N.W.A., and changed his style to start sounding more like him. After that, he started liking Brad Jordan from the Geto Boys and started sounding like him. Brad Jordan is the last person that Pac tried to emulate.

Around '92, Pac became his own person and he didn't sound like nobody but Tupac. By '94, people were trying to sound like Pac. That's when he *became* Tupac. *Me Against the World* is when I really started paying attention and listening like I was the one learning something. Up until then, he wasn't teaching me anything. I felt like, "Yeah, you decent." He was on the level of King Sun. It was cool and political, like Brother J from X Clan. I thought he'd be respected, but I didn't think he'd be like LL or any kind of superstar with what he was putting out. That's how I felt. But right about then, Cube was just breaking out. N.W.A. and Snoop were just starting to shine, and the Geto Boys put out that record, "Mind Playing Tricks on Me." All of a sudden those niggas who spoke that street gutta English were having hits, so Pac suddenly became relevant. With "I Get Around," he killed 'em. But really it was the movie roles in *Juice* and *Poetic Justice* that helped him to get noticed. Without that, record companies were passing on Pac. It wasn't until they saw him in the video for "Same Song" with us and in those movies that they started taking him seriously. "Oh yeah, that's that kid from digital underground," "he's that dancer," everybody used to say, only because they saw him dancing on the videos.

But he wasn't a dancer. Pac was not a dancer. He was an artist. Just like Treach was killing time with Latifah until he could get Naughty By Nature off the ground. Tupac was killing time with us, until he could get his group Thug Life off the ground. I will admit, I didn't think he was this genius rapper at that time. I didn't even go through everything he said and his writing with a microscope until after he died, like a lot of people. I always liked him, and I thought he was good. After "I Get Around," I thought he was better than average. But I didn't recognize his greatness until like the late nineties, to be honest. I thought PeeWee was better than Tupac. I really thought

PeeWee was gonna break loose and kill 'em, but it didn't turn out that way. PeeWee turned out to be this really shy brother, where the more recognition he got, the more famous he got, the more he clammed up. And Tupac, the more recognition he got, the more he opened up. So Pac just kept growing and growing. And the rest of us stayed right where we were at. We didn't really grow. We made more records, but we didn't really grow.

Pac kept adding facets to his personality and challenging himself more and more. The wordplay he was doing, I didn't really notice enough at the beginning. I also didn't take time to notice the things he *wasn't* doing, like he never really bragged about his money or jewelry or cars. He never really talked down or clowned anybody. He was more like, "Why are we acting like this? We should rise up and act like this . . ." He would talk about how tough he was, but he didn't have diss records. He never put another artist down. I'm talking about before he went crazy. From when he got involved with Death Row Records and everything after that, that ain't Pac anymore, that's Makaveli and that don't count. In the beginning, his first albums, it sounded more like he was trying to have a hit album, like everyone else. I didn't know he cared that much. I just thought, *I'm trying the humor angle, and he's trying the Public Enemy, X Clan angle*. We're all just trying to have hits. But if you really look at it, everything he said had meaning in the struggle. Every little song talked about what he was trying to do. Little did I know that Pac was actually crying inside.

Pac and I weren't really tight outside of music. With music we was tight. And chasing girls, we was tight. But when it came to just hanging, if it wasn't full-blown clubs, studio shows, or going to a party, we weren't hanging. If it was just our downtime, home-alone time, helping someone move or go to a movie and shit, we didn't hang like that. He was too wild for me, and I was too organized for him. He felt to me like he was still out there trying to do it. I felt like I'd already done that. I'm going the Martin Luther King way now, let's read and study history and go by the book. He was like, *That shit don't work no more, let's bust in with a .44*. By this time, I am already twenty-five, twenty-six years old. I had already put the guns down. I realized that bringing guns everywhere does not help nothing. He was just getting his guns. Every time we got to a city, I would want to hang out with the older chicks, the cooler lesbian girls in the penthouse doing ecstasy, and Pac would want to run the street with the thug chicks and go see where they're selling drugs in the hood. That was every new city we were in. When you get to be twenty-five or so, you've seen enough of that. I knew we'd end up going to jail or get into some fights with some cats. When you have to protect someone, that is different. But when you talking shit just so people see you the one talking shit? I'm done with all that. Pac didn't know when to turn it off. So that caused us not to be tight back then. He wanted to kick the door in, and I wanted to kick back. He didn't want to slow down to that speed, and I didn't want to run crazy at his speed. So once the party was over, we went our separate ways.

He had that same speed in the studio too. Once he laid a track, he would be done with it. He wouldn't look back. No coming back to fix it up. I'd say, "You can't tell what you're saying right there. You said three words over each other." He'd go, "That was last week." Everyone loved Pac on those records, but they didn't always love the arrangements and the mixing. He wouldn't let us take the time to get it right,

Shock G at the board recording at an Oakland studio with JBeatz Jackson, 2012.

so you could make the whole album sound coherent, so you could just leave it on. You couldn't turn it up, set the bass right, set it once so it sounds good, turn it up loud and leave it on for the whole album. There were songs that if one sounds right, the next one is killing the speakers. You had to run over and turn it down a little. Then if that one sounded good, the next wasn't loud enough. Or the vocals were too loud and the music was too low. He was just from studio to studio and however it wound up, he would leave it that way.

I'm a little bit that way, but I'm a little bit Dre too. Dre is the epitome of the opposite of that. You put a Dre record in and turn it up to what you feel is the perfect bass and everything and have it bumping loud and it holds together for the entire album. Pac's records weren't like that. I strive to be like Dre, but I think I'm more in the middle. I tried to make it match up. That's what Virgos do. We are perfectionists. We're always perfecting little by little finding the next piece of the puzzle, refining who we are, what we're about, trying to get it right. We're not haphazard, and Gemini is haphazard, so you won't find many Gemini, Virgo, long-life all-to-the-end friends that spend every waking hour together because they're going to clash. Pac didn't like to rehearse. He didn't have a show order. What's funny is Pac never went on tour as Tupac. He did a few shows here and there, but he never got his own tour. He never was an act on a lineup of a solid tour. He never got around to that. There's a few live recordings of him doing a one-off show here or there, but he never was in a steady tour with a bunch of cats that might've taught him some consistency; he hated being chained into that. He hated rehearsing and all that shit. I think he thought life was going to catch up to him too quickly to waste time doing all that. He just had to keep running. That's what he believed, and that's what happened. It may have happened because he believed it would.

Not everybody gets to swing at the ball though. That's why I try to do my part to make sure that everybody gets a chance at bat. Now whether you knock it out of the park and make a super home run like Tupac, or you strike out and miss the ball totally like other people I've helped out, that's on you and how ready you are. It's on you to be prepared. But some people never get the chance to even swing at the ball. There are a lot of dope people out there who will never get the chance to make it. They could be working at Walmart right now, or selling drugs or whatever, just sitting on that talent. I'd say that "at bat" is very important. But this is why I don't take credit for it when people say, "You discovered Tupac!" Yeah, well, I also discovered DJ Assassin and Mac Mone. Pac's the one that hit that ball out of the park. But what I did do is let him get that chance at bat. If I deserve credit, it's for giving people a shot. I wouldn't say I have a special eye for talent or nothing.

WALKING WITH PAC

"Hell yeah!" was Tupac's response over the phone from L.A. "Can ya fly down and lay it tomorrow? I wanna do it tomorrow." During the making of *Me Against the World*, I had sent him a tape with three new tracks on it. One became "So Many Tears," another became "Oregano Flow" for digital underground, and the third wasn't ever recorded. Which is why his next statement made no sense: "Yeah, I like the first one and the fourth one." I said, "I only sent three." He said, "No, the fourth one. I wanna use the fourth one." I thought I was losing my mind and brought every MPC disc and all the music scraps I had to L.A. with me. Turns out, after the third beat ran out, and after a good ten seconds of silence, some old throw-away stuff I had taped over popped on, and that was what he liked most. It was the beat that became "Fuck the World" on the *Me Against the World* album—a goofy-ass, Prince-styled remake beat I had tried years ago, inspired by the song "Innocent" by Alexander O'Neil.

OPPOSITE: Tupac's early business card from the d.u. era. **ABOVE:** Shock and Pac in the limo.

Pac was the hottest artist in the game, his new group Thug Life was rising fast, and our past collabs were still getting major play. Seeing him again had me juiced. I just hoped the studio wouldn't be a yack'd-up, smoke-filled nightclub already. Pac's sessions were often packed with dozens of homies, puffin' purp, swiggin' cognac, and wildin' out. Not the best atmosphere to lay coherent music tracks in. Sometimes the hip hop posturing and the pressure to keep it gangsta was so thick around Pac's entourage that I could barely focus on the craft. But before I could slip into too much worry, the juiciness of Southern California washed over me and flooded my senses. As we curved out of LAX in a black Lincoln, L.A. worked its magic. Palm trees, bright cars, that skyline. I relaxed into it, ready to dump tracks, as we used to say.

The studio looked more like a luxury resort than a sound studio. It was a large, gated property that cut into the side of a steep mountain, with two separate two-story buildings divided by a climbing, lopsided parking lot. Huge oaks and pine trees overhung the buildings, creating a hidden-in-the-forest atmosphere. A studio manager led me through the facility to Studio B, where I met the engineer assigned to our session. To my relief, Tupac hadn't arrived yet, which enabled me to get the track sounding presentable before anyone else heard it. Kenya, a really quiet and peaceful brother, had slid in from Sacramento and started setting up his guitar rig with the engineer. Kenya's real particular about his tone, so we had to mic his amps a certain way and tweak the input 'EQs'? to perfection. Right as we were ready to record Kenya's guitar, the door flew open, and Pac and Stretch came bouncin' in, all bright-eyed, loose and casual, like two playful teenagers.

"Shockalock!" yelled Pac with a big smile as we all dapped up. Stretch gave his usual, "What's the deal gawd!?" and extended his signature spread-eagle hand for a loud cracking palm-slap.

"Yo, you remember Kenya?" I asked Pac as they exchanged pounds. Kenya came to L.A. in hopes that Pac would let him put some guitar on it. Pac was down with whatever I wanted to try musically, so after I laid my programmed drums, original bassline, original keyboards, and the Stevie Wonder keyboard and harmonica samples, we rigged up the guitar and plugged it into the board. A brother named Lay Law re-laid a live bass on it, and the group No Face did background vocals with us, but Interscope either lost or decidedly didn't print the credit that we turned in with the final mixes and simply printed "Produced by Shock G" on it, with none of the musicians or interpolation credit. Oooh, I hate when that happens. Glad to finally clear that up here.

Kenya and I were being real respectful of the basic track and were trying not to crowd the arrangement. The line I asked Kenya to play was a straight, simple, long sustained note at the top of every bar, the same note every time, as if it was part of the

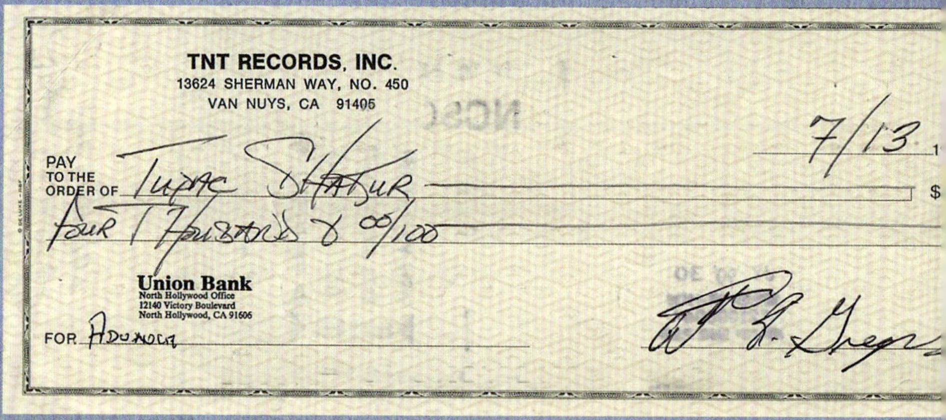

programming—more of a sound effect than a melodic guitar part. (So lame in hindsight.) Then Pac walked over and said, "No, I don't want it to sound high, I want it more active," and freed Kenya to play from his heart, which resulted in those magical guitar riffs on "So Many Tears." Pac meant "not high" as in not laid-back and intoxicated but with more feeling and urgency, like his life was and like the lyrics for that song were. The engineer dropped the beat, and we all instinctively nodded. Pac's face lit up as he recognized the parts of what would become "So Many Tears." That first pro-studio playback can sometimes be a letdown—but this time it hit.

Occasionally, Pac and Stretch would dip outside to puff a cigarette or check on the Cutfather session. His usual MO was to shuttle back and forth between the studios, the pool room, and the liquor store, barging in from time to time: "Is the beat ready yet?" At one point, perhaps during a food break, all six of us wound up bullshittin' and shootin' pool in the greenroom, and as we joked and laughed, I noticed Pac and Stretch's guns were out on one of the countertops. I felt a flicker of insecurity for not carrying anymore, wondering if I should've followed them into that shimmering mirage of gangsterism. But the good vibes took over, and we kept laughing.

When it came time to record, Pac stepped in the booth and laid the entire song, start to finish, three times—no punch-ins, no dubs. Most artists lay one verse at a time, but Pac knocked out all three takes back-to-back, straight from his notebook. Each take was about 70 to 80 percent consistent, a true testament to his skill. Still, there were mismatches in the phrasing, so the engineer and I pulled from all three to build one master vocal. Sometimes we'd lift just a breath or a syllable to keep it fluid. Over four hours of careful editing later, we had a seamless vocal track—pure, uncut Pac.

Pac didn't love his voice—he thought it sounded too boyish—so he usually doubled or tripled it to disguise what he perceived as a thin, youthful voice. Also, weed and cigarettes made him run out of breath, so layering helped ensure no lines got lost. That gave his early work a raw, layered sound fans came to love. However, this left engineers and producers struggling over the decision of which words to feature in those spots where two or three different words landed in the same space. Sometimes these glitches slipped by in the studio because the rest of the song was so hot that nobody noticed or cared. Other times we did notice and purposely left those overlaps in there for the sheer humor and rawness of it. A good example of this happens in "Keep Ya Head Up," when he says, "Ya know what makes me unhappy?" on one track, and then on a second track he says, "What's that?" The two sentences overlap and combine to create: "Ya know what makes me unhaps that." But the song is so lyrically heartfelt and musically appealing in other ways, it didn't even matter, so it was left that way. This time, his voice didn't need backup—it was strong and deep. His "balls had dropped," as we joked. We wanted to showcase it, center stage, with almost no effects.

The engineer and I took pride later in the seamlessness of the final track. It was a grueling process but worth the effort as we all eagerly anticipated hearing the neat-n-clean finished product. We specifically didn't want another "I Get Around" or "Keep Ya Head Up" style multiple-lead vocal this time. Don't get it twisted, we really love those songs too—those are classics and I wouldn't change a thing about either of them. It's just

TNT Records early check to Tupac for an advance payment.

that Tupac's voice was sounding so rich and powerful over the music that night that we wanted to showcase it bold and naked for a change, dead center, and with very little reverb or special effects. And, lucky for us, and for Tupac fans worldwide, it worked—it turned out to be the right touch for that record that year.

When he heard the final mix a few days later, he nodded: "Yeh, they feelin' it. I like it. It's dope." This was high praise coming from Pac. He hardly ever stopped to comment on finished projects or congratulate his producers. Outta sight, outta mind, yesterday's work was yesterday's work, his conversation was always about tomorrow, and his thoughts were usually in the future. But even though Pac's voice was in rare form that day, we still couldn't tell if we had made something great, or if we had accidentally assembled the weird obscure cut (seems like every album ends up with at least one head-scratcher). Either way, we did think it was artsy and we were proud of that aspect of it. Plus, it had a mysterious seductive appeal about it in that we liked it a little more each time we heard it. But trust me, it wasn't a no-brainer that it was gonna win people over as much as it did.

Another example of Tupac's brilliant ear and intuition was that the track originally had a high-pitched keyboard string track looping throughout, similar to the keyboard part in "Thuggish Ruggish Bone" or in the Dre and Cube song "Natural Born Killers." After all the vocals and guitar parts were laid, and on his way out of the session, Pac noticed me at the control board popping the mute button to that track on and off, demo-ing it with or without, trying to see where it fit best. Calmly but with conviction he said to me, "Yeah, I like it better without that," and that was it. His comments about the keyboard and about Kenya's guitar were his only two musical inputs to the session, but they both turned out to be heavy contributions to the finished product. It was little subtle details like these that brought the best out of so many artists who worked with Tupac, and left many of us scratching our heads trying to figure out what was missing on the non-Pac-related productions by the same artists. I myself have been accused by other rappers of giving Pac my best stuff, but in actuality it was Tupac's effortless brilliance bringing it to its highest potential.

The vibe in the studio back then at most Pac or digital underground sessions was upbeat, optimistic, and drenched in camaraderie. Every TNT Records event between '89 and '94, large or small, had the feel of a festive family reunion, which was further enhanced by a shared sense of being on the right team. But this session I could never forget, no matter how many obese Cali blunts we coughed through that night; it got saved in my "best of real life experiences" folder on my Shock G mental desktop.

FIRST SEEDS OF A BANGER

I always wanted to do something with "That Girl" by Stevie Wonder. It has such a unique texture to it, unlike any other song. It created its own fiber. It swings nicely too. But it's mostly the texture I jacked it for, that almost metallic bell sound of the pianos. That crunchy, early-eighties digital, synthetic sound of the drums and handclaps. With that in place I started fooling around over it until I found my own bassline and rhythm, and sprinkled in some drums wherever it helped the pattern move

Tupac and Leila Steinberg in the Bay Area, 1992. Photograph by Kathy Crawford.

but without crowding it too much. I often do the drums last, after I hear how it's trying to move on its own. Usually after you've matched a sample or two with a few new instruments, maybe a chord or a bass line, if you listen closely, it'll already have a ghost drum pattern deep in there trying to come out, and all you have to do is accent that pattern.

"I Get Around" was done like that too. After lining up the Roger Troutman sample and the Gang Starr sample, I played a chord over it, and it rang out so harmoniously that I holla'd out to my empty living room, "Holy shit! This is gonna be a monstah!" I immediately backed everything up on disks, washed my face and hands, turned my phone ringer off, and commenced to figuring it out for the rest of the day, eliminating the weaker pattern combinations, and fine-tuning it to its highest potential.

"So Many Tears" originally had five verses—Pac's four and one from Stretch. But after the NYC Quad Studios shooting, Pac suspected Stretch was connected and told us to cut him from the track. I'll never believe either of them had anything to do with each other's deaths. They loved each other like brothers. They had a falling-out, sure, but it was like a fight with your mom—painful, temporary, never fatal. They were played against each other. I hate what life did to them. It hurts me real bad. They were the best of friends.

PIVOTAL ARRIVALS

The night *Me Against the World* came out (March 14, 1995), Pac was still doing time at Clinton Correctional Facility in Dannemora, in upstate New York. I was in L.A., staying a week with a manager friend of mine named Kevin Hill who lived in Inglewood. Kevin had brought me out to produce his girl group Shay for Babyface's wife Tracy Edmonds's Yab Yum label. We would normally get home from the studio around 1 A.M., and in Inglewood the car systems boom through the neighborhood all night every night of the week. They pass by, trunk-rattling, so often that eventually you don't even notice anymore, it's just part of the normal soundscape.

That night, I stopped Kev, midsentence —"SHHHH! Wait-wait! Listen!" Faintly, through the open window, from about six blocks away, we heard the muffled bassline of "Tears," gradually getting heavier as it got closer. We could tell when the car stopped at a stop sign and then came close enough that we began to hear the drums and the rumble of Pac's voice. It cleared a hill about two blocks away, and suddenly all the highs and mids kicked in for the first time and Pac's words became audible. Those exciting few seconds of mini-concert volume as it entered our block, the crispness of the treble, the night-air reverb as it bounced off all the walls and fences, and that peak vortex sound warp as the pitch bends and the entire song goes down a whole-step right at the crossover point when the car changes from getting closer to getting further away . . .

Usually we talked over these passings, but this time both me and Kevin waited in attentive silence until the last sliver of sound trailed off some seven blocks away. I leapt up from the couch—"Oooh, that was 'So Many Tears,' Kev, that's one of the ones I did for 'im!" Any time a car went by playing Pac it had a ritualistic, almost revolutionary intensity about it, especially that year because he was locked up at the time. But this night it felt like a straight-up religious event, like Malcolm X returning home from Mecca. You could feel Pac's spirit in the L.A. air that night. Half an hour later, another car drove by blasting it. Then another. I stood in the dark, goose bumps rising. I was in disbelief. *This must be the same car drivin' around in circles,* I thought, but I went to the window, and another brotha rode by bumpin' "Tears"! On everything! I swear on EVERYTHING!

I was walkin' around Kev's livin' room in the dark with my fist up to my mouth whisperin' to myself, "Holy shit, nigga, you got the banger on Pac's album AGAIN!" It was twice now, since "I Get Around" on the *Strictly* album. Pac was quickly becoming the most loved, hated, respected, feared, idolized, basically the most popular rapper in the hood—and I was coming to the realization that I was his Bootsy. I always relate my musical life to P-Funk. Before I crashed that night, I counted four cars rockin' Pac out of the total six cars that went by with boomin' systems, and *all four were bumpin'* "So Many Tears." And the album hadn't even been out twenty-four hours yet! It wasn't even the single—"Dear Mama" was the pre-album single. This was so special because unlike "I Get Around" or "The Humpty Dance," we couldn't tell how "Tears" would be received. The song was dark, introspective, experimental. The snares were tiny, and Pac's vocals were so low-key in the delivery. We weren't sure people would get it. But that night I realized the streets had chosen it. To be in L.A. that night, to experience that with my own ears and eyes was priceless. I was totally undercover at Kev's place too, nobody knew I was even in town, much less staying there. Like I said, usually we snuck in around 1 A.M., keeping ourselves on the low. So, personally, it was a strange, rare, and lucky occurrence, a blessing. I got to be a fly on the wall in the hood while "Tears" was getting handpicked in the streets. It was the equivalent of receiving ten Grammys. My younger brother's first reaction to the song had been "Daaaaaamn, he's calmed down a lot." I remember a slight bit of worry coming over me after that, wondering if the fans were gonna embrace that change in Tupac's delivery.

This is why I stood up with goose bumps in the middle of the night in Kev's living room, with one hand over my mouth and the other over my head in disbelief as the third and fourth cars came through bumpin' it back to back like that. They were just lone cats, navigating the night in Lexuses and Hondas, no one to impress, just regular heads in a rough world, absorbing the deeper lyrical side of a dissatisfied humanitarian who had been imprisoned by the world's misunderstanding of what he stood for. It was just too much for this fool in zebra print to wrap his twisted dread-head around.

BIZARRE RIDE FROM THE PHARCYDE

By 1990 hip hop was in a race to claim the last great funk and soul loops before they were all used up. James Brown, George Clinton, and Sly Stone breakbeats had been flipped a thousand times, so when an act found a fresh way to rework a sample—or even skipped samples altogether—it was exciting for both fans and industry insiders alike. Whole new divisions were being born right in front of our eyes, branching into party rap, political rap, Miami bass, gangsta rap, freestyle/cypher hip hop, college rap, backpack rap, Midwest rodeo style, and so on. Southern bounce hadn't formed yet but was on the brink. Suddenly hip hop was no longer just an East Coast game, and artists were sprouting up all over the country like leaves on a ferocious outta-control beanstalk. What's most amazing is, no matter how golden, how silver, how mature that beanstalk gets, it never ceases to catch the industry by surprise. Just when u think every trick in the book has been used, some new kid finds yet another virgin way to flip the script and push the envelope even further.

Bizarre Ride II the Pharcyde was one of those left-field albums that blew our minds. We were in the studio working on "Wussup Wit the Luv" when Saafir barged in, popped in a CD, and hit play on "4 Better or 4 Worse." The intro hit us with the drums and horns, then dropped into an echoey whirlpool of rich keys and vocals. *WOOOAAHW!* I thought, instantly reminded of "Summer Madness" by Kool & the Gang. As a keyboardist, I was mad I hadn't thought of it first. J-Swift's production was fire, and the humor in the lyrics had us cracking up. The line, "You taste so intelligent" was especially funny to us at that time because hip hop was getting so much shit for being misogynistic. This was their way of playing off that. We stopped everything and rocked the whole album right there in the control room. That almost never happened. It was a wild and unexpected ride.

Needless to say, when we later heard that Pharcyde was coming to the Bay Area to do a show at "The Stone" in San Francisco, with our homies APG opening—we knew we had to go. As a group we sometimes went out places in low-key mode, which meant down-low attire, hoodies drawn, no bling, and we'd slip in the back door. Other times we went "full-blown," which meant we pulled up front in our stage outfits, our recognizable video imagery, with personal security, the whole nine. This was usually decided by a myriad of factors that included our mood, our momentary financial status, how much we loved the particular act or the event, the location and venue itself (places that had the "no brothas allowed" tone to their dress code, we'd boycott altogether), how much juice we cared to give them (d.u. juice was valuable back then, our stock was high). And of course, we considered how much publicity was there to be gained by *us* as well (will it look good for d.u. to be there?). The theater sat smack in the middle of the mini-Hollywood or baby Vegas section of Frisco, at Broadway and Kearny, where a three-block clusterfuck of bars, strip clubs, and restaurants existed. It was always lit up with neon lights, peep show booths, and foot traffic, including a constant flow of tourists with cameras out on every corner. It was the perfect place for a flashy digital underground public appearance. Plus the planets had aligned this particular night, 'cause each group member individually had the nightlife itch, and we all agreed to roll out full-blown and make it a big hometown spectacle.

Tupac, raiding my wardrobe, threw on one of my stage wigs. "Lemme rock this tonight," he laughed. "Ha, you look like Rick James, nigga!" He snapped back: "Yeah, okay, Fabio!" I had one on too. Pac and our homie Mac Mone continued raiding my wardrobe, while Nzazi prepared himself for the night. He assessed the various weapons in his special gun closet, clicking and snapping various holsters and ammo clips together before making a final choice and locking the door shut. "They're here, let's go," he announced as he watched Big Money Odis and PeeWee pull up outside my balcony. We all headed downstairs and loaded up for the city. "It's on tanite!!"

Shock, Mun, and Pac perform at the Oakland Coliseum, 1991.

At some point during the concert we met and connected with a clique of girls from the East Bay who invited us to a house party in the Berkeley Hills. I don't know if it was because we were digital underground, or because Pac and I looked like Tupal Sharpton and Shock Geesus Christ in our long wavy doos. We must've looked fun though because big cheeky smiles hijacked the girls' faces every time they looked in our direction. Whatever it was, it was workin' 'cause a house party in the Berkeley Hills was as good as it gets, and it had "Gutfest 92" written all over it. Leaving the Stone, the convoy was Car 1: Schmoov driving his Subaru coupe, with Pac as passenger; Car 2: The four girls in a Honda; Car 3: Big Money Odis driving his Cherokee Jeep with Nzazi in the front passenger seat, and me and PeeWee in the outer back seats with our road manager Sleuth crammed in between us.

A little ways up Pine, Schmoovy and Pac waved us to pull up beside them. They yelled out the window, "Pull over, we're gonna get some liquor." After an unusually long wait, we became restless and began arguing over what to do next. Schmoov's car goes blaring by us at 70 mph *swoosh* with a taxi right behind them. *Swoosh!* "HA! Them niggaz are clownin! Go! Go! Catch 'em!" We tore after them, catching air at every intersection. Thick white smoke filled the street. When we could finally see anything, it was clear that Schmoov's car was wrecked, its engine lying on the road. A smashed SUV was against a building. We saw Schmoov get out and pace up and down, hands on his head. Pac took off running down the hill, cursing at the taxi screeching away. Before we could process what was going on, two white GMC vans pulled in, doors flying open.

"FREEZE! POLICE. GET DOWN ON THE GROUND NOW! NOW! GET DOWN OR I SHOOT! DOWN ON THE GROUND! EVERYBODY!! FACE DOWN ON THE GROUND!! NOW!!" One by one they kneeled into our backs and cuffed us, with all of us yelling different intoxicated versions of "Wait!! I ain't do nothin'! What am I being arrested for? Yo, get the fuck off me! Yo. *Owww*, that's too tight! The handcuffs are too tight! You're making a mistake! We didn't do nothin'!!" Meanwhile, the cops, who were trying to get a handle on the whole mess, were yelling back: "EVERYBODY SHUT THE FUCK UP NOW! I SAID SHUT UP NOW!" The cops were swarmed around us, guns drawn, knees digging into our backs. Pac started yelling the loudest and hardest: "YOU FUCKIN PIGS! YOU FUCKIN RACIST PIGS! YOU BITCH-ASS COWARDS!! YOU THINK YOU TOUGH JUST 'CAUSE YOU GOT A GUN AND A BADGE? FUCK YOU!! YOU PIECE-A-SHIT RACIST DEVILS! ALWAYS FUCKIN WIT US JUST 'CAUSE WE BLACK! FUCK YOU, YOU FUCKIN'." With each word they got madder and madder, and pressed harder with their boots on the back of our necks, until I felt the bones in my neck start to creak. I looked Pac straight in the eye and yelled with all my might: "PAC! SHUT THE FUCK UP! NOW, OR THEY'RE GONNA KILL US!" But he couldn't stop. As I lay there with my cheek against the cold asphalt, and the heavy twisting boot against my neck, I had to wonder, *Why was SWAT here for just a car crash?* It didn't make sense.

Turns out, this all started at the liquor shop. Pac and Schmoov got into it with the cashier, who called for security. They were feelin' good and loose with the girls in tow, a house party in the midst, and a few drinks in the system—so they took their time and pondered the possibilities out loud: "Let's get some rum, nigga. Naw, Hennessy . . . No wait, how much is that tequila? Chicks like tequila." Apparently this made the cashier, an older Middle Eastern man, become impatient and uncomfortable, and he said, "Move out of the way please," looking to help other customers. This, of course, angered Pac: "I can't ask how much something is? Yo, why aren't you helping us?" Things escalated and suddenly a backdoor flew open and a trembling, shaking younger man (who was the cashier's twenty-something-year-old son) armed with a baseball bat came running out, yelling "GET OUT OF THE STORE NOW!"

Pac turned to face the young dude and started screamin' at him. "WHAT? YOU COMIN' AT ME WIT A BAT? YO, WE JUST TRYINA BUY SOMETHIN! WE JUST CUSTOMERS, YOU STUPID MUTHAFUCKAS!!" Schmoov ran outside, grabbed a golf putter from the trunk, rushed back in, and accidentally clocked the old man in the head. Then they bolted. A nearby cab driver, who saw them running out of the store, takes off behind them while making a 911 call on his radio, reporting "AN ARMED ROBBERY IN PROGRESS! I'M FOLLOWING THE SUSPECTS NOW!" Thus explaining the two cars blazing past us up Pine Street, and why a SWAT team came crashing down on us like that.

Back at the scene, our bodyguard Nzazi defused things a little. The police listened to Zi because he had already hit it off with them as they were handcuffing us. When they went to handcuff Zi, he offered, "I'm their bodyguard. I'm armed. In my left shoulder harness is a loaded Glockenspiel 9-millimeter hand pistol, safety-on position, and in my right leg holster is a .22 semiautomatic mini-Ruger, also loaded, safety on."

Zi was ex-military and knew the official codes of surrender, so he said the appropriate things and assumed the universally recognized position of nonthreatening surrender. As usual, he earned the cops' respect right away and was the first one they uncuffed and the only one they listened to. "We like this guy here, he knows what he's talkin' about. The rest of you can shut the hell up until we tell you to speak!"

Hours later, the store owner showed up and ID'd Schmoov and PeeWee because he didn't recognize that it was Tupac. They eventually let most of us go. Schmoov got booked for assault and battery, but his lawyer later beat the case because a flaw in the owner's testimony exposed him as a prejudiced man with biased fear toward African Americans. Nzazi did a little time for an unlicensed firearm. He always felt like he took the heat for Pac's wild nights and foolishness. And me? My biggest regret? Never making it to the Berkeley Hills party with those cute chicks. Damn, what a wasted night! For the record, ladies, in case any of you ever read this, *that's* what the disappearing act was all about. I was reeeaaally lookin' forward to that house party! We just had a hell of a detour. My bad.

THIS FLYER ADMITTS TWO
GUYS NEED 3 CHICKS TO ENTER!!!
THIS FLYER ADMITTS TWO
THIS FLYER ADMITTS TWO
TONIGHT!
"CUM" CELEBRATE LIFE WITH US!!
digital underground
mini-FREAK-Nic
LATE-NITE AFTER PARTY
FREAKS AND TRUE FAST-LANED LIBERALS ONLY!!!
ALL MEN MUST BE ACCOMPANIED BY AT LEAST THREE WOMEN!!
HOSTED BY:
DAMOND
(OF d.u. AND THE ELEMENTS)
IOWA STATE UNIVERSITY CAMPUS HOTEL ROOM # 504
PAJAMAS PREFERRED
NUDITY O.K.
FROM MIDNITE TILL DAWN
B.Y.O.C. (BRING YOUR OWN CONDOMS)
OVER-DRESSED WOMEN WILL NOT BE ALLOWED!!
LEAVE YOUR EGO AND DISCIPLINE AT THE DOOR!
IF YOU ARE STUCK IN THE LOBBY CALL ROOM 504 AND WE'LL CUM GET U!
SPECIAL APPEARANCES BY THE FREAKS OF THE INDUSTRY ..."SHOCK-G" AND "MONEY-B"
GUYS NEED AT LEAST 3 CHICKS TO ENTER. (LADIES WELCOME)
THIS FLYER ADMITTS TWO

LEGACY

There's a little grocery store not too far from Greg's place. We head down to stock up on a few necessities. A couple of his neighbors are in the aisles too, and while meeting them, I get a feel for the comfort of this regular life. I can see how he craves it, and why he likes it. They just know him as Greg. "Hey Greg, what's up?" It's so chill. There's no need to impress, entertain, or to be any particular type of persona. Everyone is just living their lives, shopping for groceries. The neighbors invite us to a little hideaway bar later that night, and we agree to meet them.

After a quick meal at the cabin, Greg takes me to Hidden Treasures, this funky little shop in Topanga Canyon, to try on clothes and wigs and things. Everything in the store is extra-funky. Loud colors and funny looks you never thought of. Greg can be ridiculously silly and fun. We try on hats, and glasses, and robes and act out different characters. In the end we wear the same old clothes out that we had on in the grocery store. We head to the bar, where we dance and sing out loud to Prince songs all night. Outside, we smoke bummed cigarettes and come up with outlandish ways to guerrilla-market this book. We make up new backstories for ourselves and others. It's random and kinda childish, but we laugh our asses off!

Later that night, or really it's early the next morning, we find ourselves on the floor of Greg's tiny kitchen, leaning up against the cabinets, still talking. We're on opposite sides of the room, facing each other, flumped on the floor, chatting. Miles Davis plays in the background, and the notes flow in and out of our conversations. Shock pauses when Miles allows for a pause in the track. It guides his own contemplations. The talk is freeform but becomes more focused.

I always wonder if by giving Pac a chance, did we contribute to his death? What if we didn't take him on? Atron said he's going to lose him if we didn't do something with him. Pac was going to take a position on the board of the Black Liberation Army. What if he had done that? Maybe he'd still be living. I'm just saying though, if Pac hadn't gotten into the music business, maybe he'd have lived a little longer. I wish I could have done more. I think I'm helping people. Maybe I make things worse.

I see tears in Greg's eyes. I remind him that digital underground may have also had an opposite effect. It may have calmed Tupac. I tell him you can't pick apart a life like that and look at every little step.

Yeah, I guess there's a lot of what-ifs. It's hard to imagine Pac doing anything calmly and with discipline. Whatever he did, it would still be him. It made him look crazy. You can't live long like that. So it just got to where his insanity took over him. It kind of overshadowed his brilliance. It overshadowed the good deeds that his words were doing because it was like, "Yo! Don't you see, you are also teaching cats how to be nuts." It made him look

so psycho that he had to sometimes tuck it. I remember being like, "What is so poetic about all this?" But, by the same token, he made my smoothness actually look like inaction. Like I was just taking it, a field nigga in comparison.

I see Greg trying to pull himself out of this downward spiral. He wipes his eyes. I see tremendous responsibility in his face. I move from my side of the kitchen and crawl over to where he is. I give him a hug. I sit next to him and remind him that he's not responsible for what others choose to do. It's wild to see Greg this way. He seems so vulnerable. I'm glad he feels comfortable enough to let me see this side of him.

We let the music fill the air, absent of words for now. I notice how I'm more able to let there be quiet space than I was before. I learned that from Greg. I don't have to fill the air with words, this open space no longer feels like an uncomfortable pause. There is a place for free and open space. After some minutes Greg says:

I'd really like to put out a jazz record. Just piano. Maybe enough time has gone by that I could do that now. Honestly, I would love to just play piano in a hotel bar from now on. I think I'd be happy with that.

This makes me think of a time a few years ago, when we were out shopping for Christmas gifts at Westfield Shopping Center in L.A., he stopped at the mall piano and asked me what my favorite Christmas song was. I didn't know it was called "The Christmas Song" so I said, "Chestnuts roasting on an open fire." He was so totally in his element then, just being a person on the keys. He must have played on hundreds of hotel lobby pianos touring with digital underground. I ask, "Did you ever feel like you were stuck in a certain style with digital underground?"

In a way, yeah. Stuck, I don't know. But it was more like we had a moneymaker, which was Shock G, Money B, and Humpty together. Humpty was for sure a moneymaker. You know how some people create albums that

Relaxing and chatting at the hotel on tour, San Francisco, CA, 2008.

have one song where it's slightly different from their main album, but it's pretty much all their same essence? For us it was different. "Kiss you Back" didn't sound nothing like "The Humpty Dance." Even "No Nose Job" sounded different from "The Humpty Dance." I felt that this was another way to put space in our music and to give us that flexible space with our creativity. I didn't really get back into the vibe of "The Humpty Dance" until I did that song with Murs, "Risky Business."

I know the mentality of Humpty. It's not that I *couldn't* get to that. It's just that I wanted to leave some space. Like Miles. Hmm, yeah. Miles used to say all you have to do is follow the rhythm and listen. He will leave a note for a while and give it space. I don't need to get to Humpty all the time. Everyone already knows who Humpty is. Look at all the records we have, as if they are notes in one jazz song. That first Humpty appearance is *Daaa!* The Humpty Dance. I don't get back to that note until I work with Murs with "Risky Business." The mentality of it. It wound up being "Doowutchyalike," "Same Song," "The Humpty Dance," and "No Nose Job." Then, once I felt satisfied, it was "Return of the Crazy One." I thought, *Okay, now I can be crazy again,* after I was able to say what I wanted to say and hit those other notes.

Meli Mel ran up to Money B one time and said, "DAMN. Where's Shock?! Good thing I'm rappin', that's the coldest pimp song ever made! How come he don't do shit like that all the time?" Even George Clinton, who I consider one of my gurus, he used to say, "That's the vibe right there. If you can keep that going." I knew what he meant. If you want to make money, you keep selling what already sold. I knew I could do that. I could turn into a pimp. But I didn't want that to be my legacy. I wasn't raised like that. I don't know what my legacy will be. It won't be apparent until we flash back. Way after my day. I'm up to something, but I don't know what I'm up to. Well, I'm a Taoist. More than anything else. More than I would say I'm a Buddhist. Or an atheist or anything else. I'm a Taoist. And Taoism means there is no main purpose or no big thing. It's more like . . . just be good and that's it. Do your share and be still, whatever happens it will happen because that's the nature of the universe. It's not that something hates you. It's not that something loves you. It's not that you're super talented or super brilliant or chosen or whatever you think you are. And it's not that you're a super outcast or hated or something terrible happens to you. It's the nature of life.

You know, the Tao is like I want to go that way, but that is blocked so I'm going this way. And we'll see. Who summed it up best for me was Fiona Apple, who also didn't do everything to stay pop. She coulda been like Avril Lavigne or Britney and kept cranking it out. But she wanted to do jazz, so she did jazz. I thought I was spinning out of control until I looked up and said, you know, "If I go by what *MTV Cribs* shows, I missed the mark." But if I look at where I live: I don't lock my door. The air is good. I've been here for a while. I'm not running no more. Whatever I was doing led me here. Not Topanga so much, but to a free place. And I have this much space in my life. I've got so much space. People don't bother me. There is no type of girl I can't date. There is no type of girl where people would go—Oh he's trippin! Because I created a life where it's like, yeah, I could date a fat chick, white chick, Black chick . . .

I never had the intention of leaving some sort of legacy or mark with my music. I was just walking around with an idea in my head and I wanted to record it. When I'm at my best, when I'm allowing myself to be at my best, I can be pretty good. But I don't always strive to be at my best. Because that's just not important to me. I'm not one of those people who is like, I need to give 100 percent of myself every minute of every day. I'm not gonna give away my happiness or my freedom just so that I can be the number-one piano player or the number-one rapper. That's gonna take all of my time and energy. And I know my sword is rusty. So I just don't battle. Big deal. I don't give a fuck about battling. That was *real* important to me when I was fifteen years old: "Who? Naw, I'll eat that nigga." Now? I mean, what do I have to prove?

I'm trying to say there are not many things that I give my 100 percent to, other than my care of others. That is something that you can't slack on. I may falter in other people's eyes. But in my eyes I'm holding my people down. Even with our distance. What I am 100 percent on is that people who I care about in my life will always get my best. If they ask a question, I will answer it to the very best of my ability. I'm never fucking with people's heads. To me that is me being my best. Nzazi thought I would carry too many people. But it was entertaining to me too, how people could be so weird. It was comedy to me. And, yeah, maybe a part of me wanted to show them the way. I just thought maybe the stability of being around Fuze, and Zi, and Atron. Us being above it all, I thought it would somehow show them the way.

Yeah, so maybe I have a purpose or maybe not. Maybe I have a legacy. Maybe I do. I just can't see it from where I'm standing. From my viewpoint. I do know that never ever, ever am I able to ignore suffering. I cannot ignore that. Whether it's a puppy or a human being. I don't wish anything bad on the people who torture animals because most of them don't understand the weight of what they are doing. They may cook a pig alive because it's cheaper. Kids, they'll crush a bug or whatever because they don't know better. But adults, we are supposed to know better. It's gonna take another few hundred years before we can understand this as a human race, but it's coming. We are maturing. But there will always be an evil element in the universe. That's the yin and yang.

Fear of a Mixed Planet—artwork in process.

HOLL

WOO

Y-

D

THE FOLLOWING CARTOON IS RATED R
IT CONTAINS: ADULT LANGUAGE
BRIEF ➡ NUDITY
AND IS INTENDED FOR A MATURE AUDIENCE.
READER DISCRECTION IS ADVISED.
STAYIN' BUSY PRODUCTIONS ®
PRESENTS:
JUNE 1996
$5.95 U.S.
$7.95 CANADA
$4.50 AFRICA
50¢ U.K.
$10.95 CLEVELAND
GREG JACOBS AND CRYSTAL SCALES
IN...
SUSPENDED TENSION
HOLLYWOOD
CAPITAL
COKE
RACKADELIC '96
BALLS
SCREENPLAY: SHOCK-G DIRECTED BY.......... SCALES N JACOBS
CASTING BY THE ALLMIGHTY/MOTHER NATURE HERSELF w/ GOD-ALLMIGHTY. CARTOON ILLUSTRATIONS BY RACKADELIC OF d.U.
BASED ON A TRUE STORY. ADOPTED FOR COMICS BY GREG JACOBS.
7F96K35BF
R
RATED.

CHAPTER 4: SHOCK G / GREG JACOBS

August 15, 2011

I wake up to the sound of a keyboard downstairs and open the door to hear Greg trying out a D'Angelo riff. Seconds later, he is bounding up the stairs in a flashy jacket, all the rings and bracelets jangling. This is Shock G. Definitely not Greg. His alter egos are a real thing that creep into his everyday life. He calls out, "You ready? Let's go!" His energy confirms it. This is very much Shock G, or even Humpty. The introspection and vulnerability of the previous night is gone.

"What? Where?" I ask, totally confused. "We're going to Hollywood. C'mon!" He sounds intense. When you go to Hollywood with Shock G, you have to wear the right "fit." Couldn't be any old thing. I style myself with long blue feather earrings and wedge sandals to match the tempo of his loud patched-together pants, a Boondocks shirt, that flashy jacket, and gleaming sunglasses . . . and we head out. His house might not be showy, but his car is. It reminds me of the Batmobile. It doesn't have winged side doors, but it may as well. We fly down the Canyon at lightning speed, and I am reminded of a trip with digital underground to Las Vegas in 2004.

Everything was bigger than life. We had to strut hard through the casinos, and we missed three flights back to L.A. while Shock made a big scene in the hotel pool, throwing money into the air until it was all floating around him. This Hollywood trip doesn't become all that, but we are definitely noticed. People call out lyrics from across the street or say, "Hey, Shock G!" A group of fans ask for photographs with Shock, and he entertains them with anecdotes. We run into Ron Jeremy—yes, that Ron Jeremy—and have smoothies with his sister and her kids. Shock is everywhere at once and speaks so that all the onlookers grasp every word as well. He tells big stories and shines in that L.A. heat. Hours later, back at Greg's place, we settle down with a pile of tofu and broccoli in front of us, for some formal interview time. Far from Hollywood now.

I thought I was holding it down and it wasn't affecting me, but all the attention was getting to my ego. The arrogance slips in and you can't even help it. When I realized that, that's when I moved up into the mountains. I stopped having penthouses, I stopped throwing parties. I stopped letting my house be a crash spot for everybody. I stopped having gold records lining my walls. My dad has them up, but I didn't need to be reminded of all that. I needed to be normal. And that's why I'm in a place like this, you know. I was trying to get off drugs too. Just trying to not drink and party so much. This put me farther from my connects. I wanted to get back in touch with who I was before digital underground.

And the neighbors out here, everybody does something, so they are not impressed. They heard I'm a musician and that's all they know. Most people in Topanga don't even listen to hip hop. They listen to jazz and opera and classical and Ben Harper and Citizen Cope. They listen to organic shit. Two doors down are the rock musicians with the group Tool. Guns N' Roses live on the top of the hill. The lady who rented this property before me used to write for FOX TV. Down the street is the editor of some radio show. They are all entrepreneurs. I was at the grocery store the other day before you came, and they were like, "You just missed Anthony Hopkins." It's nice because you can be a regular guy. I get enough of the other stuff on tour. On tour I *become* Shock G and Humpty Hump. Because those people are really me too. So is the Piano Man and Rackadelic. He's an art head, Rackadelic. He has *Mad* magazines and grew up loving jokes and cartoons, drawing Warner Bros. cartoons and all that. Listen—I've got separate bios for everyone! When I come back from being on tour, I can leave that all behind. And just be Greg. Leave the AKAs at the door! Shock G, Humpty Hump, Rackadelic, the Piano Man, Peanut Hakeem, MC Blowfish—they are not allowed in this house! That way, when I walk in here, I can just breathe.

Drawing those boundaries started to be important to me around '99. I realized I don't really know none of the girls I know. I don't know none of the dudes I know. None of them knew me past digital underground. Nobody I knew from '89 on really knew who I was or what made me tick or even supported who I was. Your friends know what you like and when you're suffering or not. My friends couldn't see if I was suffering or not. They couldn't see if I was happy or unhappy. They would just be like, "Come on, Shock!" I had to be Shock G constantly. Everybody knows that Humpty Hump is a character. But Shock G is a character too! That's me being a b-boy. That's me being an emcee. But what about just me? You know? "Greg, Kent, come on in and eat!" you know? That's who I really am. "Greg Jacobs, keyboards, can I help you?" That's who I really am too. "Take your brother to the store, he needs shoes," and me being like, "Okay. Well, come on let's go," you know?

That became important to me when I looked up and saw that I was becoming one of these Hollywood, pill-popping, coke-snorting, just like long-hair-fake-tit-girlfriend-having-Ferrari-driving-too-fast dudes. Everything I did, I had to do it big and loud. I had to ask, "Where is this heading?" I didn't want to lose who I was because who I was enabled me to create all this in the first place. It enabled me to create Shock G

Shock G and Humpty Hump for *Elemental Magazine* cover, issue 62. Photograph by B+. 2005.

WORT 89.9 FM welcomes
DIGITAL UNDERGROUND
with
RAW FUSION
and
GOLD MONEY
WEDNESDAY
APRIL 1 7:30 PM
in association with
STAR
Students Against Racism
BARRYMORE THEATRE
2090 ATWOOD • 241-2345
tickets available at the exclusive co. (state st. & high p
centre), star liquor, green earth (next to barrymore)

and Humpty Hump. I wanted to still be able to create. Creating is where it's at. Not living it, *creating* it. That's the funnest part. My favorite place to be is connecting the dreamer who just wants to do it to the record company and then watch them do it. After that, it's like peace, you don't owe me nothing. Have a fun career. People ask me, "Why you doing beats for all these unknowns?" Well, because I'm trying to get them *there.* Because that's the greatest feeling in the world. When I looked up to see people happy doing their dream or getting closer to their dream. When something happens for them and they become stars, like in the case of the Hughes Brothers, or Tupac, or Mystic getting nominated for a Grammy. That's the best feeling in the world.

OPPOSITE: A flyer for a d.u. concert with Raw Fusion and Gold Money, 1992.
THIS PAGE: Shock tries a guitar bit during a recording session for Murs, Brooklyn, NY, 2012.

When I read an interview and they say, "The first time I ever was on a real drum machine was when Shock G let me come over and showed me how to work an MPC." *Those* kinds of things make you feel fulfilled. More fulfilling is the look in someone's eyes the first time they are backstage. Or the first time I give them some stage. More than if it was every day I run with Lil Wayne and Drake. I know what they are doing, I did it too. I know what Snoop's life is like. I don't need to have more money and be on the top of the charts all the time. To be able to spark it, to help someone else to do their thing, that's a great feeling. There are a lot of people we don't get credit for. The Luniz. Some of their first big audience stage times were with us. For some people all they need is a little behind-the-scenes to see.

Shock G is just a regular dude. All he does is see what the song needs. "Right here it's missing something. Put something there." I feel like anyone who is halfway decent can make hit records. You got to have the skill. Get your skills straight first. But then, it's a lot about the opportunities you have. Also, you got to be a likable person. An asshole can have a minute of fame. But sooner or later it's gonna get you. Whether it's a police shootout or you're getting locked up or your girlfriend burning your house down, or who knows. You can't thrive as an asshole for too long. Every successful person, people like 'em. Whether you're a shoe salesman or you own Macy's or whatever.

You know what I'm the most proud of? It's that I get respect in my field, but I can walk the streets. I get respect in my field, but I don't need security everywhere I go. I like that too. And somehow I wound up having a really famous alter ego that I can use to my benefit. Like Humpty is just my puppet. I can pull him out when I need him or want him, but I don't have to be him 24/7. That's the difference, like Tupac or Too $hort, they can't take that face off. It's burned into them. It's too famous already. Fame is a cage, more than it's a freedom. The more famous you get, the smaller the world gets. The less places you can go, the fewer people you can date. I still have that wide open world.

There were years where it was very hard to put the nose on. Tupac was the first person to give Shock G a chance. When he did "I Get Around" and he wanted me and Mun on it, I showed up ready to write as Humpty. But he was like, "Naw, I want Shock G." [Tupac's first manager and mentor] Leila Steinberg told me, "That's because he wanted you: the person he knew, the person he trusted on the album. Not some character." But up until Tupac let me do that in '93, anytime from '89 to '93, anytime I guested on somebody's album it was, "Yeah, let me get Humpty." So I stopped assuming that Shock G would ever do anything besides digital underground. I fought to have space on digital underground records and that was my only outlet for Shock G. Tupac was like, "I don't want this to be funny, I want this to be real." From there, the Luniz asked me to do "I Got 5 On It." Once those two records existed, I came with my own creation, "Kiss You Back," which was me forcing Shock G on people. We were hot coming off of two hot Humpty records. "The Humpty Dance," "Doowutchyalike," and "Same Song" all three had Humpty. Now the DJs were like whatever we give them, they gonna play because we were hot. I did "Kiss You Back" purposefully with no Humpty in it. That was my way of getting Shock G on. But still it was within the gates of digital underground. Outside of digital underground, nobody was asking for Shock G, until then. I was frustrated. I thought, *If I die, especially if I have a heart attack on stage with the nose on, the casket or the tombstone is gonna say Humpty Hump!* I thought they are gonna bury me with the nose on. Like, "Wait, wait! Nooooooo! There's more to me than that!"

Humpty was fun, though. One time, at Green Acres Mall in Long Island, New York, me and Flavor Flav turned that mall upside down. We just walked through it. Me as full-on Humpty—fur coats and everything. Security walking with us. HP (Humpty Patrol) with the hats and jackets, digital underground entourage with us. And Flavor Flav with all his clocks and the yellow outfit and the whole nine. We were like, "Let's walk through this mall one time." This was like '91. Man! When we started, it was like fifteen people in our little entourage. That walk pulled everybody out of every store and made it a parade. By the time we got to the other side of the mall, two or three hundred people walked out with us. We just drained, emptied, that mall! Like, dragnetted it. Just walking and talking with a loud Humpty voice. People taking pictures, walking with us, the whole nine. Then we jumped in Flav's van and went and got arrested right away. I forget why, I think we had drinks with us. We went as a whole crew and bailed Flav out because he was the driver. He had a cool van with disco lights and all that in it.

Can you picture it? It's '91. Flavor Flav and Humpty Hump, full blown with an entourage walking through the mall with a parade of people. It looked like a Dr. King March. The more we walked, the more people just fell in. I'm telling you, we drained that mall! Right at prime time. Pulled it all out into the parking lot. Said goodbye to everybody, took pictures with everybody, got in the van and left. That shit was crazy. The police department has pictures of that day actually. I think it was Green Acres in Long Island. But, yeah, the police department has the mug shots. All the staff came out from behind the glass and took pictures with us. I kept the nose, glasses, the fur coat and everything on that whole time, just to keep it popping. I had the jewelry and the ties. Yeah, that shit was fun!

Portrait by photographer Victor Hall, for Tommy Boy Records, 1990.

CHAPTE
HUMPTY

5

August 16, 2011

Shock has to mail an old-school leather digital underground jacket, so we head out to FedEx. While we are there, two big guys walk up to him. Fans. "Hey, it's Humpty! The one who put the satin in your panties." Do they realize how awkward that sounds? Shock is kind. He takes pictures with them, signs a hat. A trip that could have taken five minutes takes more like an hour. As we walk away, he says he doesn't mind at all, but he worries that the jacket may get lost.

My relationship with Humpty was as if he existed. If I put the clothes on and everything and got in the mirror and looked at myself, it was just a different energy. My uncle Tony Red was kind of how I used to think when I was doing Humpty. But yeah, my relationship with Humpty is like Bruce Wayne and Batman or like Clark Kent and Superman, Shock G is Bruce Wayne. Everybody knows me, but everybody doesn't know I'm Humpty. So if this looks like a job for Batman . . . "Excuse me, I got to go!" Well, it was kind of that for the first five years. I'll show up at the party as Shock G sometimes, but right about twenty minutes before it was time for me to go onstage, it would be like, "Excuse me . . ." and I'd slip out and go find Humpty and everybody would be like, "Yo! That other dude just showed up with the nose! Hey, where did Shock go?"

Nobody would seem to notice. Even the people at the record company. Tom knew, Monica knew, Laura Hines [the publicist], Rod Houston, and a few other people. Rod was there once when I was changing clothes, but really they didn't have time to stop and explain it to everybody. A lot of the staff at Tommy Boy actually thought Humpty was the fifth person in our group. We just kept that going. If they didn't know, we wouldn't tell them. Humpty used to fuck niggas up! One time, Kent was playing Humpty on *Arsenio*. And he is there talking to Eazy-E as Humpty. Eazy doesn't

know it. He thinks he's talking to Shock G as Humpty. Then I walk in and go, "Yo. You seen Zi?" I'm just like, "Hey Hump, look, when we go onstage, I want you to walk out like this and then me and Tupac can go out like this . . ." We could see Eazy-E was *tripping*. We could always notice when people were tripping like that, and we'd act like we didn't notice. We'd stay in character and act normal. Like, "Yeah, yeah, alright, that'll work. Hey. Let me borrow a couple of ties. Like last week when we did those twins." "For sure." Then before they could begin to figure it out, we would walk away. We just left Eazy standing there in a fog because he *knew* I was Humpty. But now he doesn't know anything anymore.

Different people could play Humpty: Kent, Mike Webster, my wife's ex-boyfriend Devin. When I was married to Melissa, her college boyfriend, Devin, would tour with us too, and he looked like me enough to do it. When he put the nose on, you couldn't tell. He had my kind of teeth. So there were like four Humptys total. Me, Mike Webster, Kent, Devin. That shit was fun, man! Who's on first. We had everybody going! They would be on the mic and lip sync. I'd be backstage: "I came for the party to get naughty, get my rocks on, eat popcorn. It's just the same old song . . ." People who saw those kinds of shows will never let nobody tell them we are the same person, because they know my voice and they was like, "That is Shock G for sure." Kent's walking around in a zebra outfit with the mic, and they are like, "That is Humpty for sure." They will take that to the grave! And we weren't going to tell

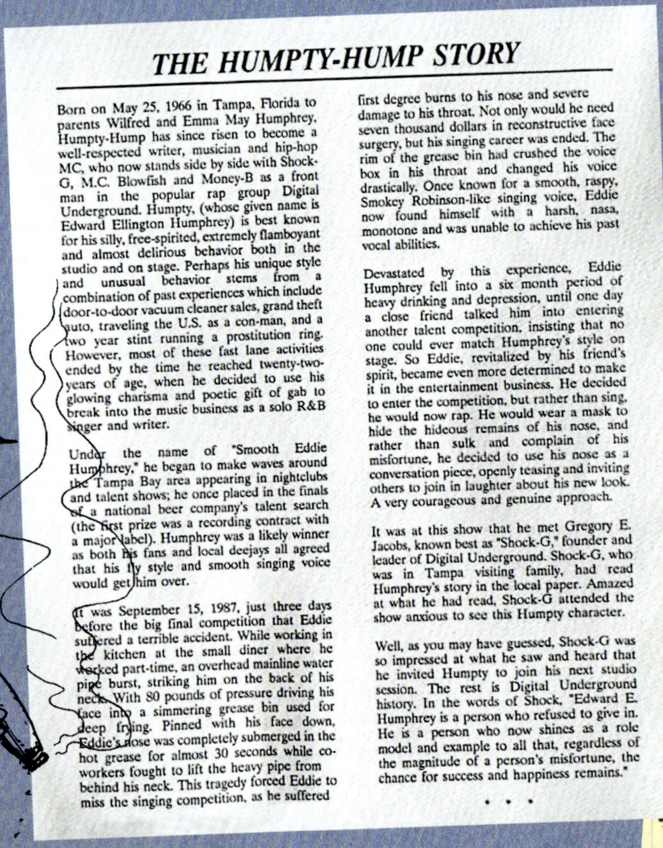

THE HUMPTY-HUMP STORY

Born on May 25, 1966 in Tampa, Florida to parents Wilfred and Emma May Humphrey, Humpty-Hump has since risen to become a well-respected writer, musician and hip-hop MC, who now stands side by side with Shock-G, M.C. Blowfish and Money-B as a front man in the popular rap group Digital Underground. Humpty, (whose given name is Edward Ellington Humphrey) is best known for his silly, free-spirited, extremely flamboyant and almost delirious behavior both in the studio and on stage. Perhaps his unique style and unusual behavior stems from a combination of past experiences which include door-to-door vacuum cleaner sales, grand theft auto, traveling the U.S. as a con-man, and a two year stint running a prostitution ring. However, most of these fast lane activities ended by the time he reached twenty-two-years of age, when he decided to use his glowing charisma and poetic gift of gab to break into the music business as a solo R&B singer and writer.

Under the name of "Smooth Eddie Humphrey," he began to make waves around the Tampa Bay area appearing in nightclubs and talent shows; he once placed in the finals of a national beer company's talent search (the first prize was a recording contract with a major label). Humphrey was a likely winner as both his fans and local deejays all agreed that his fly style and smooth singing voice would get him over.

It was September 15, 1987, just three days before the big final competition that Eddie suffered a terrible accident. While working in the kitchen at the small diner where he worked part-time, an overhead mainline water pipe burst, striking him on the back of his neck. With 80 pounds of pressure driving his face into a simmering grease bin used for deep frying. Pinned with his face down, Eddie's nose was completely submerged in the hot grease for almost 30 seconds while co-workers fought to lift the heavy pipe from behind his neck. This tragedy forced Eddie to miss the singing competition, as he suffered first degree burns to his nose and severe damage to his throat. Not only would he need seven thousand dollars in reconstructive face surgery, but his singing career was ended. The rim of the grease bin had crushed the voice box in his throat and changed his voice drastically. Once known for a smooth, raspy, Smokey Robinson-like singing voice, Eddie now found himself with a harsh, nasa, monotone and was unable to achieve his past vocal abilities.

Devastated by this experience, Eddie Humphrey fell into a six month period of heavy drinking and depression, until one day a close friend talked him into entering another talent competition, insisting that no one could ever match Humphrey's style on stage. So Eddie, revitalized by his friend's spirit, became even more determined to make it in the entertainment business. He decided to enter the competition, but rather than sing, he would now rap. He would wear a mask to hide the hideous remains of his nose, and rather than sulk and complain of his misfortune, he decided to use his nose as a conversation piece, openly teasing and inviting others to join in laughter about his new look. A very courageous and genuine approach.

It was at this show that he met Gregory E. Jacobs, known best as "Shock-G," founder and leader of Digital Underground. Shock-G, who was in Tampa visiting family, had read Humphrey's story in the local paper. Amazed at what he had read, Shock-G attended the show anxious to see this Humpty character.

Well, as you may have guessed, Shock-G was so impressed at what he saw and heard that he invited Humpty to join his next studio session. The rest is Digital Underground history. In the words of Shock, "Edward E. Humphrey is a person who refused to give in. He is a person who now shines as a role model and example to all that, regardless of the magnitude of a person's misfortune, the chance for success and happiness remains."

• • •

them. "That's what you think. He's got you fooled!" A friend of mine said he argued with his uncle all night, and he said, "There is no way I could tell my uncle that you was Hump because y'all fucked him up at that show! Fucked his head up!"

I didn't always have a good relationship with Humpty, though. I felt like he was taking over. There are only so many times you can hear, "Can you put the nose on?" There were times where girls on tour wanted to be with Humpty and not me. It's hard not to feel a certain type of way about that. There was one time where we were a featured guest on a sitcom, *Drexell's Class*. After filming we all had girls with us, the actresses from the show. Everybody had a girl. The one who came with me was real pretty. Just when it starts to get all touchy-feely, she looks right at me and says, "Wait! Put the nose on!" I thought she was messing with me, but she was dead serious. I had to get up and go put the nose on for her, and I could see that her whole body language changed. I had to have sex with her as Humpty.

That was the worst. Everybody was laughing too hard the next day, they was like, "Man! Humpty fucked one of your chicks, man!" I did not think it was funny. I shouldn't have told them. To me, Humpty was just a cartoon. You know like, before the real movie comes on, the Warner Bros. cartoons are just the warm-up. There are always those people who just like the cartoons. If your attention span is quick and short, and you kind of got American pop culture energy, the cartoons will do you better than the actual film. But the film should rightfully come after the cartoon. Humpty is the cartoon, for sure.

Humpty is my toy. He's my plaything. Humpty is my imaginary friend, and if I kill him in two albums, I realized it won't be as fun anymore. Something changed for me in '08 or sometime around then. Maybe it's because I stopped drinking so much. After being a bit more sober, I had more time to sit and think. I was reading a lot of books, positivity books. I realized that you can really fix any type of situation. Rather than sulk or dwell on the fact that things aren't working out for you, there is almost always a way to make it work for everyone involved. You'd be surprised. If you sit and meditate on it, there's always, always a way. And you can have some fun with it too. It's that stillness. If you are quiet long enough, the answer will fall right into your lap. So I did that. With Humpty, I meditated on it and I realized, *Why am I fighting this?* It's actually incredible. I got Humpty Hump at my disposal. I can do anything with him, whatever I want. I am the only one who has him like that. He can rap about whatever, stand for whatever. He's my hype guy, but he will do whatever I want, any time I want. That's pretty incredible. I thought, *Okay, what do I want to do right now?* And it was The Shock G Trio. Perfect. Let Humpty be the special guest who opens for us. That is dope. Humpty can promote us. He hasn't opened for anyone else ever. He's hard enough to find, let alone open up for a group. I don't even need to buy an extra plane ticket for him.

MONEY B:

I always liked Humpty. I think Shock probably gets tired of Humpty because he has to be it all the time. But I never get tired of it. I think it probably got to a point where especially in the heyday with "Humpty Dance" and everything where people only wanted Humpty where Shock would be like, "Wait a minute—I'm Shock G!" But he *had* to be the Humpty character. I know he got tired of it. But for me, I never had to be Humpty, so it was just entertaining to me. I remember Shock saying that Humpty is corny and a clown and he didn't want to have to do that. But I never thought of it like that. I liked Humpty. He still makes me laugh.

One time he actually got stuck as Humpty. He turned into Humpty and couldn't get himself out. We had a show and it was somewhere like whatever state, and we had to do an after-party in New Orleans that night, which was about a three-hour drive from whatever state and city we did the show. It was Shock, but he was being Humpty. Shock's brother Kent was gonna be Shock G, and Fuze and Jimi were there. So we are driving for three hours, and we had drinks in the back of the limo the whole time. After a while we are drunk, and Humpty is all out the moon roof in the limo throwin' shot glasses out onto the street and everything. He is just all out there like, "Aaaahhhh!"

Finally, we get to the event and he starts throwing up everywhere. And it's so much that the throw-up is coming out through the Humpty nose—I'm just sitting there dying, like, oh my god. But he's choking and it's so bad, but I'm laughing because all he had to do was take the nose off but he couldn't do it. He *wouldn't* do it. He was just a mess. He was like heavy breathing, going *heh heh heh . . .* I almost died. I was like, "Dawg, all you had to do was take the nose off!" He's like, "But I'm Humpty, man." By the time we got to the party, they had to drag him out of the limo. Like, his feet were dragging on the ground. I asked him, "Yo, you gonna be able to do this?"

Just then, the back door of the club opened, and I guess they were all waiting for us. So Shock went in. It was a table right there as we walked in, full of glasses, like half-empty glasses. They filled the table. He was like, he said "I'm Humpty Hump!" and he just went *swoosh* and knocked all the glasses down. Smashed all the glasses down on the ground. The crowd went "Aaaaahhh!" You know? They loved it. And so we went in there and he did "The Humpty Dance." He did the first verse like three times. The same verse. The brother couldn't rap his own lyrics. He was stuck. He was just Humpty. He couldn't even try to be Shock G, even onstage.

OPPOSITE: Humpty with Humpty girls, Blue Martini, Tampa, FL, 2012.
RIGHT: Just after Shock G's verse, Humpty hides behind a piano on stage giggling. He is still humored by the whole act. Playboy Suite, Las Vegas, NV, 2008.
BOTTOM: Image of Humpty created by Overton Loyd for an unreleased video for "Bounce 2 This" by George Clinton and Parliament-Funkadelic.

The whole thing was just so funny. I mean, he got it together enough to perform. But he just didn't realize that he could take the nose off and get out of that character. The funniest part is it's like his big fear too. He's got like, I don't know what you'd call it, Humpitis? Humpphobia? Fear of dying as Humpty. Whatever that is. I was going, "What's wrong with you?" But he does really become that character every time he does it. This time he was stuck in it. He became Humpty for real and he didn't know what to do. Humpty is definitely a separate person. There are things that you would only expect Humpty to do, but Shock would never do. It's like when he's Humpty it's okay for him to do it. But when he's Shock, it's not okay. I think eventually, over time, he realized that he can use Humpty to his own benefit.

Humpty Hump at LA Live in Hollywood, CA, 1989.

KENT RACKER:

Humpty was fun! When I would play Humpty at a show or whatever, we would plan it all out so that if he was Humpty and he just walked out of a room, he would tell me what they talked about and who was where, where certain things were in the room, so that I knew everything when I would walk in as Humpty. He'd give me the fit and after I walked in and stayed there a bit, he'd walk in as Shock G. You could tell they were stuck trying to figure it out because you could see them looking back and forth from me to him to me to him. But we would just keep going and act like we don't notice.

CHUCK D:

Shock is a complete introvert/extrovert. He had these dynamic characters that he could kind of hide in. He could become a different character. I thought they were perfectly crafted. They were crafted so well that he would be jealous of his own creation. He would get jealous of Humpty! Sometimes he would come out performing as Shock G, getting down and rhyming and whatever, and then he'd come out as Humpty and there'd be pandemonium in the crowd. When he'd come back out as Shock G, he'd be pissed off with the audience like, "Yo, man, I'm more than the Humpty!"

I would see Shock getting mad at his own creation! It's like you gotta go with it, man. There would be times that Genuine would be dressed as Humpty for fun, and Shock would come out and see him, or Shock's brother Kent would be on tour with us, backstage dressed as Humpty and being kinda quiet but getting some la-la and Shock would go, "Yo! What's up?" You know, "These are my characters!" He had made these characters to fuel his musicality, but he didn't want others to just use them for fun.

One-story-tall giant head used in the music video, "Return of the Crazy One." The head cost $50,000, which to this day is not that funny to Atron. It was used a few other times, but it was too large to use on many stages and even banned from some so as to not upstage the other acts. For years it collected dust in a parking lot, because that was the only place it could live. It matches the spirit of the Parliament Funkadelic influence on Shock and digital underground. Atron gifted it to the Bronx Hip Hop Museum in 2024 (but as of publication, it hasn't yet been moved).

LOS
ANG

ELES

CHAPTER
WAY WE S

S; THE ING

August 17, 2011

Greg and I are both up early to continue projects from the past couple of days. We rummage around his place looking for old tour photos, ticket stubs, and memorabilia. Most was lost in a house fire that was part of the Oakland Hills firestorm of 1991. All of digital underground lived together and stored everything in that house. They lost a lot. We're getting ready to drive to Rialto, east of L.A., to visit Money B for an interview, and so that Greg and his girlfriend can play around in Mun's pool. Money B's place is a bit more like I had originally pictured Shock G's—large, brand-new Cali-looking place with a giant pool in the backyard. Every year they host celebrity pool parties at the end of summer for his birthday.

When we arrive, Mun's longtime girlfriend, Tonia, makes everybody fruity mixed drinks, with their small dog tucked under her arm. Mun and I sit on stools at a tall kitchen table to get ready to tell stories. He has so much to say right off the bat, he's trying to get it all out at once, so some stories overlap or happen like tangents one right after another. Money B is hilarious. He has such a distinct voice (the same voice he raps with onstage), and a great cheeky laugh that is contagious.

The entire time Mun and I are talking, Greg walks back and forth through the glass doors, dripping with the pool water and calling out, "It's all lies! Don't listen to a word he says . . . lies!" But it's like, you brought me here in order to talk to Money B. Eventually we are all sitting together around a little round table, and everyone's memories and conversation mix together over sushi and our fruity drinks.

Mac Mone, Clee, Mun, Shock, and Fuze at Starlight Studios in Richmond, CA. This is where the Sex Packets album was recorded—the group spent numerous hours here, recording for digital underground, Raw Fusion, Tupac, and "clowning in the reception area" as Mun says.

MONEY B:

Studio session with Jimi (Chopmaster J) Dright, Mun, Fuze, and Shock G, 1990.

Okay, I'll tell you what is true . . . We were in Virginia. Virginia Beach. And we all went out to go to this club. But they looked at us and didn't want to let us into the club because Pac had on all these gold chains or whatever, they were making judgments. But while we're standing at the door, we could hear that they were playing "Kiss You Back." Pac was pissed and he says, "Give me my fuckin' record then!" He's like let us in or stop playing our shit. He was outraged that they would stop us at the door and not even know that they were playing our music inside. Eventually they did let us into the club. But by the end of the night people were telling us, "You should go see some real shit. It's in Norfolk." This was like forty-five minutes away, but it was in the hood. Black folks. I think it was myself, Saafir, Tupac, Shock, and I want to say DJ Jay-Z.

So we go to the club in Norfolk. Tupac's walking around. I was just too wasted to do anything, so I fall into a corner and watch everybody. Eventually this one guy goes up to Pac and threatens him. It turned into this whole thing where the whole club including myself spilled out onto the street. But, like I said, I'm barely registering what's going on here. I could see they were passing pistols and all that. I was drunk, so you'll have to ask Shock what he said exactly, but I do remember he said something to kind of ease the pressure. He was like, "Yo, peace everybody. This is what we gon' do." He was trying to be a peacemaker. That's how we got out of there! I was in a daze at the club but when we got back, I remember thinking, *Wow, that could have been real bad.*

But Tupac, of course, was not having it. He couldn't let it lie, he wanted to go get a gun and go back to the spot. On the way back to the hotel, we were all hyped up with him. We were saying, "Yeah, let's all see what we can get and meet at the park in one hour!" But after the long drive, we finally got back to the hotel and we forgot all about it. We got out of the car and we were like, "Alright cool, good night, see you tomorrow." Tupac couldn't believe that. He did not want to let it go. He *couldn't* let it go. He wanted to go and get Nzazi's gun. I think Fuze had a pistol, PeeWee had a gun, and Nzazi had a bunch of guns. So, he goes around asking everybody if he can use their gun. This made everyone at the hotel jump up thinking there's actual present danger. Then he says, "Come on, we gotta go back to Norfolk!" So everyone goes, "Come on, man, get out of here!"

Mun, Shock, and Too Fly Eli backstage at the Red Devil Lounge, San Francisco, CA, 2005.

Oh, this made him even more upset! He was like, "Y'all some punks!" He could not let shit go. He would never ever want anyone to get the best of him, or for anybody to think that somebody got the best of him. He was never deceitful or vicious. Bitter maybe from being attacked so much.

Nobody really ever fucks with us, with digital underground. They're all so busy talking about "The Humpty Dance" and "Oh, my daughter listens to you! Alright, you're good to go. Just drive a little slower, okay?" That's what the cops tell us. Our records don't cause them to worry about us. There is a lot of shit I wanted to say on record. But now, I feel lucky for some of the stuff that I *didn't* say. I never got the chance because I was like, "Well, that doesn't fit our image." I thought, *Next time Pac asks me to rap on something, I'll say it.* But in the end, I'm glad we didn't get too militant, violent, aggressive, rude, thuggish, revengeful, mad, or bitter. I'm just glad all that didn't make it onto any record. "Digital Lover" is one track where we slipped a little something in. It's the one where I was going, "You need a digital lover, digital lover." Then there is one where we say, "You need a nigga to love you." We slipped that one in. It's kinda rude.

The "I Get Around" video shoot was probably the funnest day of my entire life. We had a ball making that video. Everybody had a good time. When we were shooting the video, I remember thinking if this video shows half the fun that we actually had that day, it's going to be good! There were a lot of goings-on at that shoot. Big Syke was there, Shock, Pac. All of the homies were there, and then a hundred-something girls. So how can you not have fun? Even though we were shooting a video, it was really like being at a big pool party—the vibe was great. No drama, we were just having a good time. We shot the video in Malibu so everyone wanted to go out and party at night, but by the time we got back to the hotel after shooting, everyone just passed out. We were all exhausted from the day. I had about eight dates set up for that night, and I was like, "Yeah I'm gon' call you, yeah, I'll call you, yeah, okay, I'll call you." Yeah right, I'll be there. Nope. Nothin'. I was passed out.

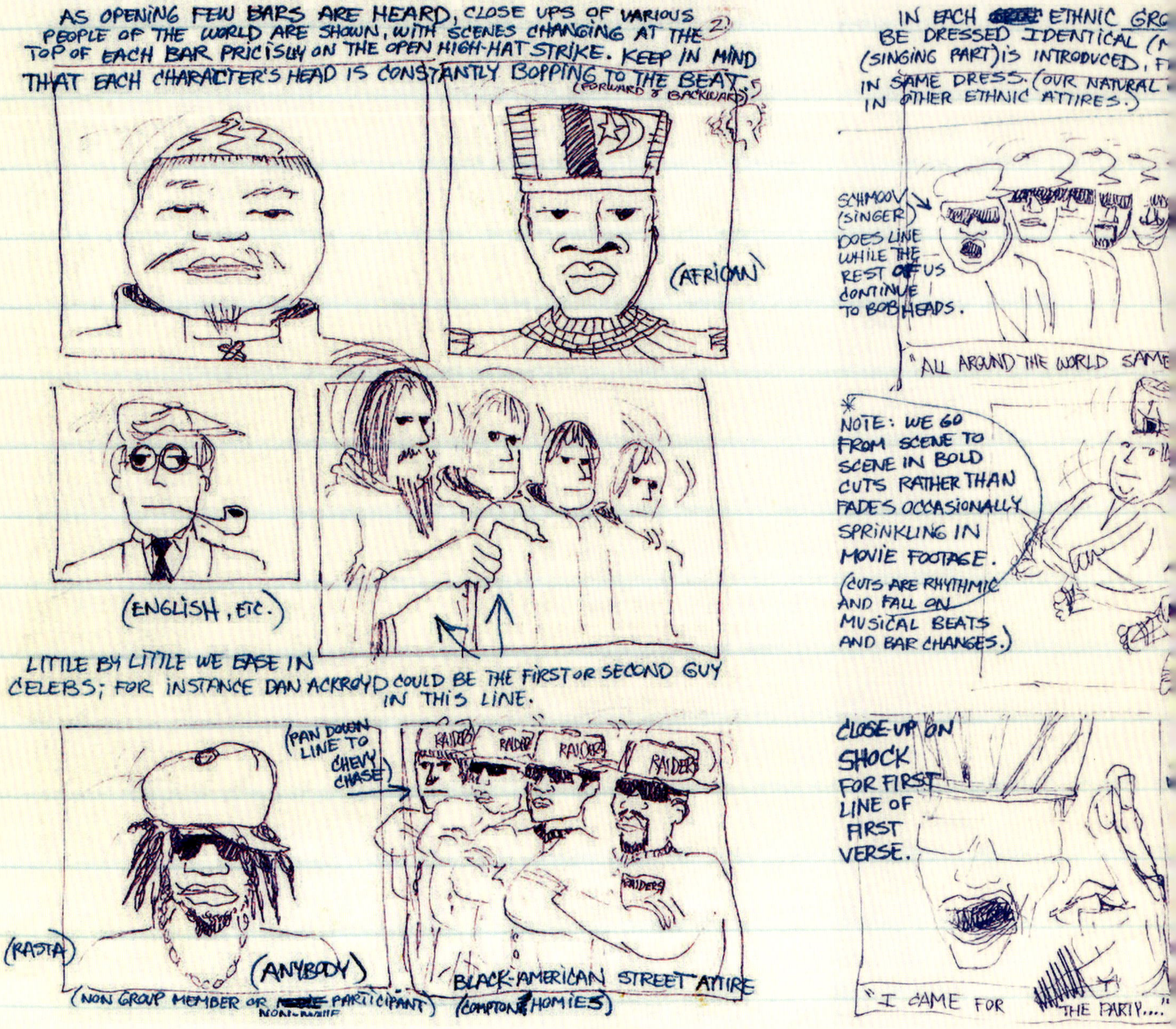

SHOCK:

For me "Doowutchyalike" was ten times more fun and memorable because in addition to the fun that would be fun for anybody—the stuff you see like the pool party, having fun, shooting a video—this was our first video shoot. It was the beginning of our dreams starting to happen. It was a confirmation that our art was being recognized. Even so far by at least one record company. We didn't know how the world would react to it, but at least Tommy Boy feels that we have something, so we had all that going on too. It was the beginning of a career. When we were on the set of "Doowutchyalike," that's when I first realized I had made it. Suddenly all these people were walking around with clipboards and walkie-talkies going, "Shock—where do you want the girls to stand?" I started thinking, *Wow, this is tight,* you know? Sometimes I would cut in and tell them if something didn't look right, but I didn't

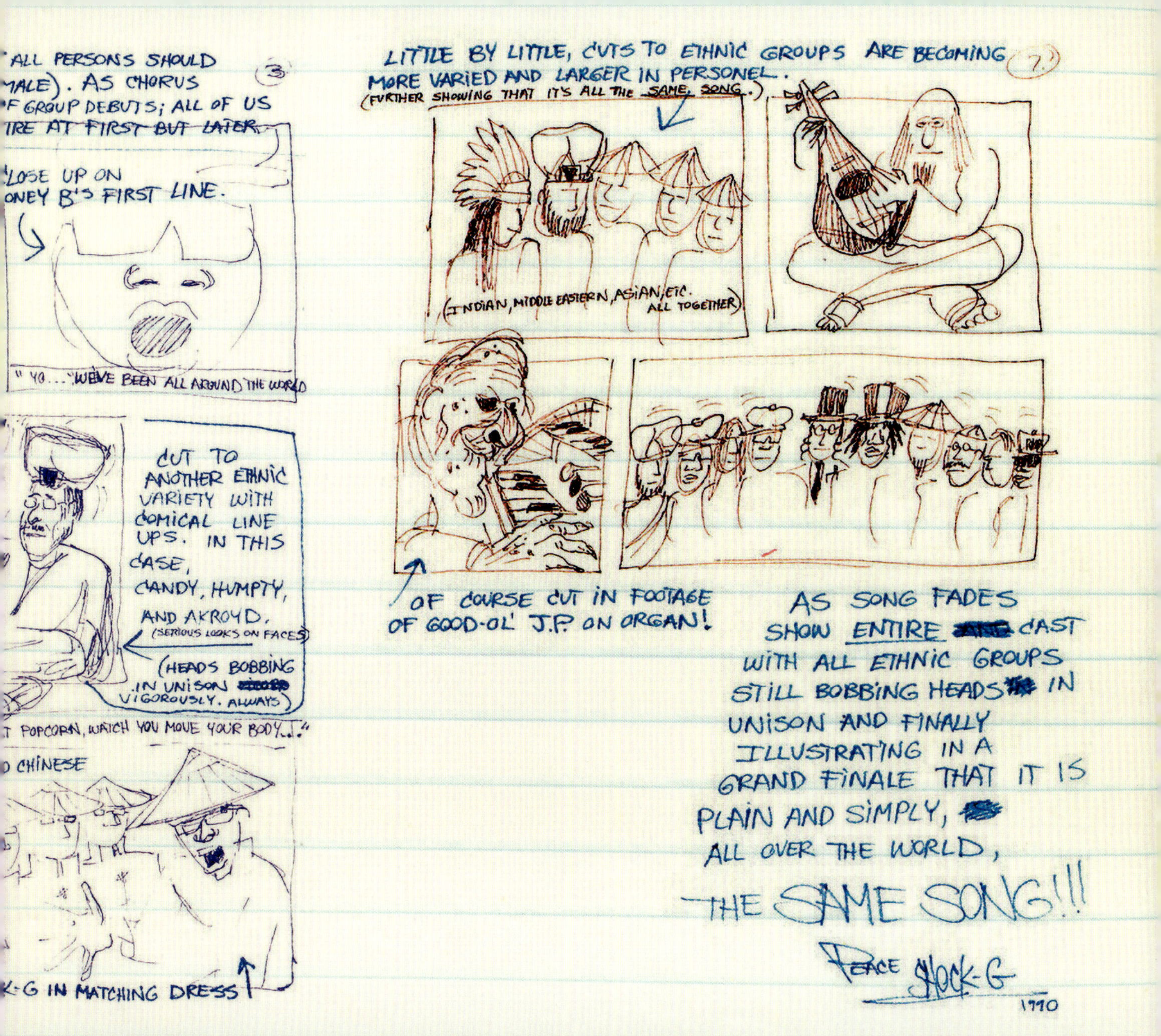

think they would actually take my opinion seriously. I'd say, "If this was a real hip hop party, the DJ would be like this," and they would change everything to make it right. "Alright, tell 'em how you want it."

I didn't want to mess anything up, so I was careful to say things at first, but I soon realized that they really valued what I said. That is when I felt the power of being an artist. I could see that the whole thing revolved around me: all of the equipment, the trucks, the lights, the models, and all of the shit. If I said, "It has to be lit this way," they would light it that way. I think they gave me even a little more jurisdiction because I was the one turning in the storyboards. I would draw everything out myself. Tommy Boy liked the scripts I sent in, so that is what was used. It was strange to see all these white people from the film industry walking around with copies of the drawings that I had sent Tommy Boy going, "Okay, we're gonna get the piano shot now." Looking at my drawings and setting the room up like my drawings! That's the moment when I thought, *This is it!* But I didn't really have time to sit back and gloat over it because we were always moving forward. It was all too fast, and we were always too busy. There wasn't time to appreciate where we were because we were in it, living every moment of it. We just felt like this is it, and for the rest of our lives it will be like this. There was no time to stop. After that, I knew exactly what to do. I always drew everything out and handed it in: This is "The Humpty Dance" video, this is the "Kiss You Back" video, eight pages, every shot already picked out.

"Doowutchyalike" turned out to do okay in the States. It was number 40, or top 100, or something on MTV. We had some love. Tommy and Danny came back from being on tour with En Vogue going, "In South Carolina, man, they playing y'all!" There were a handful of cities around the States that were into us. But not as much as Europe. Europe was really on to us! That's when Tommy Boy came to us and said, "You got a fifty-city tour in Europe: Germany, France, Austria, Finland, Italy, everywhere." We went to Europe on tour with "Doowutchyalike," but we were still just ragtaggin' around. We had our equipment in boxes. We didn't have any money. We weren't famous yet. Then during the time we were overseas, "The Humpty Dance" came out. We had no idea it was doing so well in the States, because in Europe they didn't really like it. Some guy with a nose didn't make sense to them. They loved "Doowutchyalike" because it was socially freeing, but "The Humpty Dance" was just an American-ass hedonistic song to them.

It wasn't until we came home from Europe that we saw something had happened. As soon as we got off the plane in New York, people were running up to us screaming, "That's digital underground, that's digital underground! Can we get your autograph?" It was the first time they were asking us. We were blown away. We used to say we went to Europe as frogs and we came back as princes. By the time we came back, the States were on us! New York was on "The Humpty Dance," the bass coming out of the cars was killing people on the streets.

It was the early nineties, and I took Greg to a mall. I walked in after him, and I saw this huge crowd in the middle of the mall. I thought, *Oh shoot, it's a fight or something.* I was trying to figure out what was going on and looking to see that Gregory was okay. Then I see him right in the middle of everything writing on paper. I said, "Gregory, what are you doing?" He goes, "Ma. This is what I've been trying to tell you. I'm famous."

—Shirley (Greg's mom)

OPPOSITE: *Humpty in Times Square, fooling around, 2014.*
THIS PAGE: *Money B performs in Las Vegas, NV, 2012.*

MONEY B:

The one thing that I think Shock doesn't know is—I mean, we've been doing this since like what? '89? The thing is, I'm still a fan of Shock G. It's funny because sometimes we will be doing a show and I'll just start watching him. And he's crazy! I'll be watching him like, "This is fun!" He entertains me even though I'm supposed to be working. I'm in it, but I'm still there in the audience watching it. He's a great entertainer. Even though I learned from him in terms of being free and open with ways to make my music, I'm probably more of a hip hop dude than he is. I still am a fan of watching his performance. I take from that as well. I'm probably more of a rapper. But as far as performance-wise, I take a lot from his performance and I apply it to the way I do my performance.

I would hope and I think that we are all fans of each other in some aspect: Shock, Fuze, PeeWee. I'm also a fan of PeeWee and Fuze, and I know that Shock is a fan of Fuze and PeeWee. I know that Fuze is a fan of PeeWee, and he appreciates what I do. So I'm assuming there is probably some of that going all the way around. We're all doing things that none of the others can do or can pull off in the same way. None of us can DJ except Fuze. I don't think any of us can play guitar the way PeeWee does. Probably nobody takes the rhyming aspect as seriously as I do. There's no way any of us can be Humpty the way that Humpty does.

Nzazi, Schmoovy Schmoov, Humpty, Chopmaster J, and Money B out driving around in their limo. Note the "Humpty Was Here" sticker on the trunk.

CHAPTER 7: THE DANGER ZONE

August 19, 2011

Over avocado toast Greg and I talk about Nzazi, or Zi, digital underground's longtime friend, security, and road manager.

Zi is the one who got me on the road to vegetarianism. He found me this place too. Becoming a vegetarian was a pretty big shock for me and a feeling of great accomplishment. I feel good about staying out of professional rehab all this time too, self-managing my addictions. But I feel mentally strong for that one. At least when I'm winning. Knock on wood. I still go in and out of phases of cigarettes, partying, and alcohol abuse; it is a difficult balance for me sometimes. For the record it was way harder to stop eating animals than it was to stop any type of substance abuse. There's some form of dead animal in front of you everywhere you turn in this society. It's very hard to take the compassionate path and vow not to eat our evolutionary cousins and homies. I owe a lot of this to Nzazi. You know—he lives down the road actually.

I ask what Nzazi is up to today (meaning, lately), and Shock tells me he has a martial arts studio in L.A. Shock calls Nzazi right then and there. We waste no time and head right out to meet him at his studio. Nzazi is smaller than I imagined, but just as fit. All muscles. He has on a skintight red athletic shirt and talks from the second we walk through the door. He's proud of his accomplishments and shows us medals and honors hanging and framed around the large open-plan studio. I can see that he really cares for Greg. That is immediately evident. Nzazi has seen so much while touring with digital underground and tells one shocking story after the next—drugs, overdoses, guns, close calls. He speaks about tough situations that Shock had to go through and a lot about the trouble Tupac put the group in.

NZAZI:

I got a message on my answering machine from Atron, and he was saying, "Zi, I have a project that I'm involved in and I need your help. I need someone to watch over this group and maybe some security, maybe some management stuff." I have a pretty solid military background and have been involved in martial arts most of my life. He presented me with a proposal and said, "Why don't you come up one night and run the security for a record release party and the management aspects of this event?" I was pretty comfortable with that. I had done government events, corporate security events, I had worked internationally on State Department work and UN work and stuff like that. So, I said, "Well, this is small compared to that." They didn't tell me until later that they expected problems.

I get to the place in the hotel and I meet these guys. My first thought was, *Okay, this thing will never fly. This is the most bizarre group of characters that I've ever encountered.* It was cartoonish. It was just bizarre. I lived in a completely different world. The show was unbelievable. The crowd, the noise, the chaos, the colors, the people. I got to meet the group. That's where I met Greg. He said, "I've heard a lot about you. Thanks for working with me." Very polite, very well mannered. He seemed to have come from a very good home upbringing. Just a really well-presented person. The other guys were basically the stereotype guys, feral people, *Lord of the Flies*-type people. And they're just wild and out to party.

Greg eventually got into the groove too, he became one of them. I saw that other part come out. It wasn't until the show began that I started hearing rumors about the 33rd Street Vagrants versus the Main Street Gremlins or something. They were having some sort of problem with each other because somebody stole a CD or tape from somebody's mother. I thought, *I can deal with this.* I've handled people before, kind of corralling them around. And then all hell broke loose. One of the Gremlins versus whoever it was, whatever—there was a fight. And I went into . . . Well, let's just say I responded in a professional way. I did my thing and I kept them safe and there were shootings and this and that. It was something out of an action movie, and we settled it all down and got them back to the hotel. That was the beginning of my relationship with digital underground. I got in the car, I drove back to L.A., went to work the next day like any other normal day.

Not much later, I got another call from Atron, saying, "We're going on a world tour and I can make it worth your while." And so I said, "Okay." On tour I got to know everybody. Tupac was the roadie at the time. He was really a bizarre kid. I wasn't associated with this type of behavior . . . I felt like if you have the opportunity to travel the world, doing what you love and getting paid quite a lot to do it, that there would be a degree of reverence for that, a degree of humility involved in that, which simply wasn't there. Greg really understood that it was kind of an honor. I think some of the others started out understanding how fortunate they were. And some just didn't get it at all. It was like they won the lottery. They acted like fate shined on them and here they are going all around the world. They took advantage of it and partied.

Nzazi, Kent (as Shock G), Greg (as Humpty), Money B, Mun's brother (Cullen), DJ Fuze, and Chopmaster J, NYC music seminar, 1989.

It was an amazing time because when we traveled to places, there would be fans, throngs of people. You go into a store and people would just give you things. Or people are bringing you their daughters saying, "Just take my daughter, do whatever." It's just very wow. Like: *What are you doing?* It was very out there. It is something that most people can never even comprehend or experience. I remember going into a store with Greg and someone handed me a leather jacket, maybe a $2,000 jacket, saying, "Please wear this." I'm just the dude that makes sure the group gets onstage, and you're just handing me expensive clothing? And you would go to restaurants and people would give you their full meal. It was really strange. It was bizarre. It's something I had never experienced. After some time many of the guys felt entitled to being treated that way. There would be times when people didn't know who the hell they were, and they wouldn't get that same treatment. That would make them outraged.

As time went on, I got into the groove of things. I got to know the guys very well, and I got the feel of everything. My main job was to make sure they got on and off the stage safely, and I kept them to the itinerary. That's it. I was actually doing more of what probably a special ed teacher would do with a group of middle school students. That's what it felt like most of the time that I was involved in corralling this group. I felt like, I'm just getting the kids off the playground from recess.

But it was fun. I have to say it was fun. In hindsight, it was the dream. I mean, for the amount of money that we made for the work we did and then what that afforded you. There were some nights that were just really, really funny. During this time the "Humpty Dance" was really big, you couldn't go anywhere without hearing "Sex Packets," in any city in the world. They were really big and having an impact, not just regionally but globally. It's not thousands of people listening to you, it's tens of millions. It was hard to wrap your brain around.

I remember Greg going through a personal evolution too. He would want to go out after the show and be in the mix of people. He may have a different perspective, but I am supposed to be his protector. So, I'm like, "You have the number-one record in this country, if not the world, you don't have to go outside for anything. You could hire Chef Boyardee himself to come to your hotel room and make you whatever the hell you wanted." We had that kind of thing at our disposal. But he just always wanted to go out, and I'd say, "Okay, this is bull ish. Why do you need to go out? You just did a great show. You got standing ovations, you did that." But again, that's from my perspective. For him, as an artist there's another energy or something he's gathering from that moment.

There were many times I almost quit. They would just make my job so hard. This one time. It's 3 in the morning. We are in some city we know nothing about, and they want to go out to get fried chicken at the corner of Hood Boulevard and Convict Street. You get what I'm saying? We get to the corner of Convict and Hood at Joe's greasy Chicken Shack, and there's of course an assortment of characters. Everybody's there with the ankle bracelets on, being monitored. There's the low-level offenders, there's all these people just hovering around this chicken joint. And, of course, Greg jumps out of a limo with the full Humpty regalia, and everybody turns and says, "Oh, it's Humpty. Wow." Greg is signing autographs and shaking hands. Then Tupac immediately jumps out and darts up and down the street in a frenetic manner, which he would normally do. Just running back and forth, literally just running, back and forth, down the street with his pants hanging low.

I'm watching all this going, *I'm the squarest of square dudes watching this.* And it's just like, *Okay, I'm in hell.* I was completely stoic and just trying to process this information. Another one of them is falling out of the car with an open bottle of liquor still drinking it, and they're all relishing the celebrity. Of course I was there to protect them and make sure they could get on the stage again the next night. I saw Greg doing his thing with his faux mink coat and the medallions and all the gold and the nose and the eyeglasses, and suddenly I see these guys going to their car to get guns. And he's looking over at me like, "Oh, look everybody loves me." But

I can see the people are signaling each other, and they see this guy dripping with all this bling and he's got wads of cash in his hand, visible. He's just throwing hundred-dollar bills at the counter in the chicken place. I had to move around the outer perimeter and set up and get ready. It's like whenever they went out to dinner, I had to think, *I'm going to have to shoot somebody tonight.* I saw the guys getting ready to rob Greg, and I simply walked around the side behind them and I disarmed them quick, put the guns away, and went up to Greg and said, "Your order is done, we need to get the hell out of here. Do you understand?" He's going, "I'm with my people. These are my folks. I got to be right in there with them. I got to keep it real." I said, "Okay. Well, this is when keeping it real doesn't work out so well, alright?" I said, "I just had to put down a couple of armed robbers and it wasn't nice and I need to get you back home before the police show up." Usually Greg at some point would pick up the vibe, and say, "Okay, let's go."

There was a night when we were in, there was some show, possibly Minnesota, and Greg was doing his thing and spinning around with his long coat doing all this sort of stuff. Somebody reached to try and snatch his coat. We had just lost one coat on the red carpet, and I said, "Look, we're losing too many of these coats." They're very expensive—in the range of a thousand-dollars-plus per coat—and that adds up. So, I was onstage posted up and watching over everything, and Greg spins around and this person reaches over and snatches the coat off of him and he almost falls offstage. I shot out, prevented him from falling offstage, pushed him back up, dove into the audience and retrieved his coat. Greg for a minute was shocked because it was all kind of weird. That's a lot to happen so quickly. I wore a kind of a black blazer, what do you call it, a duster? I had all my guns and everything under the duster. I flew into the crowd and this thing opened up with all these weapons in it, and I just dove off the stage, on somebody, and I think I broke someone's arm or something. Felt like slow motion. But I got the coat and hurled it back on stage. Funny thing, Greg never missed a beat. He retrieved the coat, put it back on, and continued to dance. I love it. It was really hilarious, especially now looking back at it. There were so many crazy nights like that.

My relationship with Greg evolved many times through the years. But as far as Greg goes, he was always able to read what was in the best interest of everyone, even if he took it all the way to the edge. I was always trying to corral everybody, and I took a very practical avenue of function. And he saw each individual separate as who they really are. He would make some decisions that were not the best professional decisions, but he rarely made decisions that weren't in the best interest of an individual person. digital underground, they were all really great guys, like decent human beings separately. Collectively, it was a mess.

You know where he got that from? That kindness toward others? I think he got it from my mom, Gloria. My mother always did stuff like that. One Thanksgiving during dinner, a homeless man knocked on the front door and she took him in, sat him down, and fed him. We grew up poor, but she would give you the coat she was wearing in winter if you needed it. Gregory was also always reading. He used to read a lot of Shakespeare when he was young and learn about different types of people. He has always loved learning about people and I think that gave him the care for them.

—Shirley (Greg's mom)

Greg always played this role of being this player but see, he never really was. That's the funny thing about this dude, really he was just a down-to-earth guy. He was the type of dude who would always remember everyone's birthday. He always remembered his mother's birthday, and she would get a card or something from him every year. He would play this role like he was this big ladies' man, like a detached dude, you know? He really wasn't. Even now, he is a hopeless romantic. But it doesn't blend well with this industry. He called me once about this girl Melissa, and it was like this long talk about what she meant to him and what was really important to him in life. Then when they got married, I spoke at the wedding about that. They had this nice wedding on a boat, and that is the part of Greg that I care about the most. He is able to be so openhearted. He was openhearted to her and he needed her so that he could be a good husband. I think, had the world he lived in been more receptive to that, he would still be in that marriage.

Greg called me one day and said, "Ma. I met her." I was like, "Who? Aretha Franklin? Who are you talking about?" He goes, "No, Ma, I met the girl I'm gonna marry." He liked her because she didn't really know who he was. She was totally honest, had a decent family. He liked her a lot. He took one look at her and he was smitten. I still remember how young they looked when they sat at the counter looking at me with doe eyes, saying they wanted to get married. I thought they didn't know what they were getting into. But had it not been for the world he was in, it would have been much easier for them.

—Shirley (Greg's mom)

Portraits of Greg and Melissa (Mel), 1989.

Greg discovered Tupac, and Tupac always had some sort of weird problem acknowledging Greg's role in his life. I remember having a long meeting with Atron about getting rid of Tupac because he was a liability to the group. Greg was the only person who argued with everybody about keeping Tupac in the group as a roadie. That's definitely what made Tupac become who he became. Greg created Tupac. Then Tupac turned around and did not acknowledge Greg at all in the end. Tupac wanted to pretend to be a self-made person. But who he really *was* was this kiss-ass roadie. "I'll do anything. I'll clean toilets just to be on the tour bus with you guys," and he was always in everybody's face. But Greg saw something in him that nobody else did. Nobody could work with Tupac. Maybe it's just that he wasn't mature enough.

People clam around and claim Tupac. But it was really Greg's investment in him. I don't know how many others he invested in, countless others. So many times he wrote for people or stayed up late at night in the studio and supported people and never asked for anything and honestly never got anything back in return. I had a friend going through a really tough time years ago, and Shock came to me with a blank check and said, "All I need is rent money." That's who he is. He carried so many people along his path. Beyond the music and the dancing, that's really who he is.

OAKL

LAND

CHAPTER 8: FA
THE UNDERGROU

DJ Fuze (and son), Shock G, Saafir, Jaybeatz in Oakland, CA, 2011.

ILY OF

D

August 22, 2011

Even though we have been working and busy all morning, there is a heaviness in the air. Greg's pretty quiet. Maybe he's tired of telling stories. Suddenly he looks up and says, "You know who you should talk to? They aren't that far away. Fuze and Saafir. They're out in Oakland. C'mon. Let's go. We could get there by this evening if we go soon." Oakland is miles away, a six-hour drive of flat nothingness. Just straight, flat, barren road for miles.

I think about how digital underground started out in Oakland and how that is miles away from what Greg's life is now. It's figuratively far and actually far. Shock's already getting ready. He says, "You don't need to bring much. We'll find some hotel to crash in when we get there." I see this spontaneity often in him. Most people would take a while to decide if this was really a good idea. They'd ponder it on and off for a few hours, maybe call the people they were going to meet, and ultimately decide it didn't make much sense. Not Shock. He knew instantly that we needed a change of scenery. For him, it's not even really about interviewing them, he's just following his intuition and instinct.

He has his small duffel ready, sunglasses on, and keys in hand. "C'mon. If we leave now, we'll get there by 3!" We are out the door and in the car within the hour. We speed down the cliffs of Topanga Canyon, like it's nothing, in Shock's sleek dark silver Camaro. The windows are all the way down. That warm California breeze that smells like palm trees, ocean, and freedom is rolling right through. Free is something I have felt often when I'm with Shock. Especially in moments like this. We pull onto the 405 and we must be going 100 mph. Normally I would be gripping the handles, but I'm not even worried right now. It's easy to feel invincible around Shock. It's the way he lives his life. We zip in and out of traffic. "We are flying!" I hear myself say. Shock responds with, "This is nothing. I can push her up to 155. You gotta drive this car fast. We can make it to Oakland in two hours if we want to."

I'm not going to tell him to slow down. We talk the entire time as he gracefully weaves in and out of lanes as if the other vehicles were not even there. I'm impressed at how casually he's speaking, zipping down the highway at this speed is nothing to him. He's lost in thought. He's starting to go down memory lane too.

We make it to DJ Fuze's house around 5:30 P.M. His place is nice, not an artsy cabin escape or a mansion, a nice house, painted white. We walk right into a dining room–living area with a wood table in the center of the space. Fuze gives me a tour of his many walls of floor-to-ceiling records, plays some of his new music, and presents us with a beautiful vegetarian meal. I ask him, "What was it like touring with digital underground in the nineties?

DJ FUZE:

Back then there were very few white people in the rap game at all. Like really in it. Today a lot of people like to argue about what hip hop is, but there are so many white people doing it. Back then even breakdancing was mostly Black, or Puerto Rican. Hip hop educated a lot of white people about racism that still exists today in America. So when we were touring, the fact that I was white drew a lot of focus to me that I didn't necessarily want. I had to come up with opinions on things I hadn't even thought about before. I was used to being in the background as a DJ. When we were touring in Europe, people looked at me like I was the head of the group even though I wasn't. They looked at me like I was the creative force and the mastermind of the group because I was white. That's some kind of racism right there. People always came up to me first to ask the questions. They would ask what I thought of Public Enemy, what my role was in hip hop, what it was like to be white in hip hop. That was the first thing that would be asked. They would try to keep that line of questioning going, and I would always have to bring them back around to talking about our group. I would have to tell them that I was not the leader of the group.

DJ Fuze at home with his record collection, Oakland, CA, 2011.

In Europe they were really into an intellectual way of listening to rap compared to a lot of Americans who listen for the political aspect of it. Public Enemy was huge in Europe. I had a lot of conversations with Chuck D. We had a good rapport and so we would stay up talking about politics and the Nation of Islam and just different levels or different ways that white people could fit into hip hop. We'd be stuck in the catering area for hours, just talking. Nzazi was also real close with Public Enemy. I don't know if I would call Nzazi a Black nationalist, but for a long time he was definitely a revolutionary or he had a revolutionary way about him. He still does, but transcending race, his whole life is a revolution. I spent a lot of time on tour talking to Nzazi and Chuck. The tour was like half ass-out crazy partying and half intellectual thought. It was an interesting dynamic on the tour bus. Tupac embodied that whole thing together. Tupac was a super-intellectual person, educated when it comes to politics, Black nationalism, intellectual thought, and he would read John Steinbeck novels, stuff like that. We could talk about that, or we could talk about who is the dopest rap group, or who is the finest chick. It was all over the place. At the time we were not conscious of how dynamic our tour bus was. It was just who we were at that moment.

Fuze comes with us to meet Saafir, and brings along his one-year-old son. Saafir (Reggie Gibson) is an emcee, producer, and actor from Oakland. He made his entrance into hip hop in part by recording and touring with digital underground in 1993. He is a wheelchair user now, and Shock helps him in and out of the car. We stop by a large graffiti mural that says "Underground" because it is too perfect for a photo of these guys. Saafir suffered a spinal injury in 1992 that has progressively become worse through the years. He was a passenger during the intense crash and fire after the aborted takeoff of TWA Flight 843 at JFK International. Shock is constantly telling Saafir that a vegan diet would help. That, and less stress in his life.

After they reminisce, we drop off Fuze and his son, and pull up to our hotel. Shock heads into the room for a bit, and Saafir and I decide to talk in Shock's car. Saafir sits passenger and I sit in the driver's seat. Throughout the conversation he plays samples of his music in the CD deck.

Mac Mone, Fuze, and Money B during filming for the video "Piano Man," which was produced by Shock G and became a big Bay Area hit, 1989.

SAAFIR:

Before I got into hip hop, before I got with digital, I was a full-time bona fide criminal. I was introduced to the streets at age twelve. That's when I got my first taste, in the late eighties. When I came into the game, it was really stunts, blunts, and hip hop. As far as the hip hop movement, I started off as a DJ. My name was DJ Ready-Bo at fourteen years old. I used to go over to this cat named Jo's place. I lived on the border between North and West Oakland. Apgar Street. There was this guy there who is part of a family called the Black Whales. Rest in peace. He just passed away about a month ago. He brought a lot of the neighborhood youngsters together and he started a rap project. Actually he did a couple of them. It was called the APG Crew. That was my first introduction into stepping into organized hip hop. From the streets to that. Before that, I used to sell weed in West Oakland on 24th and Chestnut. Right there on the corner. That's when I first touched down, and I ended up migrating to another place called Ghost Town.

Saafir, Oakland, CA, 2011.

I migrated there, selling weed and doing my little street thing. DJing was more like a hobby at that time. My man Jo lived a few houses down with the DJ setup. He was an older dude. He was mad cool. He used to be like, "Reg, what's good? You want to get down today? I got the tables." And I'd say, "Yeah, well, okay." He'd smoke his weed and be doing his housework, and I'd be over on the turntables with the earphones on. I'd be doing that every day for at least a year until I got really good. I got my cutting hand right, and I'd be cutting and scratching. I really wanted to be a DJ. I was listening to Kurtis Blow, the Breaks, Sugar Hill Gang, of course. There was a record called *Clear.* I forget the band's name. I know it wasn't Kraftwerk. (The group Cybotron and the song sampled a Kraftwerk record.) It was like a pop lock song.

Straight hip hop. Back in the day, in the streets it was distinctive. It was like either you was an entertainer, you was rappin', DJing, breakin', or you was in the streets. At the time I was trying to integrate into everything. Hip hop came from the streets. But what happens is you can't be a superstar and still be *in* the streets. Hip hop pulled me from the streets. Not so far as to make me leave the streets altogether. But it pulled me from dying in the streets. It gave me an out. I didn't really believe I could make it in hip hop until I heard LL Cool J's "I Need a Beat." That was *the* record. Once I heard that, it gave me goose bumps. It made me feel something I had never felt before. I was like, *What the fuck? Why am I feeling like this?* It was like speaking to my soul. I knew from that moment that I was gonna be doing that for the rest of my life. LL Cool J is the reason I am rapping today. He was the hardest thing going at that time. He could really rap. He planted the seed in me, and I took it from there and cultivated it. So when I got with my cousin Mac Mone and he introduced me to digital underground, Money B, then Pac, and then Shock, it was like it was nothing. It was natural. I had already been in it as long as they had been in it. When I connected with them, it just felt natural. I just fell on in.

The variety of musical influences that digital underground came from is what made digital unique. They merged musicianship through hip hop. You got programmed beats along with live drummers. You got the programmed beats and samples along with live keyboard and piano integration. Shock integrated hip hop with musicianship. It was like a live band, and he put together a show, man. He did something that wasn't being done at the time. And he was immortalized for it. As far as I'm concerned. He did something that nobody had done at the time. That makes him a forefather in this hip hop shit. And he has to be respected for that along with Money B too. Money B is right there with him. Really Money B, Shock, Fuze, and Tupac. That was the core. And legends. Legends are made outta that. You know Shock G discovered Tupac. In actuality, Shock G was the founder of a guy who went from regular entertainer, to icon, to legend. If you are in a position where you are discovering legends, you have to be considered a forefather. A pioneer. Just like Dr. Dre is considered a pioneer. Eazy-E discovered Dr. Dre. But Dr. Dre discovered Eazy-E too. Shock G is in there with them. The pioneers of the West Coast. Man, he is a major factor in this shit.

SHOCK:

Saafir would not get comfortable with digital underground. I remember saying, "Man. I'm getting old. Too old to run this shit myself. Why don't you take it over?" And he was like, "What? You passing this to me?" I was like, "Yeah, I might. You lead it. If you want, you lead it. I got it going, but I never thought I would keep it going forever." He was like, "Bud. I don't want to run this. It's too much responsibility. I don't want to lead it wrong." I tried to tell him, he's smart enough, young enough. People look up to him in the group. He did think about it. Tripped on it a bit. But he just said it's too much responsibility. I remember him saying it just like that and I was just, wow.

For me, I wasn't trying to pass it to him because I thought it was too much responsibility. I thought the payoff is lovely if you hang in there. The respect and the money and everything is balanced with the responsibility. I thought he was younger and more hungry and that he would bring in the next three years of good ideas. I brought in enough for us to get through three charting albums, and my thought was if he took it over, he can get us through another three, and we would just keep passing the torch. I thought it's bigger than if we just had separate solo careers. I thought we would Wu-Tang out. Be a super group like Funkadelic. I always pictured that digital underground would be something that was always there, and the main chief would change. I would be one of the main chiefs, but not the only one. I thought, *Let's see what happens when the cream rises to the top.* Maybe it's me, but maybe it's PeeWee or Clee, or Saafir. I don't know. I just thought we needed new writers.

Shock, Fuze, and Clee at the DNA Lounge, San Francisco, CA.

CLEETIS MACK:

I joined digital underground when I was fifteen. I was always around because Money B is my cousin. So, one day we all meet up at this club and Shock is there shooting pool. He turns to me and he's like, "Clee, man, what are you even doing in here? How'd you get in the club?" I said my Uncle Bobby [McCall]. So, then he pulled me aside and we sat down and he goes, "How would you feel about being the new lead rapper for digital underground?" I go: "What took you so long?" That's what I said. But I was extremely happy. Around that same time, Saafir got in the group and I remember asking him how he got in. He said, "Well, Shock asked me, How would I feel to be the new lead rapper for digital underground?" I'm like, "Oh, okay . . . so that's like his pickup line, huh?"

Shock and Clee.

Both of us were on *Body Hat Syndrome*. I remember Shock would call me all the time to apologize for that record. He said, "You deserve more. I wish I had done better for your first album." That's just who he is. Imagine someone doing so much for you and helping you carve out other paths for yourself and then they call to say, "I didn't do enough." I told him, "Whenever you think about me—just only know how much I appreciate you."

He's a one-of-a-kind person. He's the type of artist that people like Sting or Prince would call when they were having writer's block. But you'd never know. He didn't care about the money or any of that. He just cared about making art and helping people.

I remember we would go do a show and he would see homeless people sleeping outside. He'd give them a room and say, "I'm sorry you're all going to have to share the same shower, but you can stay here as long as you need. And he'd give them money. Sometimes I'd watch him give them more than I was making on tour. But that's just who he is. When you're young, you don't understand. But now that I'm older I see how much that changed me and affected me watching him. It became much more than just making music.

Mystic, 4rAx of the Mekanix, George Pye, Jaybeatz Jackson, Numskull of the Luniz, Clee, Dialect, and Fuze (center).

MYSTIC:

Shock is my brother. He put me under his wing when he brought me into digital underground. Who knows where I would be had he not been so present at that time. He saw the light in me when I was still a broken young Black woman. Shock is also a big part of what gave me the courage and freedom to walk away from my record deal to go back to school. But that wasn't really the core of the conversation. It was that I was deciding to go back to school to be of service to children. What struck me about his instant support and excitement was that he, too, had unfulfilled dreams and passions but did not feel he had the freedom to claim them for himself. He wished he could pursue other art forms (drawing and writing, piano playing). But being in the music industry and being successful in it can complicate how we pursue the totality of our dreams. Shock carries a weight of responsibility for others. He could not, in that moment, have the same freedom I was claiming, but was no less thrilled for me. The stage may always be a party at a d.u. show, but life is not. I'm forever grateful for the quiet moments.

Mystic performing on tour.

RAY LUV:

The first day that I met Shock was at this house digital underground had in West Oakland. It looked like all of 'em lived there. Tupac and I were part of a group at the time, "Strictly Dope." It was Pac and I and Mark Dorado (DJ Dizzy). Anyway, Leila Steinberg sent a video of us to Atron Gregory and that's how we ended up going there. Tupac and I went down to the house and they were working on some music for *Sex Packets*. Shock was the first real rock star I ever knew. My grandfather was a big performer back in the day, Cab Calloway, but I only really knew him after—in his seventies or eighties. I can still remember so clearly that day that I met Shock. The TV was on and it was the D.O.C. premiering his new video on Ruthless Records. We all stopped to watch it. Everybody was speechless. I was thinking, *The D.O.C., that's what I want to do, I want to do stuff like that.* So watching that around them and standing there next to Shock, hearing what they were working on for *Sex Packets*, it was unreal. Everything that I wanted to be as a musician, Shock was.

Digital underground was like a godfather in the Bay Area. So when we went to the video shoot for the Humpty Dance, me and Pac, it was one of the most amazing things that I ever saw. Everybody was there, Eazy-E, Sir Mix-a-Lot. And I remember us being young and broke at the time. So when we get there, we go right to perform. I'm telling you, this was one of the biggest moments of my life. I looked over while I'm performing and I see Shock G. I'm like, wow. This is the dude I look up to. The guy who I think is the star of all stars is watching me perform right now. It was amazing. I remember Tupac turned to me and said, "One day, man. I'm gonna be the man! You know what I mean? That will happen to us." After meeting Shock, I decided that I would be doing music for the rest of my life.

After all these many years I look back at that time period as the incubator for my path. That's one thing about Shock is you feel very comfortable to be yourself around him because he is shamelessly himself. He carried a whole group of people on his back. He brought the Ray Luvs and the Tupacs and all the digital underground babies on his back. He really brought us all something. He brought fun back. Right now, today, the world needs a Shock G more than it ever has.

PEEWEE:

Shock is a few years older than me. What really made the vibe is him and Schmoovy Schmoov were some serious funk fans. I mean, those dudes, we'd sit around and have a drink and play a bunch of Parliament, Sun Ra, and just really, really good music. I was, like I said, a few years younger, so I didn't even really drink at the time. So hanging out with them two dudes, it'd be like hanging out with a couple of my uncles, but just really being free, having fun, and cracking up at them dudes. We kind of grew into old men like that. But it's still this big brother, young uncle type vibe.

I got this super-silly, dark sense of humor and Shock and Schmoov, they share the same thing. So there would be a lot of times where we could just take a ride or call each other on the phone and say all of these silly concepts. I mean they would be real-life things, but turned into this silly stuff. I know Shock took one of those silly nights and ran with it. You know how you get sleepy and just start saying anything? So we were sitting up talking about people, and I'm like, "Man, dude's an asshole, and she's an asshole. There's just big fat assholes and skinny assholes and crazy assholes." He ended up making that concept into a full-out comic book. I was like, "I thought we were going to do it together." But, man, one day I go to the house and he's got all these pictures of all these different assholes. I look at it all spread out and fine-tuned and I'm like, "Hey, man, that's some assholes, man."

This one time, we were doing the Humpty Dance, and he gets to that part, "And if you missed it—'Just grab them in the biscuits.'" So we just jamming, and the crowd's going. He gets to that part, and he doesn't say the lyrics. He says, "And if you missed it," and he turns around and shows his ass to the crowd and then turns back around and starts finishing the singing. I'm just like, "Man, this dude blows my mind all the time." People think, "Okay, man, I'm going to get up. I'll learn these moves. I can imitate Humpty, and I can do this and that." I was like, "Nah." First of all, the reason why you can't do it is because he's not acting. Shock is really crazy. I think Greg is when he's purposely trying to be nice, like the little boy, "Get a haircut. Sit down, little boy. Okay, do your schoolwork." That's Greg. Greg gets tired, and then Shock and Humpty and all these other fools just come out, man, with, "Fuck Greg, man!" It's really the doowutchyalike thing.

Crazy as all of that stuff was, one thing I learned from him, and from Schmoovy Schmoov, is how to just live, to just be free. You're not jacking yourself up, but just live. What is it to just . . . I wake up in the morning and I tie my shoes and then I eat my eggs. I sit in my car, and I get to this place. I do these things, and then I go home. I pet my dog. And then I go to sleep. No, man. Let's go. Actually live!

TOP: PeeWee, Shock, and Mun at Tupac's birthday celebration, Yoshi's, San Francisco, CA, 2012. **BOTTOM:** PeeWee, Ray Luv, and Fuze at the same event.

TOPA
CANY

NGA

YON

WHO'S
WHO'S
WHO
WHO'
WHO
WHO
WHO'S
FACE YOUR FEAR...
...OF A MIXED PLANET
CLEA

CHAPTER 9: RACKADELIC

August 24, 2011

It's the day after our Oakland trip and I find myself sitting crisscrossed on Greg's floor surrounded by his artwork. I'm going through his framed work, posters, some finished, some in process. The trunk we bought is still here filled with photos from when we followed one creative tangent. He's a few feet from me at his easel, working on a new bright starburst piece as we chat. The smell of the paint and art supplies is lightly filling the air. This is the largest room in the house. The ceiling is two stories up; it's bright and filled with inspiration. He pauses to open up all the sliding glass doors to let in the soft afternoon breeze. It's just enough to cool us a little without rattling the papers too much. On one side of the room is the old, painted, white upright piano with stacks of art, magazines, and paintbrushes underneath it. On the other side, behind me, are the two stacked keyboards. Everything is light, colorful, and overflowing with creativity.

Early sketch of Donna Summer by Greg Racker from the 1970s. He kept this drawing at his home in Topanga Canyon. **RIGHT:** Shock G performs at the Whisky a Go Go in Los Angeles, CA.

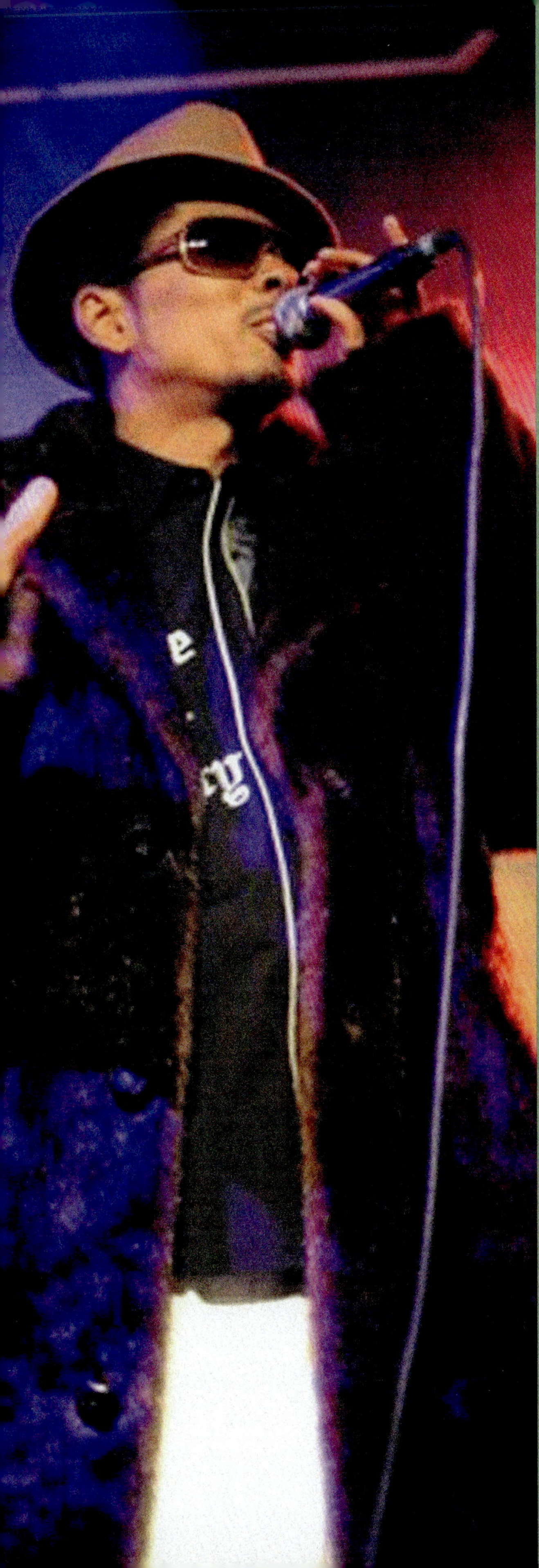

I used to draw nasty stuff, X-rated stuff, I got a whippin' once for drawing a life-sized orgy scene on the wall of our shed in the backyard. It was a way to plant it in the minds of the girls without having to actually say it to them. Instead of risking grossing them out, I'd just show them drawings of sex and play off their reactions. I could read the interest in their eyes, some girls would look at it longer or differently than others. It helped me identify the freakier ones, I could see it arouse them.

My all-time favorite artists for comics were Sergio Aragonés and Don Martin from *Mad* magazine. Them cats were hysterical! It was all about the way they drew expression and emotion—the surprised, shocked, or embarrassed looks on the faces! They used to have me folded over in the back of the class crackin' up! Then in junior high, in Queens, New York, it became superheroes, all day. My favorites were the Marvel characters—Iron Man, Spider-Man, the Black Panther, the Silver Surfer. My mom took me to meet Rick Kirby and Stan Lee of Marvel Comics when they had their Public Expo in New York one year. We liked Marvel over DC because they were cooler and non-racist. DC comics only seemed to cater to whites. DC had no awareness of other ethnicities in their strips, not even background people, much less superheroes.

Marvel on the other hand introduced Black Panther, the first Af-Ameri-hero, and they also occasionally had non-whites in their stories as background characters. That may not seem like a lot, but it was a breath of fresh air in a strictly white cartoon world. Sure, Fat Albert existed, but that wasn't my reality as a kid either, my reality was a mixed world. I grew up in mixed neighborhoods, and most of my family is mixed. I have half-breeds for all four grandparents. Mom's mom is half West Indian, half East Indian. Mom's dad is half Jewish, half Puerto Rican. Dad's mom is half African American, half Irish. Dad's dad is half Guyanese, half Bajian (of Barbados Islands). That makes me an eighth of all of the above, a multiblooded variety pack. A calico cat.

This sketch was created by Shock G for use on the Shock-G.com website, which Da Noses created.

More than superheroes or X-rated stuff, what I drew the most was my teachers. If, say, my teacher was fat, I'd make him into a fat superhero, with a new story each day based on something wack he said to me. If I thought a teacher was dumb, I'd draw her as "Idioma, Queen of the Idiots." Stuff like that, just to get back at them. My mom started keeping my cartoons and asking around for people to publish them. When I was only ten or eleven years old, she tried to publish a humorous comic strip I had created called "Looney Dap"—something about a goofy dude who used to ride a bike with his girlfriend. That's all I remember. None got published, but some almost did. I think it was too weird back then.

NOSE
JOB
OVER
NEW
WORLD
ODOR
MARKER
DRAWING
BOTTOM HALF
OF 4AM COME-
DOWN DOODLE.
WWW.SHOCK-G.COM
IMAGE
VIEW
JENNIFER
W/ WHITE
TIGER
SKETCH
DS AND FAMILY
WHIPS
HOCK'S ART
PENTHOUSE
6 AM
BRITTNI/SHOCK/PAC
COLLAGE
ICE
CUBE
GREEK
MASK
SHOCK

It's evening now and we're milling about Greg's kitchen, grabbing late-night snacks. This will be my last night in Topanga and I can't help but feel a little sadness or worry about going out on my own with this book. I'm leaving the bubble we created. Greg sees a troop of ants marching past. "Here they go again, marching through having a parade in here. The best way to get rid of them is to put soapy water on all the entrances. Then they don't even want to come in." Shock is talking to the ants as he prepares the soapy water. "Hey, you don't want to stay in here with me. Look out at your world, you got all this out there. GO . . . live your lives!"

I can't help but feel that Greg is talking to me. It is time for me to go. I head to my room and gather the last of my things. In the midst of packing, I plop on the floor and sift through the large stack of material he gave me to take home. I find a paper with some words that I hadn't seen before, written about art. It's interesting to look through the words he has written about art alongside his actual drawings. The art is wild, free, and silly, while his words are thoughtful and reasoned. They show the careful and decisive planning that went into everything Shock did.

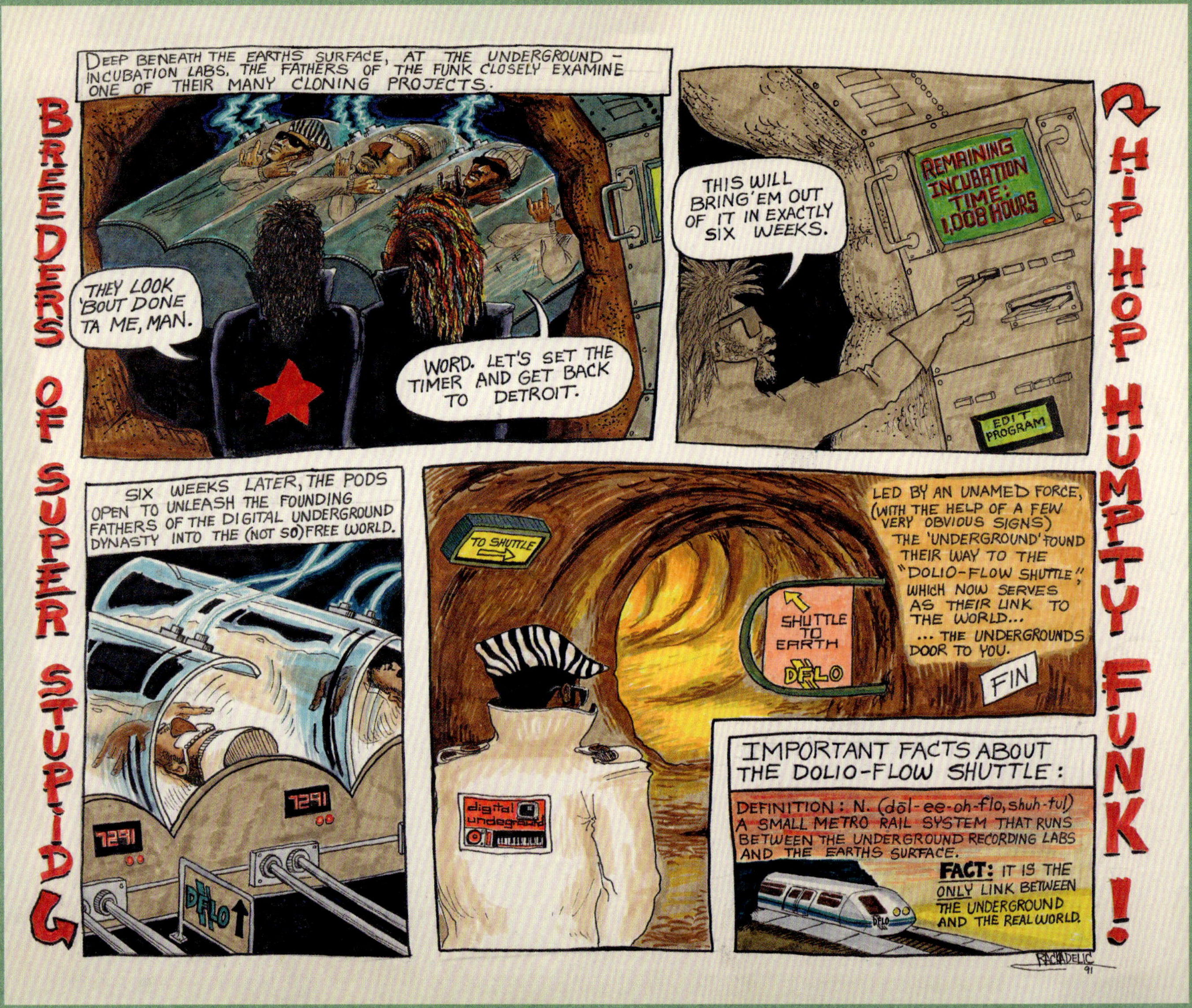

The Master Poet, J.Period's snapped photo of the original framed artwork in Rakim's studio. The upper right corner was ripped out and stolen—it was Tupac's signature.

"Shock G is quietly one of the most groundbreaking artists of all time. Let me tell you a story . . . I once went to Rakim's house, and on his studio wall, he had an amazing poster-sized cartoon of himself on top of a giant cement block, crushing all the other emcees beneath it. At the top, it said, 'The Master Poet.' When I looked closer, I couldn't believe my eyes. It said, "Shock G." Rakim told me the story: In 1989, a kid had waited outside his dressing room in Oakland for an hour after a show, hoping to give him this giant cartoon. The 'kid' was Shock G but digital underground hadn't come out yet. Three months later, 'Doowutchyalike' blew up. Rakim kept that drawing on his studio wall as inspiration . . . for years. Let that sink in. The greatest emcee who ever lived kept Shock G on his wall for inspiration—to this day. That's how important Shock G is to the culture." —J. Period

SEE THE MUSIC, HEAR THE COLORS

Music and visual art—it's all the same thing to me. I hear art shapes, and I see music in my head, the same way that people hear music with their ears. Much like when people see written words, they hear the sound version in their minds. Drawing is the visual equivalent to singing or playing an instrument, while the rhythm of vision is a dancer. For instance, if I drew three skyscrapers in a row, each getting equally taller, it's the same mental process as if I sang the bit from "Sorry Ms. Jackson" when he says, "Forever, for eva eva? For eva eva!" It requires the same ability to identify shapes, visualize sizes, and place them where they belong in order and at

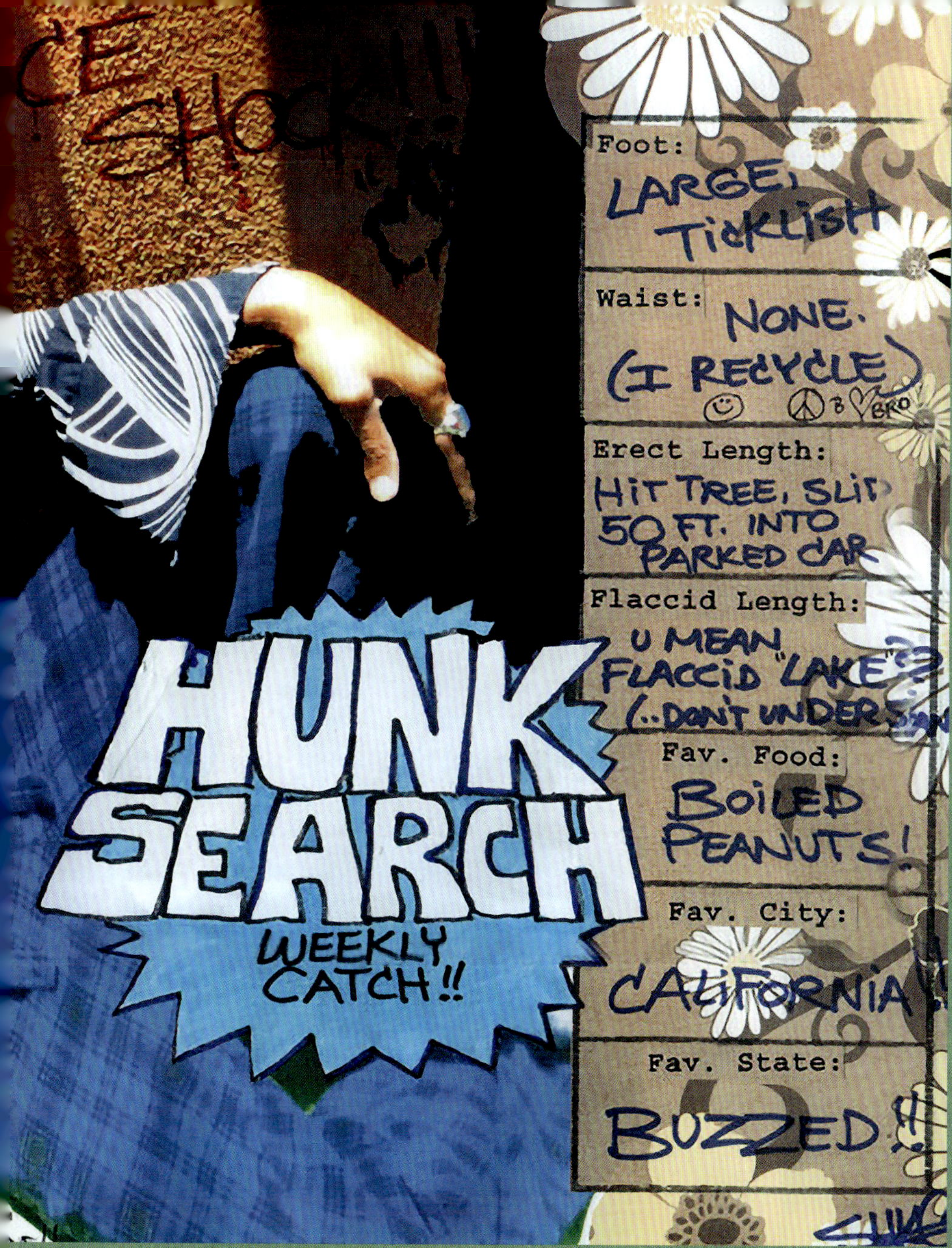

Shock originally wanted this image to be a large pull-out poster for the center of this book. The humor of it really tickled him. Original photograph by Kim Shady (as noted), 2011.

the right increments. There's harmony in vision, it has rules and tendencies just like sound does. Turquoise can be considered the third harmony to indigo, purple the seventh, and so on. Most musicians I know see the music. And most visual artists actually hear colors when they paint. I often ask singers for specific colors rather than notes in the studio, just in case their note for that color is different from mine.

When an artist is involved with as many facets of their career as possible, it's just less room for error or mistranslation by some label-appointed geek who doesn't get it, and less chance of the concept or style being lost. Sometimes it's better not to hoard the work though, sharing with other artists always brings more variety to the package. But if you yourself are, say, a singer but you also draw, you'll be better equipped to choose, approve, critique, inspire, guide, and direct whatever artist is doing work for your project. I storyboarded all the digital underground videos, co-directed

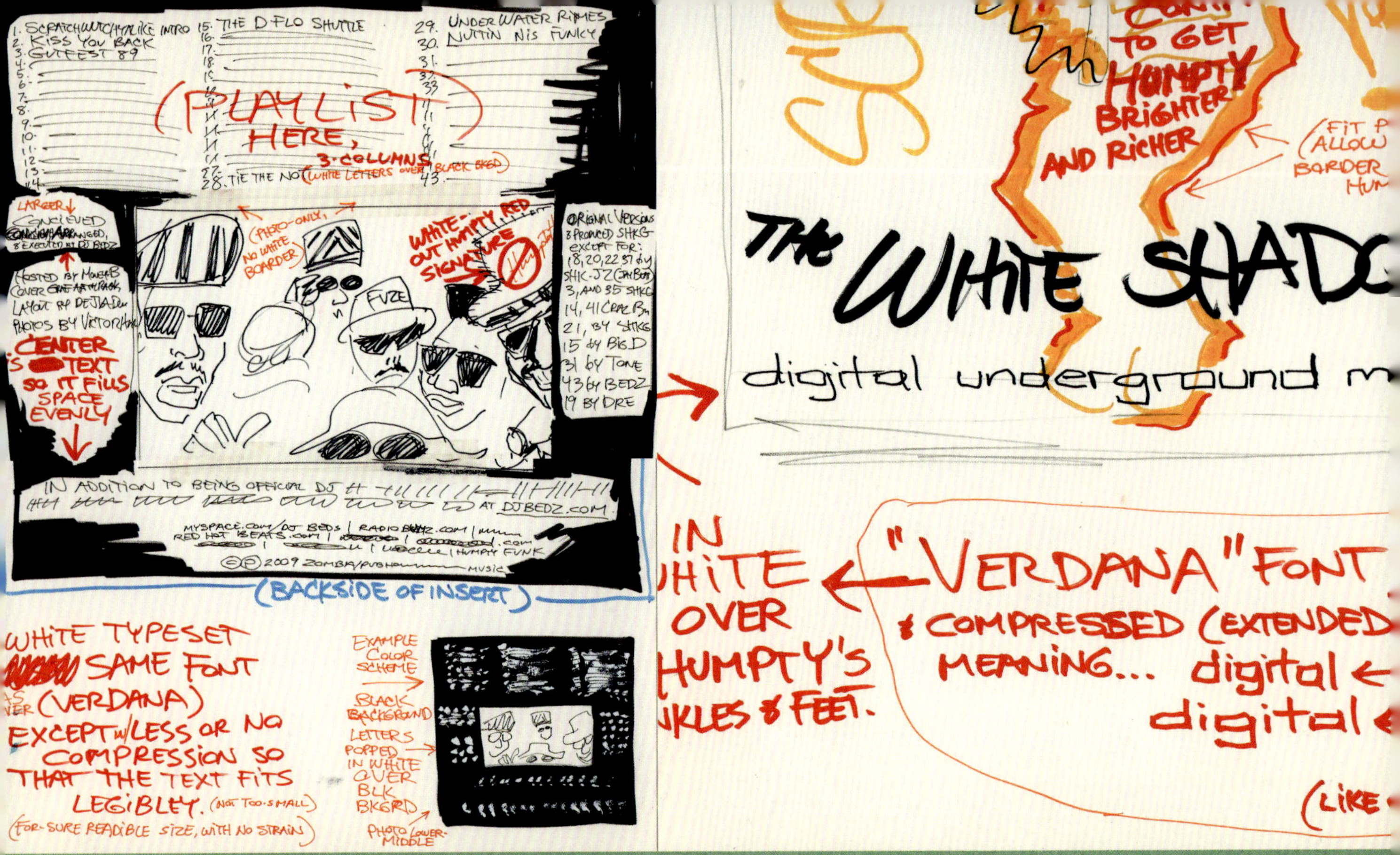

the shooting, and edited the footage along with Money B and Fuze. We felt like a label-appointed video director, fresh out of film school, wouldn't know why Humpty's walk in a certain take was more hip hop than the next. We sat there breathing down their necks through the entire grueling editing session, making sure they used the takes we insisted on, even though many of the shots went against their standards because a grip got in the shot, or because some camera wiring was exposed. They would say to us, "But we can't use that, the camera shadow's in the shot!" And we'd say, "No, make sure you use that take, it's fly."

Steve Miglion was head of the art department at Tommy Boy back then, but for the life of me I can't remember us hammering out any projects together. We didn't interact much, so I didn't get to know him too well because Monica or Tom would probably inform him that we have the digital underground cover figured out already, we're gonna use one of Shock's drawings, and he has the typeset all picked out and everything. There probably wasn't much left to do, I imagine. I do remember working with him on the "No Nose Job" cover—I think he designed the layout. It usually took me the best three or four hours of casual prime time of whichever day I set out to do it. I normally reserved a free afternoon for it, and then made a fun day out of it, after which I'd gawk at it, and take that feeling of pride and accomplishment with me into the club that night, which boosted my confidence with the ladies. I usually didn't have to send it in to Tommy Boy until the following morning, so I enjoyed at least one night of leaving it on display at my drafting table to "dry" and to juice me and my company whenever we looked at it.

"Yeah, that's gonna be the cover to the next single. Let's have another drink." I rarely ever restarted a piece, because I sketch the ideas in pencil until I was sure of the design, and then went over it with markers—color

first, black outline last. That way we all agreed and approved the pencil draft first, before I go to ink with it. I've long missed the joy of drawing for plain ol' recreation, unless trapped somewhere with time to kill, doodling on a plane, like, late-night on the tour bus or sitting around the coke table at an afterparty at someone's house. That's when the cool ish jumps off. Outside of that, hardly ever, almost never. I only draw for hire, or to illustrate a concept toward a project I'm involved in. No time as an adult, ya know? Each time I have a project in front of me, I set out to get materials, in whatever state, city, or side of town I'm in. This causes me to work with a wider variety of artists, studio engineers, types of paints, markers, whatever, and forces me to learn new mediums all the time. This can be both a blessing and a curse. I do kinda evade it to sorta never really obtain it, from a slight fear of getting trapped behind an art table and having to end my lifelong exploration adventure.

CREATIVE FLOW

Miles used to say, "If you listen to the music, it's already there." I know what he means. That's how I make beats. When you pay attention, you can see there's a drum beat already there. Or with painting, you can look and know what is needed. You just have to put it in. Stevie said it too. We don't write the music. You can look and know what is coming. That's what shamanism is to me, just being there and catching the message. My favorite mentors are funk and jazz musicians. Sometimes it's hard to translate what they say, how do you not "play" so much. I felt like maybe it's not forcing anything. Space is the mentality. The space is the points you want to make.

I finish packing and suddenly remember my rental car still parked in that same spot, threatening to slide forward the inch or two that would pull it straight down the canyon. Tomorrow morning, I'm actually going to have to find a way out. Reality is starting to hit. These past weeks, I've grown closer to Greg. I can see into his brain. Like learning a new language—I think "in Shock G" sometimes. My perspective has shifted. I hear the screen door open and close and see that Greg has moved from the kitchen to the wraparound porch. He lays flat on his back and stares up at the star-filled night sky. I quietly walk over and lay directly next to him, so close that our arms are touching. I feel such nostalgia for this moment in time, even though I'm still here.

Did you know we are actually all descendants of aliens?

Ha! I laugh out loud. I know he is completely serious about this, and we are about to get lost in another Greg-tangent pulling us into another dimension.

NEW YORK CITY

CHAPTER 10: B

Greg Spero, Shock G, and Ski Beatz recording for Murs's album, Williamsburg, Brooklyn, 2012.

...CKSTAGE PASS

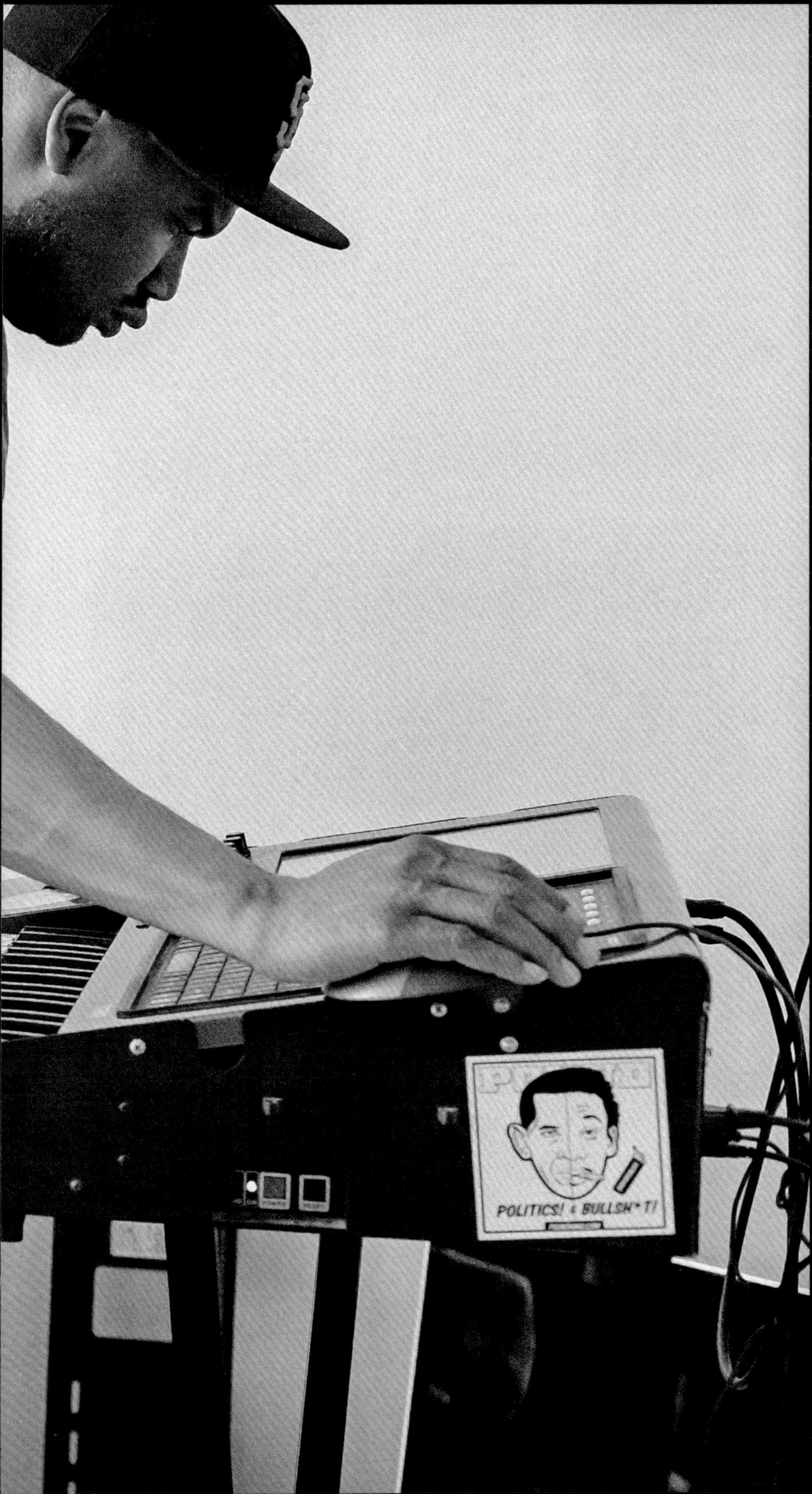

August 2011–May 2012

I arrive back home late at night, armed with hours of recorded conversations and folders filled with photographs, words, and memorabilia. I lug my bag past the flickery neon "Niels' Diner" sign and up the familiar carpeted steps of my walk-up on the Upper East Side. My neighbor's dogs are yelling at me as I walk past their door. New York always feels a little grimier than I remember when I come home. It's like I forget. It still has that energy, though. Seeping up from the concrete. It's that feeling that something is brewing. Anything can happen. I can still hear Greg's voice and laughter as I mess with the triple locks on my door. He was here with me once before. I remember sitting with him smoking cigarettes out the window and thinking about how much I love it here, feeling free and like true artists in a bustling creative city. As I enter my apartment now, that same window looks quiet and bare.

As the days creep by, the book project is constantly on my mind. I take every opportunity to talk with anyone Shock knows or anyone who may have a story. I have my recorder with me at all times, just in case. I find myself backstage a lot.

October 2011

I run into Professor Griff and DJ Lord of Public Enemy at the ATP Music Festival. I originally came here with my Canadian cousin, Vincent, but somehow we lost each other in the crowds. So I sit with the two of these guys on stools at one of the festival bars. We talk casually for a bit, but when we faintly hear that stunning and distinctive voice of Beth Gibbons, we decide to head up a dark stairwell and sneak behind curtains backstage to watch Portishead perform. I tell them about the book project with Shock G and give them my number for Chuck D to call me. Two months later, in December at 3:07 A.M., I get the call. "Hey, this is Chuck. Is now a good time to talk?" I'm thinking, Well, this is a wild time to call *but, "Yeah, of course!" Heavy D had just passed away, and Chuck was suddenly flooded with memories of an era. It was the perfect time to talk.*

Chuck D, photographed by Lynn Goldsmith, New York City, circa 1991–1992.

CHUCK D:

December 2011

I always knew that Shock was a musical visionary. I knew from the combinations of what digital underground had brought to the table. I really became enamored by the fact that he was able to reproduce the funk sounds and give it to us in a hip hop type of way. Shock was the orchestrator that made it all happen. Digital underground came out with "Doowutchyalike," and in 1990 we had the pleasure of actually touring with them as Public Enemy with Heavy D aboard a national tour. digital underground was a major feature on that tour because they had just come out with "The Humpty Dance"—that was a big-old national hit. From that point on they had it set with the *Sex Packets* album. With their music you got the reach into Jimi Hendrix and reach into George Clinton and there was a reach into hip hop, and it was like Shock G had taken all these musical worlds and combined them into one statement that was funky and that everybody could get with. I just remember the joy that he brought to twenty thousand people when he would go onstage and they would do their thing. It was absolute happiness when Shock and the rest of the crew were performing.

As they would get down, I would be in the crowd watching a digital underground show with the rest of the fans, and I know they would do the same for us. That was the beauty of hip hop at that time. Everyone supported each other, and everyone supported each other's show even with us all having a different point of view. I think it was an enjoyable tour for Shock because with guys who are musically gifted like he is, the music isn't enough. You gotta be able to give them a stage. You got to give a guy like that everything he needs to actually live and breathe music.

That's the beauty about Shock; it's like a record is not enough for him, a stage performance is not enough. This dude is a one-man orchestra consistently trying to get out. That's always been a cool aspect of him. Shock had this musicality on tour. If we were in a hotel with a piano in the lobby, there were two guys that would actually be able to play piano songs on it: One was Flavor Flav and the other one was definitely Shock G. I remember the time we were in Kansas City at the Hyatt Hotel, and Shock gave a whole performance playing on the piano in the lobby. You know his musicality had to get out somewhere. The stage wasn't enough! Shock is a guy who got into his music. He was married to his music. I can't see him getting mad at anything other than maybe something musical.

My relationship with Shock is the same as it was with Heavy D. Heavy is one of those people where we would always pick up exactly where we left off. We knew that the time together was always good and will always be good, and it was the same thing with Shock. Picking up right where we left off is an important part of our whole peer group of the nineties. We had a sincere love for each other's craft and a love of the music and the craft as a whole. Shock G and digital underground were quite liberating too. They allowed us to breathe easy on our show and just have a good time. It was always in the realm of having fun. They had Tupac as their dancer and backup roadie back then, so when we granted our love for digital underground, Tupac was a part of that. We really enjoyed being able to go around the country and help other artists like them go around the country with us, so they could play where they might not have played on their own at the time. That was the beauty of being a headliner.

At one point we were in Oklahoma City and somebody had run into our locker room while we were onstage and took my jacket. Pac said he saw the guy try to leave the arena with it. When I asked if he had seen it, he's damn near putting this guy who is like 6-foot-8 in a yoke. That's when I saw these dudes are really all love! See, we were older cats, so we would always give advice to the younger guys, and looking at that day when our locker room was compromised and violated, Pac was not gonna allow that to happen. I saw they were all loyal to their people. And we were too. We were all loyal to our people that we were on tour with, man. I mean, I tried to not let it go too far because I didn't want to see anyone get hurt. But I saw that he was in full support in that moment! The whole digital underground crew, they were all cool cats. Beautiful cats. They always wanted to have fun! Trust me. They only wanted to have fun! You got to understand though too, I was married on that tour. And it was very important when someone comes along that's nineteen, twenty-one, twenty-three, you know like Pac and Shock and all of them, Fuze. I mean, I smile because these dudes were having a ball, man. And just doing music. I wanted them to be safe and okay, and to not get arrested and to keep on playing their music.

We laid down the law at the beginning of the tour. I said, "Yo, this is not a headlining tour. Public Enemy is not headlining. What we're doing is just closing the show out." There was no "big I, little u." It was not like, we are established and you're the rookies. None of that. Everybody was respected and acknowledged. And this went from the very top to the bottom and from the bottom to the top. We really enjoyed the respect of each other and the respect from the audience. We loved that whole period. I don't think that period of time is recognized enough as truly being the strongest period in hip hop ever. It was very special times. The thing that's probably missing now in hip hop is things like that. That Shock G would stand in the front row and see our show, and we would stand in front and see his show, and we had that undying support for each other and for whatever point of view they had. These dudes had the *Sex Packets*, which was all about being young and getting busy! It was crazy! It still puts a big smile on my face. We would go onstage and be like, "Alright, let's watch this," and they would go, "*Yo, we got your packets, man!*" I mean, what can you say? It's sex, right? What are you gonna do?

It's too easy to say that Shock is a disciple of George Clinton. Shock is really a disciple of music itself. Prince, George Clinton, Jimi Hendrix, Jam Master Jay, I mean, it's all in him. Larry Graham, Sly and the Family Stone, it's all in Shock G, and we are all very fortunate that some of him has gotten out. To me I think digital underground is perfect for the digital age, and nothing should stop them from producing two or three albums every year. They are a group that could have, seriously, seventy or eighty albums. That's how much music Shock has got in him. I hope he doesn't have any fear. All he has to do is just breathe deep and release. Nobody knows that better than him. There's nobody that really compares to Shock G and digital underground, so he should have no pressure to breathe deep and just make some music and let us all get it! Shock G already made himself who he is and we are all thankful for it. Whatever Shock decides to do, we all benefit. He's got a hundred years of good music in him, and I'm getting on my knees saying this: "Yo, dog, whatever you do, just let me know!"

He was always bleeding musicology, and his crew too was a diverse band of characters who really seriously meshed and complemented where Shock G wanted to go. Their sound and what they represent allowed people to be free and be comfortable to do their own thing.

SHOCK:

After a show we would always be at the piano in the hotel lobby. As long as I was playing the piano, someone would be rhyming. Sometimes we would play until the sun came up. There would be nobody left in the lobby but us. That was fun. Flav, [MC] Serch, Pac . . . It would be us four mostly. Every once in a while, Jodeci or someone might sing a song, but they were so busy chasing the girls up and down. But for us, especially if we had a crowd around, we would do that first until there was no one left. And then go upstairs. If there were any girls left, great; if not, oh well. The music was more fun to us. But the R&B groups on the other hand! "I'll cry for you . . ." Singing all that shit. They would make three or four trips to the lobby. Or they'd send someone down to get the girls. "Hey, Devante said he'll take two, you right there in the blue and uh you right there. Let's go." The girls would go, "Ooo! Girl, I got to go! Take my purse. Oooo girl!" and hop in an elevator. That is sick. I don't think I ever sent Nzazi to go to the lobby like, "Yo, pull a couple a cute ones up here." Fuck that. Ain't that crazy?

Sometimes hundreds of people would be in the lobby, bar spill out after the show. These guys used to walk around with a pizza box going, "Hey, you want a pizza?" Then when a girl would open the box, his dick would be in the box, just by itself with nothing else. We got so used to the girls going, "Ahhh, he crazy!" and running around. We'd go, "Well, shit, he did it again." I mean, it'd be like, how many cities are we gonna do this? They just love that dick-in-the-box trick, yo! When you're in this business and in the environment of it, girls will let you do that. But if you were in the parking lot of a club, someone would call the police on you. At that time hip hop was so new that anybody who was on that stage was like a different kind of brother among brothers. It was rare. Most adults were like, how does that even work? How do they make those sounds? Is there another record playing in the record? It was such a cutting-edge thing. Maybe it was like the days when they did the first electric distortion on the guitar. It took people a long time to figure out hip hop. Now everybody is an expert. Everybody knows what it's supposed to be. Even grandmothers are saying, "What do you think about so-and-so's new album?" Hip hop just came up and took over, like a vine, baby! That's beautiful.

Tillman's

March 2012

I heard that Murs would be at a jazzy restaurant/nightclub called Tillman's in midtown Manhattan. I call him up and we plan to meet for an interview after the show. I first met Murs at a studio in Brooklyn. Shock had come out to record a track for his new album. Their mutual respect was palpable, filling the air as they tried different beats and guitar riffs or milled about writing lyrics here and there. I knew how important Murs was to Shock. His name is tattooed on Shock's arm along with Tupac, the Luniz, and digital underground.

The show wraps up at about midnight, and Tillman's is preparing to shut down for the night. Murs and I decide to record the interview outside. Murs, his wife Kate, and I huddle under the awning, just barely out of the heavy Midtown rain. It's one of those insistent NYC downpours where you have to raise your voice to be heard, voices already raspy from hours of shouting over music. The sidewalk glistens, slick with rain, and the air is filled with the smell of hot wet concrete, and that familiar sense of late-night possibility. People spill out of the club calling out as they pass, "Hey! Wassup, Murs. Nice show," "Yo. Murs! Alright, man." He fist-bumps, nods, raises a hand in easy recognition.

MURS:

I hadn't even known Shock that long when he agreed to go on tour with me. That was insane! Not only that, it was for little or no money. But the fact that he thought I was cool and came on the road with me probably kept me from either killing myself or doing something even stupider. It's like I may have only sold three thousand records, but I'm on the road with Shock G! And he's playing "So Many Tears," and he's telling stories and being cool with us. He knew everybody's name from the tour and we were nobodies. He looked up everybody's music. I do that now—I talk to everybody and find out their interesting stories. He taught me that. There's so much value in that.

I picked him up from the airport with my goddaughter's mother. The entire tour was crazy. No matter what, the man never, ever, ever, ever, *ever* missed a date. Never was late. Ever! I'm paying him shit money, we're playing shit clubs, and he showed so much respect. I mean, this guy plays stadiums with the biggest names. He discovered Tupac, for crying out loud! And here he is on tour with me and showing respect to all of us. That meant a lot. Shock has always been at all the important moments in my life. I like having him there also because he's important to the ghetto without actually being ghetto. Shock would teach me things about being on tour too. He would sometimes be like, "You guys are so mean to the guys who want to hang out with you, but if there's one guy with four girls, let the guy get on the bus. Be super nice to him. See what happens." Duh. He kept me so cool on tour. I think I would have got into a lot of fights on that tour if it wasn't for him. He's just so calming. I still think I may have broke somebody's nose on that tour, but he's kind of a peacemaker without even really doing anything in particular. He just made me feel better about myself. Like there is no need for all that.

Shock, Ski, Murs, and Alexis in the studio recording for Murs's album, *Love & Rockets*, 2012.

You know, there is one moment that really sticks in my mind because it means so much to me. I drove to drop Shock at his house with the wife of another producer who grew up listening to Shock G and really respected him. When we get there, Shock takes off his coat and she just slaps me again and again like "Did you see that?!" I mean, she was socking me! "Did you see that!" I was like, "What?" She goes, "He has your name tattooed on his arm!" I didn't know. He didn't ask me. He didn't tell me. He just took off his coat and I'm like, "Whoa!" She's not even playing it cool 'cause she is super hood, so she's just hitting me and being loud about it! I was like, "Oh my god, are you shitting me?" Then she said something really awkward that made the whole thing even more awkward than it was. He said, "No, I put your name because working with you is really important to me." At that point I just wanted to cry.

We linger there a while, conversation drifting easily between us. Kate's surprised to hear about the tattoo. "Wow, really? That's amazing! I guess it's good he came to our wedding then." We laugh, and the talk flows—loose, curious, playful. There's a kind of freedom in it, like the kind that emanated from Shock. The rain begins to ease, the night stretching out around us. When Murs speaks again, there is a shift in energy.

Kate and Murs in the rain outside of Tillman's, 2012.

There is one other Shock G story I want to tell you before you go. It's a *Risky Business* story. We were shooting the first day for that video. We had just partied all day. I had literally drunk about a fifth of tequila. We started at 8 P.M. and went until about 3 A.M. I know Shock was wasted. Crazy girls on the set. I was just going home 'cause I know I gotta get up in the morning. Shock rides off on a motorcycle with some chick from the video! I'm like, "We have to be back at seven, G!" thinking there is no way. I show up at 10 hungover, like *uuhhh* . . . I was like, *I know there is no way Shock is here.* I say, "Can we just shoot my parts right now?" They go, "No, we are gonna go get Shock." I was like, "What? Where is Shock?" I go into the mansion and head up to the exercise room, and I'm thinking I know he's just passed out up there. Nope. He is in a completely bent over backward bridge pose. I was like, "Yo, what's up man!" And he's like, "Oh, what's up, brother? I'm just doing my morning yoga."

I'm thinking to myself, *I know for a fact that you did cocaine last night. I know for a fact that you got wasted because we got wasted together. And I know for a fact that you probably fucked that girl because she was out of her mind. How are you up at 7 A.M. doing yoga?* And he was bent over backward. The real thing, not some punk-ass yoga! He is talking to me upside down, G! I mean, what?! Like, he didn't move, he wasn't startled. I come in like "YO!" and he's calm. He is a yogi. He says his office is the boulder on the top of Topanga Canyon, and he sits cross-legged with the computer and does his work. And lizards crawl on him. These are the stories I think of most when I think of Shock G. Man, I love him.

COSMIC DIALOGUE

SHOCK G AND GEORGE CLINTON TALK IN THE FUNKIVERSE

May 2012

I meet with George Clinton at BB King's in Manhattan and speak to him for a while backstage. This section is from that interview, interspersed with a phone conversation I had with Shock around the same time—fitting that George Clinton and Shock should have a fictional conversation over different points and places in time.

SHOCK:

One of my first bands from junior high was [called] Parliament II, if that says anything about what I think about George and what he was doing. At that time we wanted to showcase the music he was doing and bring it out more for people to hear. He was the Tupac of our generation. He was about self-empowerment, *one nation under a groove, shine some light on us.* Even when we started doing digital underground, I wasn't really thinking about me at first. I was thinking about getting George's sound out there more. We talked first by phone. He was at Tommy Boy Records, and I think De La Soul was there working on the "Me Myself and I" record. This was the same day that Tommy Boy received "The Humpty Dance." So they let George listen to it. Then Marcie calls me up from the label and says, "I have a surprise for you," and she put George on the phone. I remember all I was thinking was, *This is George Clinton!!* Then he goes, "Yeah, man. You got something here." That was it. But to me, it was *huge*!

GEORGE CLINTON:

When I first heard digital underground, I was at Tommy Boy Records. They were asking my opinion on what song to put out for their first single. I said, "The Humpty Dance"! I didn't even know it was one of our records that they had sampled at that time. I just knew it was the shit! That shit was just so, "Rrrrrrooowww, Rrrrrroooooouup!" That song was just yelling out, "Oh hell no! This is it! This is the one!" Oh shit, everybody knew that was it! "The Humpty Dance"? It's like "Atomic Dog." When it comes on, they ain't no doubt about it. Your ass is getting up and getting on the dance floor. You ain't got no choice! I remember, I called Shock and I woke him up. But as soon as he answered the phone, he knew my voice. I didn't even know him yet. But he goes, "George fucking Clinton!!" Ha. That was great.

SHOCK:

All that year we stayed in touch. Members from Parliament Funkadelic came to the studio and sang with d.u. That was first. Then, in 1991, I flew out to Detroit for three days to work on *Sons of the P* with him. Four years later he invited me to perform at Woodstock with him.

GEORGE CLINTON:

Shock and the whole group came to Detroit in '91 and we did *Sons of the P*. I found out all of them could play keyboards and jazz and shit. Man, they knew everything about us. They were like walking P-Funk historians. Shock's mother once told me that he had a life-sized cutout of me! He used to carry it around everywhere, bumping into people on the subway. But we were also learning about them. They were a band, an actual band. I didn't know they could play all these instruments. It was gospel. We were like, "You don't need to sample us—we'll sample you!" Matter of fact, we did use them during that same time to play on a track of ours. It's called "Shadows on the Wall." Digital underground was one of the premier groups to sample us. They really brought it to life. "All Around the World," "Same Song." I feel like they're part of our group. Funk is the DNA in most hip hop. But they are like the first-run clones. They are part of us.

George Clinton and Sir Nose De Void of Funk perform at BB King's Blues Club, NYC, 2012. **BELOW:** George Clinton and Carlon in Humpty noses—backstage BB King's, NYC, 2012. Shock G and George Clinton chatting at Shock's place in Topanga Canyon.

When I think of Shock, I think of Humpty. I make him put his nose on. He just makes me laugh! Humpty is a character. We talk about having different characters all the time. He got ashamed of being Humpty at times. But, I was like, "Oh hell no! This is theater. Get that nose out. That is your act. That ain't got nothing to do with you as a person." A lot of people don't know, but "The Humpty Dance" is the most sampled song in hip hop. It was sampled by Will Smith in "Wild Wild West." It was sampled by LL Kool J in "Mama Said Knock You Out." It's in the movie *Happy Feet*. A lot of people don't realize the influence that "The Humpty Dance" had on hip hop history. Shock was the Bootsy of hip hop.

1999. We landed the mother ship at Woodstock and Humpty was with us. This was my birthday too.

SHOCK:

This was Woodstock '99, nothing like the first one. It was not about peace and love. This was when they were throwing used tampons up onstage. It was insane! Girls were getting thrown above the crowd to crowd-surf, then pulled down and raped, and then thrown back up again crying and screaming. It was the opposite of the first Woodstock. But for me I didn't see any of that. We were all separate from that. For me it was great! I was hanging out with George and having the time of my life. He almost missed his performance at Woodstock, though. We were in the bus, all set to go. Everyone but George. He was so late and we couldn't figure out where he was. Then his assistant came down and said she couldn't get him to come down because he was looking at *The Assholes*—a book that I made, a comic strip. He didn't want to put it down! Everybody was trying to get him to come, but he was like, "One more page, just one more." He couldn't stop laughing, and he almost missed his whole performance! Everyone was in stitches!

George Clinton and Humpty perform together at Tupac's birthday, Yoshi's, San Francisco, CA, 2012.

GEORGE CLINTON:

You seen *The Assholes*? [*laughs*] "From one asshole to the other. Damn, your breath smells like shit." [*laughs*] It brings in that element of humor again. Oh my god. Man, the things they say to each other! He gave me the first book off the press at Woodstock when we did "The Humpty Dance" together.

SHOCK:

After Woodstock, I called my mom, and I was like, "I just did Woodstock with George Clinton! What do I do now?!" I was *done*. After that I was like, *What more can I do? What else could I want?* But, yeah we keep it going, even today. Actually behind the scenes is even stronger than in the public eye. This one time in '06, we did a House of Blues show and I didn't even know he was in town, but when we were doing "I Get Around," he just appeared onstage. He walked out from backstage and joined in! I was on the keys, so we moved into more of a funk sound. But he'll do that. Just show up. It was all crazy. It was dope and it went down. You don't even know what it's like for me to know him this well. It's like being Jackie Chan and having Bruce Lee on speed dial!

Mama Humpty (Shirley) and Greg in Humpty noses, Tampa, FL.

I took him to see George Clinton for the first time in Hermosa Beach. He went nuts! He was just blown away. He was about thirteen years old at that time. I said, "Gregory, you could do it yourself if you want to." Then I remember a couple years later, we went into a music store in Manhattan and he comes over with this life-sized cutout of George Clinton. I said, "They are not going to give that to you"—but they did. I was like, "How are you going to walk around with that?" But he was just obsessed.

We used to listen to a lot of music in our house. Whatever was popular at that time. Stevie Wonder, Chaka Khan, Luther Vandross. When he was about five or six years old, we were watching Stevie Wonder on TV and he was just moving and dancing around to it. I remember thinking, *Oh, yep. He's got the fever!* He used to do Stevie Wonder all the time. He was an entertainer from the start.

—Shirley
(Greg's mom)

TAM

PA

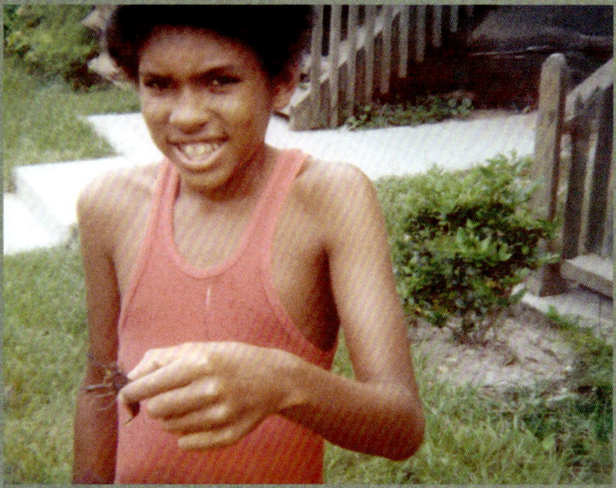

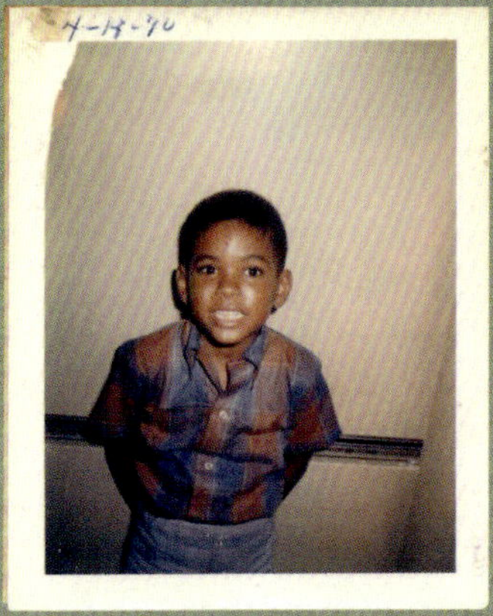

TOP ROW, LEFT TO RIGHT: Young Gregory caught something; Greg plays around on friend, Toby's guitar, Tampa, FL.

MIDDLE ROW, LEFT TO RIGHT: Greg and Kent with cousins Julie, Steven, and Jeffrey on a stoop in Brooklyn, NY; Fists with Pops on the way to Disneyland; Kent, Eddie, Greg; Little Gregory, 1970; Greg acting tough in Far Rockaway, NY.

BOTTOM ROW, LEFT TO RIGHT: Greg with a goat; Kent, Grandma Gloria, and Greg.

CHAPTER 11: THE RACKERS

June, 2012

I arrive in Tampa early in the day and spend the next few hours going through old photo albums with Greg's stepmom, Sonya, and getting tours of the house from Greg's dad, Edward (Eddie Racker). His dad designed and built this house, and the whole family is proud of that. It is all one level with a semi-outdoor pool enclosed in glass at the center. As you walk in the front door, to the left is an office, and if you pass that and keep going left, a long hallway leads to bedrooms. To the right of the front door is a door to the garage and then immediately after that you enter the open kitchen, living room area. Straight ahead, sliding glass doors open onto the patio with the pool. The kitchen is separated from the living room by a bar with barstools and a little strip of tile. The living room has leather couches, what feels to me like a wall-sized TV, a pool table, and the family bird, a talking African gray parrot, named Afro. Eddie calls the bird Rooster when it's acting up. Afro mimics everything. He meows like a cat all day long, or sounds like a landline telephone ringing. Sometimes he yells out, "EDDIE!!!" and sounds exactly like Sonya.

The walls of the house are lined with framed family photographs and images of family members standing with famous politicians or basketball players. Shock's gold and platinum albums hang on the walls as well. We sit down at the barstools, and Sonya hands me one of her famous Kahlúa and Creams. She's having one too and says, "It's not too early, is it?" Laughing, she leaves Greg and me to talk. Greg reaches above the fridge and grabs a box of Lucky Charms. Something he would never do back in Topanga Canyon. It seems out of character for him to have sugar cereal. In Tampa, in his father's home, he seems a younger version of himself and he stays that way.

The next morning we head into the city. I get the full Gregory Racker tour of his old life: the house they lived in when he was a kid, where he used to bike the streets, all the little pranks he used to play, his high school, and an old girlfriend's house. We visit some long-term friends, we eat boiled peanuts, and we head to the recording studio and that first radio station where Greg played the full fifteen-minute version of "Knee Deep." Shock had posted a plaque for Kenny-K on the door, and he's excited to see it's still there.

Later in the afternoon, we've returned to Eddie and Sonya's home. I sit at the barstools again. This time to interview Eddie, Sonya, and Shock's little sister, Liz. It's so funny to talk with them all together like this. When people know each other well, there's a lot of, "No, it wasn't like that. It was this . . ." Or long periods of "What was his name again? Michael? No, Tommy? No, that wasn't it." Every once in a while it's, "No, don't tell that story. Tell that other one, the one about the snake . . ."

UPPER LEFT: Kent and Greg in the '69 Camaro. "Greg and I remember, when Shirley would drive it, people would pull up next to her and try to race her. It had so much horsepower. Eddie would race all around Tampa. When the cops would chase him, he'd pull right into the garage!" —Kent **ABOVE:** Greg holding an alligator, Tampa, FL. **OPPOSITE:** Greg in Hermosa Beach, CA. Photograph by Kent Racker.

EDDIE RACKER:
To put it mildly, he was different.

SONYA RACKER:
He was special.

EDDIE:
One of the earliest times that Gregory demonstrated that he was working off a few extra cylinders than most kids his age was when he wanted to get a snake. He came to me and asked me, "Could we get a snake?" I initially said no off the top of my head. He said, "Why not?" I said, "Well, they're dirty, dangerous, and expensive and your mother will never go for it." He said, "Okay," and went away. Later he came back and asked, "Can I get a snake?" I said, "They are dirty, dangerous, expensive, and your mother will never go for it." He says, "Well, I already asked Mom, she says it's up to you." So he took away one of the four reasons I'd laid out. I said, "Well, that surprises me, but they're still dirty, dangerous, and expensive." He says, "Okay."

He comes back a week later, says, "At the pet shop, they've got a sale. I can get a baby boa constrictor with a tank on sale for sixteen dollars or something like that. They stay clean in the tank." I say, "Well, they're still dangerous." He asks, "Do you know Mr. Josh Anders?" "Of course," I answered. "Well, I work with Josh Anders and his daughter has a pet boa." Josh was very conservative compared to me. I'd say quite conservative. So, hearing that, I say, "Okay, well then, let's go and get a snake." So we went and we bought him his first snake. He found out why I said no, and then he just whittled away at each one of my reasons because he knows I'm not just a "No, because I'm your father. I'm bigger and stronger than you" type thing. I go by reason. He took away all the reasons. So he got his first snake.

Someone at the school he was at suggested that we take him to NYU. NYU was testing kids for extraordinary or genius whatever. I think he was only about three years old and they tested him. They said, "Well, he's not quite to where we would say 'genius' but he does have extraordinary or unusual use and understanding of language." In other words, if you asked him about something and he didn't understand it, he'd keep going at it with, "Well, is it like this or is it like that?" Until he could find something that it was like, so he could understand what you were talking about. And they said that was rather extraordinary for a child his age. So we were moving out of New York at that time down to Florida. But we did a survey of where they had the best elementary schools in the Tampa Bay area. And we made sure to find one that was very highly rated for Gregory. We went by that to find a place to live.

SONYA:
School was easy for him. He just breezed through school. I think he was probably underchallenged though because he left and then later had to come back. Looking back, I think he was just bored. Kent was always involved playing basketball, and he and his friends would go play sports together. Greg, while he did those things, would also disappear for our entire evening, and he'd be in his room sketching or drawing or playing music. He would spend so much time working on things like that. Greg would sometimes hide out and work on a project. He has always known what he wanted. I'm not sure he always knew how he was going to get there, but he stayed focused. I guess, deep down, when Greg left, he left somewhat under the terms that I wouldn't have wanted to see him leave home. But he was adamant that he was going to make this thing happen at any cost.

When you look back, it shouldn't have come as so much of a surprise to me when he finally made the decision "I'm out of here." We were very, very concerned when he left. I recall there being a period of time that we didn't hear from him at all. When we did get to the point where we were hearing from him, I don't think he was feeding us the real story of how things were going. I think it was a pretty rough start, but he never called, he never complained. He never said, "I think I made a mistake." He just followed through. He was always very, very focused and very, very deliberate about how he spent his time, who he spent his time with, and what he wanted to do.

EDDIE:
Still is.

SONYA:
Greg was focused, very, very focused.

EDDIE:
Narrowly focused.

SONYA:
He wanted to be in the entertainment business. He wanted to pursue his music from the time I met him. I came into the picture in about '78. Greg would have been about fourteen, fifteen . . .

EDDIE:

When he was younger, he would doodle, he would draw things, and we noticed that he was extraordinary at that. He would draw action figures, and when he started making music, he did the covers. He drew the covers for the albums or CDs. I remember he'd get little pieces of paper and he'd be drawing something on it, and then he'd go to the next page and draw the same thing. To me, it would look like the same damn thing on every page. He'd do it over and over and over, I'd say, "What the hell are you doing?" Then he'd flip it, and you'd actually see the thing moving through there. A flip-book, he called it. Yeah. He just improved on his own, and he didn't really practice it so much as he did it as relaxation. Like somebody else would read. He would sit down and draw.

I knew the editor of the *Tampa Tribune*, and I guess we were all sitting together telling stories about our kids. I said something about Greg drawing, and this guy mentioned that they had an opening in their graphic arts department. They wanted him to draw one picture that encompassed all sports, as a test. I guess he drew this one picture and they were very impressed by it. Especially because of how he drew hands. Most people don't get the hands, they said. They went ahead and offered him the job. He just brushed it off. I was very disappointed because I felt like the guy went out of his way to get him an interview and everything. He can walk in without a major degree or any previous accomplishments and everything and work for the most prominent newspaper in town, and he just blew it off. That's when he first told me, he said, "I can do music on demand." He says, "I can only draw when I feel like it."

SONYA:

We would suggest to him too, "Well, Greg, why don't you go to school for the arts and critique your skills?" The same with his music. His father and his mother tried to get him to take piano lessons, and it was like, "I don't want to be like someone else. I don't want to model myself after someone else and their techniques. I just want to do this on my own." That's how he was about anything in the arts. He rejected that vehemently.

EDDIE:

Yeah, I think it got in the way of everything, actually. I don't think he did anything else to excel or to the level he probably could because he was always preoccupied with music. He probably could have got better grades. He could have done a lot of other things better if he weren't so preoccupied with music. I first realized this may actually work the first time I went to his school to watch a performance. They were having an assembly, whatever they call it, different groups were going to do different things, and I guess he organized it. I remember sitting in the audience, the school crowd was very rowdy. They wanted to hear him and his group, and they were chanting and doing things that they do. The principal came onstage with a handheld mic trying to calm them down, and they seemed to just get louder and louder.

OPPOSITE, LEFT: *A rare photo of Kent and Greg (seated at the piano he learned all the deep jazz tunes on) with their Doberman, Pitch.* **MIDDLE:** *Greg and Nadina at prom, 1980.*

Then Greg walked up to the principal and took the microphone away from him. When he did that, they cheered and they just shut right up and calmed down. I said, "Okay. He's got that, that charisma, that thing that people notice and they listen to." I was very impressed with him that day, and I never questioned him going forward to work on a stage or in front of a group again after that. That moment resonated with me. Being able to control a mass of people like that when they were out of control just by simply looking at them and with a few gestures, that's it. Even if you're liked, it's still hard to control a group like that. So, to me, I'm looking at it from a completely different perspective. I couldn't critique his music because I'm not someone who makes a living critiquing music. I know what I like. So, who else was in the show, he can probably tell you. What the show was, how long it was, what they did, how well it was applauded or whatever, I don't remember any of that. I just remember him walking up on that stage and taking that microphone away from the principal of the school and managing that audience.

LIZ:

I have one story that I remember when I really felt like, "Okay, my brother's doing something major." It was when I was in elementary school. I was getting on a bus. I didn't even know my brother was in town at that point. "Humpty Dance" had already been out. All the buses were stacked and we were right in the middle of the pack. All of a sudden I hear all these kids starting to scream in the front of the line. I'm looking, I'm like, "What is going on?" I see each bus getting louder and louder and louder as it gets closer to our bus. How he knew where I was in the line, I don't know. But then I saw everybody just rush over and hands are all out the windows, screaming. He gets on the bus and was like, "Come on, I'll take you home." He wasn't in costume, but it was his normal, crazy clothes. I remember getting off the bus, and all the kids were hanging their hands out the bus and screaming. And we get into this, I think it was a blue top-down car, and we drove off. It was just so unreal.

I asked Liz, "You were on the 'Doowutchyalike' track, isn't that right?"

LIZ:

Yeah, we were just talking about that. I don't even know how that came about. I think Kent recorded it here at our old house and then sent the tape over to Greg.

EDDIE:

"Daddy, can I go out and play?"

SONYA:
And if I remember, we didn't know what they were doing until that album came out.

LIZ:
I don't remember actually doing it. But I remember going, "Okay, that's my voice," when he sent over the record. I guess it was a tape that he sent. When "Humpty" came out, I thought it was brilliant. At that point music was so hard, and I thought he brought some fun into hip hop. It was something positive rather than always something negative. I'm always learning more about his characters and who or what influenced them. It's really mainly our family. My dad's side and my mom's side. Which is really funny to me. I think one of his uncles is in the Humpty character. Who was that? One of Mom's brothers?

EDDIE:
Oh, I don't know. Oh, maybe Crazy Frank.

LIZ:
Crazy Frank! My brother has so many [characters]. There's a character from I think my great-aunt or somebody. It's just so funny how he collects everything from all these different people and develops something that really takes off. He completely does a transformation. He was always very supportive of me too. He went to my graduation when I had a senior collection for my fashion design. He definitely influenced me. He was born with a gift to just know music, hear music. The way he taught himself piano. I had a passion for fashion, but I had to grow into it and develop myself into what I am doing now. I think he was just born with it. So it's different. For him it's running through his veins. His ability to draw and write, and he's smart . . . Well, sometimes.

SONYA:
Well. The thing was, Gregory left abruptly. Then after being in California or wherever for two or three years, he decided to come back to get his GED and he breezed through. He was in and out. But that second part is when Liz spent the bulk of her time with him.

LIZ:
It was just always filled with adventure, fun, craziness. A lot of times I was around his boys. But I was really young. So they remember me running around in diapers. They watched me grow up. But when I got a little older, he would trust me to be around everybody even if he wasn't there. I remember I had a little crush, an innocent crush on someone, Dot. I'd always be like, "Where is Dot, where is he?" Later I found out that Greg had told everyone not to let him around my sister. They all protected me. If he wasn't around, he told all of these people, "Watch out for her. You can go by her, but make sure she is okay." Somebody in the crew told me that later.

Gregory Racker Presents
CHAPTER • ONE
MEET, Mr. BANKS
STEP ON IT, KID! I WANT TO GET TO MARTIN'S PLACE BEFORE HE CLOSES.
RIGHT, CC.
SOMEWHERE IN THE LATE-AFTERNOON N.Y. CITY STREETS, AN ALL WHITE LINCOLN TOWN COUPE' MOVES ON.
CREATED WRITTEN & DRAWN BY GREG RACKER • SEPTEMBER 10, 1979
1

Greg's brother, Kent, taking an old-school selfie. He was the photographer for the "Demo Engineers." **BELOW:** The Master Blasters: Omar, Gwen, Phyllis, Cush, Greg, MC K Bar (Kenny Rollock), and Roland Owens. **OPPOSITE:** Promo Shot for the "Demo Engineers" (Greg and Kent) in YBor City, Tampa, FL. Photograph by Kent Racker (Canon AE-1, timer, and a tripod).

Years later, in August of 2024, Greg's younger brother, Kent, and I finally have the interview we've talked about doing so many times. Me in Seattle, Kent in Oakland. As Kent is talking, he strums a guitar here and there and hums a tune. It's surreal talking with him, because this feels exactly like what it was like chatting with Greg by phone. There would often be the sound of the keyboards or him drumming on something in the background. Not only that, but Kent sounds so much like Greg. His laugh is identical. I can see how it was easy for him to play Shock on the road. He helped keep that Humpty mystery alive.

KENT:

Greg and I, when we were in our early teens we would cut grass. That's just what you did in Florida. And we were surrounded by wildlife all over the place all the time. There's bugs and snakes. An alligator will cross the street somewhere where you're driving, like you're surrounded by it. But we started to get really into snakes. I think he just thought they were cool and whatever he did, I did. So we would go snake hunting and we'd catch the snakes and then sell them. If we didn't keep them, we would sell them to the pet stores. You get ten, fifteen, twenty bucks for a good-sized snake to a pet store back then even. That was good money. We got pretty good at it. We knew which ones were poisonous and all that, and we would go way, way out.

We were nature boys. Florida nature boys. It would be Cush, Greg, and I. Cush was from New York too. All of our childhood friends were from New York. But we were nature boys. We would bass fish or just catch things. A lot of times, what we caught our families would eat for dinner. We were three years apart. Three years is a good number. You can be close and reflective and at the same time, the older one can have a bit of, "I'm going to protect you." If you're too close, you'll be going through the same stuff at the same time. Like two years is not enough time to earn some wisdom. We were very close, and then he reached the age where he didn't want me around anymore. I used to sneak into his room and play with the equipment while he was gone. By the time he came back, I wrote a song. It was this reggae tune. I played it for him when he got back and he just laughed. He thought it was so funny.

We knew we were both going to be doing something with music at that point. We had this little beat-up upright piano. And we always had so many records to play and listen to. Our dad had a really

Greg's sister, Liz, holds up a d.u. jacket he sent her, 1992.

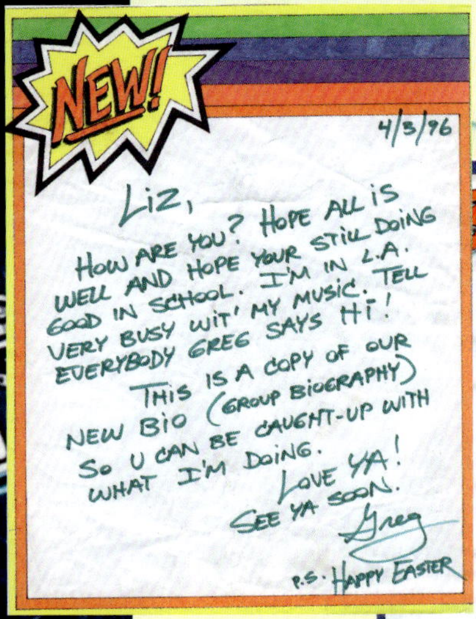

4/3/96

Liz,

How are you? Hope all is well and hope your still doing good in school. I'm in L.A. very busy wit' my music. Tell everybody Greg says Hi!

This is a copy of our new bio (group biography) so u can be caught-up with what I'm doing.

Love ya!
See ya soon.
Greg

P.S. Happy Easter

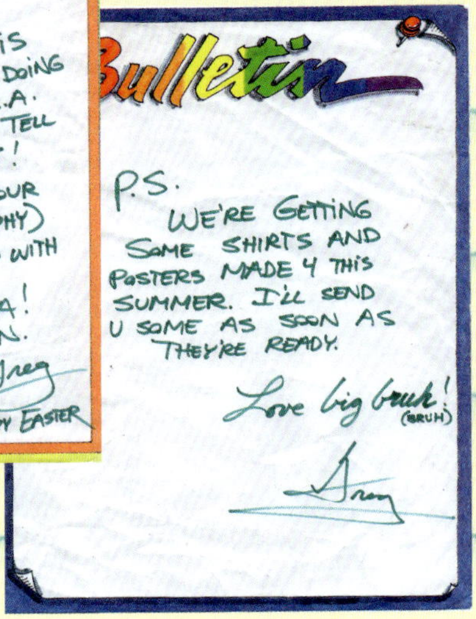

P.S.

We're getting some shirts and posters made 4 this summer. I'll send u some as soon as they're ready.

Love big bruh! (bruh)

Greg

cool and expansive record collection. I think we had Miles Davis, Jimi Hendrix, lots of Parliament. So then when hip hop came out, we could tell where the break beats were coming from. We would always try to figure out the break beat. We would chop it up like Siskel and Ebert. One of the things we would talk about, and you can hear it in the records, is how East Coast hip hop, the funk that it took was from James Brown, Parliament Funkadelic, the older stuff. You know what I mean? The West Coast hip hop came up on the later funk, post P-Funk, you can hear it in the records. East Coast hip hop, the snare sounds and the kick sounds have to have some organics, got to have some break beat record grit somehow on it. That comes from the nature of the records that it all came from. Those recordings are gritty. You listen to those old James Brown records live or in studio, they're kind of gritty. Greg never wanted to do R&B because it was too polished, had to have a certain groove to it. Hip hop to us was like rock and roll. It's total freedom, and P-Funk laid the foundation for that.

Back at the Rackers' Tampa home, I settle into my room for a bit. When I come out later, I see the house is filled with new faces. A bunch of Liz's friends have come by to watch Planet of the Apes *on the big-screen TV, and the whole atmosphere has shifted into a more lively and energized scene. Friends are treated like family in this house—lots of smiles and warmth. Greg grabs Sonya and me and pulls us over to the pool table, where he lays out a deck of cards. I see the young Greg sparkle in his eyes. He's been dying to show us three-card monte. He's loving this moment, so we humor him. He's in full character, brought back to his days of playing this game for money. Sonya is laughing and having so much fun, but I'm sure when he was actually working this magic on the street, she was not so happy. The next day we get up early to pick up Dwayne from the Master Blasters and visit an old friend of theirs who had a stroke a while back and now lives in a care facility. Now a wheelchair user and unable to speak, this friend is full of life and laughter when he sees us walk in. Greg tells everyone to treat him well—that he's digital underground royalty and deserves the best respect. "You know who this is?" he says to everyone we pass by. Greg plays the facility piano for a sec, then we all head outside to tell stories and laugh hard. I'm amazed at Shock's ability to make this moment feel so normal, fun, and comfortable. It's just old friends reminiscing about old times.*

Later, we meet up with Cush at Hooters. Another original member of Shock's first group, Parliament II. I'm here to finally hear Cush tell the one story that Shock won't tell me. He says Cush tells it best. I've been looking forward to this. I can see exactly how these guys were when they were in Parliament II. It's like no time has passed. They're just some kids cracking jokes and having a great time. They keep getting stuck in laughter so hard that it takes a while for Cush to get all the way through this story.

CUSH:

When we were in the ninth grade, we had a little crew. It wasn't a gang. It wasn't a rap group or nothing like that. It was just a few fellas who used to all hang around each other. And that was Sam Tims, Dwight Willson, Darryl Brown, myself, and Greg (who later became "Shock G"). We had this one female who pretty much bogarted her way in the group. And we couldn't do nothing 'cause she was much bigger than all of us! It was just like, okay, she's in it, but not really in it. Nobody would tell her.

Well, what happened was there was this talent show coming up at the school and we knew we wanted to get in it, but we didn't know what we would do. We knew we'd sing, but it was like, what record? You know, what group? Greg and Darryl Brown wanted to do Brothers Johnson, "Strawberry Letter." And Sam was a big Parliament fan at the time. Sam was way ahead of us when it came to Parliament. Dwight was a big fan of Parliament also. Greg thought Parliament was a dumb group at that time. I was in between because my sister listened to Parliament and Bootsy Collins and stuff like that. Well, Sam had so many records, and after you listen to Parliament for a while, you get hooked! So we all decided to emulate Parliament. We made our name Parliament II. Greg was always a good artist so he started making posters, and we would post them all around the school: "Parliament II is coming!" "Be ready for the concert of your life!"

After about two weeks of this, everybody's like, "Who is Parliament II?" People began to think this was a real concert. They started telling each other, "Yo, Parliament's comin'!" So word spread. I'll never forget this moment when we were in the hallway between classes and these guys came up to us, and they said, "So you guys supposed to be Parliament II, huh? Alright so, you get onstage and you guys are wack, we are gonna just clown you for the rest of the school year!" They put us on the spot. That's when we really started practicing. Well, it would always start off as practice, but then some of us started falling asleep. See, our school was split into double sessions. The ninth graders went to school from 6:00 to 2:00 and the eighth graders went from 2:00 to 6:00. So, being in the ninth grade, we had to get up so early in the morning and we were tired! In Florida too, with the heat and everything like that, we would get so tired. So then we made up this rule that whoever fell asleep first would get hot sauce on them. My father used to grow his own hot peppers. The practices started off real slow, and someone was always getting the hot sauce. Then one day we had our dress rehearsal, and we were putting on whatever we could think of to emulate the look of Parliament. Sam wore the diaper, and I dressed up as Dr. Funkenstein. I'm pretty creative too when it comes to getups and stuff like that. So I had this aluminum foil thing. I put it all around my arms and legs and everything. I had an old motorcycle helmet that I made into an aluminum helmet with aluminum foil all around it. It was pretty cool.

The day of the concert, Greg's mom bought us some dry ice. So we had dry ice all on the stage. I was so nervous peeking out, looking at everybody out in the auditorium. Word spread, so other schools were there in the auditorium. It was a full house. The first act went on, second and third, and we were the last act. We finally went on. Greg was out there first, 'cause he was on drums. I was one of the singers. Dwight had a guitar. Darryl had a keyboard, I believe. I can't remember what Sam had. So the show starts. Greg's on the drums. Dwight came out; he had on this satin bandanna around his head and an Afro, looking like Jimi Hendrix. He came out. Darryl came out. Then Sam came out and he had the diaper on. I was so nervous. I had nailed pieces of two-by-fours to make me even taller, so I was six feet tall. I came out and I had these big glasses on and the suit on, I looked like Dr. Funkenstein. I had also put all this powder on me so I was all white, and I'm pretty dark, so it was like Shocka Zulu. I came out and I see everybody's screaming! I was so nervous, my palms were sweaty, and then the floor was wet from the dry ice.

Well, what happened was, when I grabbed the mic, I got electrocuted! And it was right on key! The song goes, "Aaahhhh 'lay me down to sleep" When I grabbed the mic, I screamed! "AAAAaaaaaaaahhhhhh," being electrocuted and all, and I threw the mic down. Then the speakers blew up! But the thing about it, when I grabbed the mic, electricity was going through me, through the aluminum foil. You could see it! Everybody was going crazy! It looked like I was on fire. I'm standing there holding the mic, just screaming, 'cause it's shocking the piss out of me! "AAAAaaaahhhhh!" I throw the mic down, "Baaaoooowww . . ." And everybody's jumping up and running to the stage. They had to hold the crowd back. All you could see was this smoke. After getting electrocuted, I couldn't really walk. I'm like moonwalking almost. I'm in a daze, all dizzy; I can barely see the light. So Dwight says, "Pick up your mic," and I'm like, "No, man. It's gonna shock me!" He's like, "No, it's not gonna shock you."

I pick up the mic again. And it didn't shock me. And we're singing and stuff like that. And all of a sudden it went through again! I mean, there was sparks coming out my mouth! I'm holding together my teeth and stuff like that, and it was shocking me again! So I threw the mic out there in the audience, and they just went crazy! It was like "Oh man!" After that, Greg did a solo on the spot with "Brick House" and everybody there was dancing and going crazy! Well, I was backstage recuperating from that experience. I was in a daze at that point. I thought I was on death row or something. But from then on we were the most popular kids in school. I mean, everybody knew who we were! Guys wanted to be like us, women wanted to be with us. It was crazy from then on. Junior high school, all through high school, we were the most popular. So that became our group, Parliament II. And that is basically the start.

Greg and Kent in Far Rockaway, NY.

Greg with the Racker family—Kent, Liz, Eddie, and Sonya—Hermosa Beach, CA. Kent, Liz, Eddie, and Sonya.
TOP LEFT: Alexis with the siblings.

CHAPTER 12: GREG

January 18, 2012

It's our last day in Tampa. After another long day reminiscing with old friends of Greg's and a night out dancing like silly schoolkids, we make it back to Eddie and Sonya's house. The entire family is asleep, but we decide to shoot hoops down the street. We are stumbling around the garage looking for the basketball, when Sonya walks in a bit disheveled. "What are you all doing?" I immediately feel like I'm doing something wrong and mischievous, and Greg is over there hiding in the corner behind one of the cars just snickering. It's so ridiculous, but I don't know how to not feel like a schoolkid caught sneaking out. At this moment I see how close this book has brought me to Greg. I've walked through his streets, I've heard his stories, and I've lived in his many worlds. And this funky, strange life of his has now become part of mine.

Sometimes, I'm like, *Oh, I'm fucking up right now. I shouldn't be here. I shouldn't be doing whatever session, whatever party.* Then, after the smoke clears, six months, a year later, that thing that I was so uncomfortable and embarrassed about was actually just what was needed for me or for someone else. Whatever it was, was just the right thing and it was just what was needed. I've found that the result is usually better when I'm not quite sure. If I'm doing it perfectly or when I'm a little too concerned about what I'm doing and I'm trying to keep it right, then, when I leave, like a session or whatever, and I'm like, *Ooh, I just killed it! I left them with something hot!* It's usually not all that. It's not special. I'm usually not way off, but it's usually not as extreme as I think. Most of the time, when I think, *Oh, that*

OPPOSITE, CLOCKWISE FROM TOP LEFT: Greg and Alexis on the drive down memory lane. Boiled peanuts on one side, camera on the other, Tampa, FL, 2012; Greg with Cush and Reggie at Hooters, telling stories, Tampa, FL, 2012; Greg playing around with Cush's sisters and nephew, Tonda, Shalay, and Shalay's son, Hakeem, Tampa, FL, 2012. **THIS PAGE:** Greg telling stories while driving around.

Greg shading in Humpty's nose in the hotel room, Las Vegas, NV, 2008.

A moment of rest, after a long night and a show. Outside the hotel, Las Vegas, NV, 2008.

session was so uncomfortable, or I'm worried about how a record came out, those are the ones that later turn out to be *the* ones. Those are the special ones.

I believe that there's way more wisdom in laughing, relaxing, partying, vibing, being free, being nice. There's way more wisdom in that than there is in being prim and proper and work ethic–oriented and groomed to the T every single time and never stepping outside the box. I don't think about phone bills, and Social Security numbers, and organizing this and that. I don't think all that shit's important. To be honest, I was off balance the entire time we did the first two, three albums, and I never got a chance to catch my breath from the time Tommy Boy first said, "We need you to put a band together by Friday. We want to see you perform for us." Then it was, "Can you be ready for a tour? Can you this, can you that?" And that went on until about '94, until I was able to go . . . *Until* me and Melissa moved up into the mountains, actually. That's when I was able to finally take a breath. Just like, I never had a chance to reflect and look at everything. Or sit and watch one of our entire shows by myself and take it in. It was always like, I only had enough time to catch one song, and even then, there were always other people with me while I was doing it. I couldn't focus on it.

Yup, it was crazy for a minute, but some people run their whole life like that. Their entire life. I refuse to ever have no downtime. I fight for my sleep. I fight for my rest. I understand the importance of sleep. I love to dream. I feel better the next day when I'm rested. It's like anything that demands me to run at full speed all the time, 24/7. I don't even aim for that. I've aimed at things that leave a lot of space in life, like music. If it wasn't music, I'd be drawing. If it wasn't drawing, if I just had to have a regular job, I'd probably be a salesperson or something because the hours aren't as important. Some jobs, it's not about how much you're on the clock, it's about what you do. When I worked at Music Unlimited, I had "salesman of the month" plaques, even though I wasn't there as much as the other salesmen. I was just more efficient with my time. I feel that way about making music too. I feel like I'm a little more in control of my career than the average artist is. It never goes too far off the path from how I want to go. At least I've been lucky like that.

Shock walks in to the old radio station he used to work at, 88.5 FM. Everything looks the same—but now there is a plaque on the door in honor of Kenny K.

EPILOGUE

This book took a few detours, and veered down multiple creative paths after the Tampa trip, eventually slowing to a full stall in 2015. Greg was most interested in style and form, thinking of interactive possibilities, and hoping to create a new and unusual piece of art. As the pages filled with story after story from his life, he was afraid that it was becoming too much like a memoir. And so we paused, took a break, lived our lives. The pieces of the book sat in files on our computers and in the very deep corners of our minds. Five years slowly went by. I finished my master's degree in education and began teaching in New York City public schools. I got married and had a baby girl. Greg moved back to Tampa. Sometimes he'd send a video message, or I'd call and we'd have a long catch-up conversation. He'd create a series of messages with wild stories about aliens abducting him or spaceship encounters and whatnot.

Then 2020 happened, and the world turned upside down. We were all in quarantine. I decided to start looking again through Shock's art, his writing, the photographs, and all of the typed-out interviews. There was so much. I saw that all the pieces together painted the portrait of a person and an artist: complicated, introspective, creative, real, and imagined. Not a memoir but a new piece of work filled with art and words. I felt the desire to get this out into the world. I sent Greg copies of this new version in August of 2020 and he liked it better—or maybe he was just more ready. We started back in.

It was only eight months later, on April 22, 2021, about 9 P.M., that I got the call. Actually it was an email. Shock started a group email for close friends and family, where he posted outlandish ideas, creative thoughts, and videos of himself—usually from a hotel room balcony. I opened the email to see what new video he might have added, but instead these words formed in front of my eyes: "Peace, I heard some disturbing news about Greg's health let us know he is okay . . ." My heart sank. I saw another message pop up: "I'm literally on a phone call right now with a friend who called to confirm that he heard Shock had passed." I dropped to the floor. I called Shock instinctively and heard his lively voice recording with a piano riff on his voicemail. I wrote him a text: "Please tell me you are okay!" I think I believed that I could catch him somehow before it became true. Keep him alive and with us, just by reaching out. Still on the floor, my hands shook and my eyes filled with water as I tried to find any information. It was like those dreams where you can't move or scream. I couldn't work my phone. I found myself muttering "no no no . . ." A mutual friend, Eddie, wrote me a text: "I think it is true . . ."

A week later I flew to Tampa, eight months pregnant, in the middle of a pandemic, my husband and two-year-old at our home in New

York. I knew I needed to be there. I thought back to our last conversation, not long ago, via FaceTime. He had teased my daughter, Anaïs, that her stuffed dino named Zucchini was his. "Hey. Is that my toy? I think you have my toy!" My dad called out, "When are you gonna make a jazz record?" and Greg said, "Tell him I'm on it!" He told me we should talk more often and that maybe he would move up to New York City for a while.

I arrived at my hotel in Ybor City, in Tampa, in the late afternoon on Friday, April 30. The Allen Temple AME Church was just around the corner. The last (and only) time that I was in Tampa was with Greg. We had come to stay with his family and interview everyone for the book. He took me all over the city to see old friends, the radio station he worked at, his old high school, where I made him wear the Tommy Boy backpack to look like he went there. He showed me where he used to bike with Kent as kids, and he knocked on an old girlfriend's door just in case she was there. We must have laughed the entire time.

That afternoon, as I walked out into the hot, damp, Tampa street, flashes of my time with Greg flooded me. I saw the stool in front of the pizza place where Humpty and I got into it. Everyone came out to help him, not me; I felt like the picked-on younger sibling who had finally lost it and ended up with a time-out from punching her brother in the nose. Down the way was the nightclub that Shock stormed out of, with no warning, yelling as if we were in a relationship and having a huge fight. Many of the patrons knew who he was, and I think he was playing with that attention. He thought it was hilarious and flew around the corner. I really thought he had actually left me in downtown Tampa, but then I caught him holding his stomach and cracking up, leaning against an alley wall. "You thought I'd really leave?!" He loved the entertainment of it.

I paced up and down East Seventh Avenue for about half an hour, flooded with memories, and finally walked into the Allen Temple Church to join the wake. The church was smaller than I expected, painted pink, and lined with palm trees. I signed my name on the guest list and walked in. I saw about fifteen people on the other side of the aisle and didn't recognize them. My head turned back toward the front of the church. I made out the smooth lines of the mahogany casket, the beautiful full, drooping white flowers. I followed the open top and the cream fabric along with my eyes.

Then, suddenly, I saw him. It was Greg's face. Still and plastic, but it was him. He had his old smirk, and I felt as if he may jump up and laugh at us all: "What y'all doing?! You thought I meant this?" I could hear him saying something like that. Saying something about the bizarreness of us all gathered there for him. But he just lay there, absolutely still. As I moved to the other side where everyone stood, I could make out faces better. I saw Too Fly Eli, who wrapped me in a hug. I hadn't seen any of them for almost twenty years. Money B, Nzazi, Atron, Ray Luv, Cush . . . all these people I'd met while I followed Greg through his life story, people from his childhood, his family, digital underground, and the music industry, all of their faces came into view. We were all a bit older now, and the pandemic masks we wore gave us a certain level of anonymity. But here we were. We mingled a bit, hugged, caught up in slight ways, and mostly just sat with the reality of why we were all there. Afterward, I was swept into a house party with the digital underground family. We told stories, reminisced, and sang out old d.u. lyrics.

Very early the next morning, I checked out of the hotel and headed to Greg's family home. It was a difficult morning. Most of the family stayed in their rooms until it was well past the time we were supposed to be at the church. Everyone tried their best to pull on the outfits they had picked out, or dot makeup. I thought how hard this must be, to have to mourn so publicly. The family knew how many people Greg had touched, and they included everyone openly: musicians, friends, fans, even the media. The procession of limos, cars, and vans arrived. Finally it was time.

The service was perfect. Intimate and human. Beautiful words were said by many. George Clinton, Bootsy Collins, Chuck D, Jermaine Dupri, CeeLo Green, Busta Rhymes, Rob Base, and many others spoke about how Greg or Shock had impacted their lives. Cush told a story and ended with, "I miss my brother. I'm really gonna miss him . . . He took on the world. And he won. That's all I have to say about now." The Luniz were there, Cleetis Mack, Ray Luv, Yo-Yo, Master Blasters, Esinchill, Metaphysical, Dialect, Da Noses. MC Serch, DJ Fuze, Money B, Tom Silverman of Tommy Boy Records each stood up to give reflections. Finally Kent took the microphone: "I've always felt so much love from everybody that he touched and no story is too small or too long, and I would love to hear every one, any story you have about him, they're always about love . . . It's been a charmed life being a brother of Shock G. You think about what he's done for friends. I was his brother! I'm going to miss him."

I had my camera, but I didn't take any pictures. No reunion pictures with digital underground, or Master Blasters, or with the Luniz, Esinchill, Metaphysical, Dialect, Da Noses. No images of the slingshots blasting his music. In the end it wasn't about that. Greg was my friend; he'd become family. And now he was gone, and I was left to finish this last chapter on my own.

The procession to the burial site was very much Shock G. Celebrities, champagne, everyone singing and dancing. It was big and loud, and showy, a party atmosphere, an uplifting celebration of his life. As we arrived at the burial site, slingshot motorcycles pulled off to the side, and friends and family silently exited the other vehicles. There were about forty of us that walked up the tree-lined path to the burial site. We stood around in the Tampa heat, spread out on the grass with Greg's family sitting all together, closest to the site. Quiet words were said as we all stood silently. I looked back to see Money B standing alone about fifty feet away. I could see the heaviness in him, in how he stood so still. As I turned back to the site, I saw the box with the casket being pushed into the granite wall. Greg was in there. Someone lifted their hands and began to seal the box permanently into the wall. I could barely hear Greg's dad say, "I guess this is it. It's final now."

A wave went through the crowd. The finality of it. The unexpected emptiness of such a strong presence, now gone. Many speak of Shock's spirituality and his ability to live on an astral plane, that his spirit is alive and free. But to me, in that moment I felt the suction of his presence being pulled away from here. Just gone. A large empty feeling. PeeWee caught me in his arms before I could crumple into a ball. He brought me into the shade so that we could hold each other and let the tears fall.

The flight home was unusually quiet, except for the soft hum of the engine. I could hear the echo of Greg's voice, his laughter. I could feel his presence through memory. It's just the rest of us now to carry these memories. I thought of how many people he has touched, how many lives he has changed. I am not unique in that he gave his heart, his time, his humor, his creative energy to so many. Each of us was special in his eyes. It's just us now to remember how he, or his story, or his art or his music has changed us. It's just the rest of us now.

—Lex

ACKNOWLEDGMENTS

Greg (Shock G), none of this would exist without you: *Forever my mentor, co-conspirator (or BP as we called it), and friend. Your stories, your laughter, and random phone-call riffs still ricochet around in my mind every day. Thank you for letting me in, thank you for allowing me to see the world through your eyes, and thank you for trusting me to help carry your voice forward. The gift of your friendship keeps teaching me long after our first sessions in Topanga and far beyond our last recording. You've taught me to see humor in everything, to be open enough to let creativity guide my path, and that the bravest art reveals our authentic selves. Your voice walks me through every choice on every page and Humpty Hump's "hypothetical, political, lyrical, miracle-whip" still makes me "laff" out loud as I edit. This is for you, BP!*

To the Jacobs, Kraft, and Racker families—*Shirley (Mama Humpty!) Kraft, Edward (Eddie) Racker, Sonya, Herb, Kent, Liz, and Gloria. Your generosity with memories, photos, and late-night fact-checks turned a pile of interviews into a living scrapbook. Thank you for opening your homes, various boxes, laptops, and your hearts so willingly. It means the world.*

To my first, fierce, and fabulous editor—*my mom, Carol Wolfe Clay. Through countless late-night screenshares and Zoom calls from Seattle to NYC, we created a pandemic-era lifeline full of laughter, hope, and purpose. You guided the creation of something truly beautiful—this book would not be the same without your attention to detail and care for Greg. I loved our freak-outs over subliminal messaging, all the giggles, and all the celebrations. The memories of working on this book together all these years, I will always hold close.*

To the voices who chime in throughout these chapters, to the image keepers, and to Shock's circle of d.u. fam. *Your stories, memories, images, and love are beautiful time capsules that bring us right into his world: George Clinton (whose cosmic funk runs throughout these pages—thank you for your mentorship of Shock), Bootsy Collins, Overton Loyd, Rene "DJ Stretch" Negron, Shawn "Shah T" Trone, Kenneth "Kenny-K" Waters,*

Earl "Schmoovy Schmoov" Cook, Neil "Sleuth" Johnson, Atron Gregory (thank you for being by my side; you are forever fam), Nzazi "Zi" Malonga, Ronald "Money B" Brooks, Tonia "Ton Teezy" Spurlock, Bobby McCall, Ramon "PeeWee" Gooden, David "DJ Fuze" Elliot, Jeremy "Jaybeatz" Jackson, Jimi "Chopmaster J" Dright, "MC Dazzlin Doc-P," "MC Scoobie D," Tom Silverman, Monica Lynch, Leila Steinberg, Tupac Shakur, Afeni Shakur (for inspiration you didn't know you contributed), Raymond "Ray Luv" Tyson, Mandolyn "Mystic" Ludlum, Cleetis Mack, Reggie "Saafir" Gibson, Michael "Meta" Russell, Demond "Dialect" Dowdy, Omari "DJ Nustylez" Edwards, Too Fly Eli, DJ Flame, MC K Bar, MC Ronnie Ron (Omar), Big Money Odis, Nicholas (Murs) Carter, Liz Suwandi, Esinchill Campbell, Chuck D, Flavor Flav, Yukmouth and Numskull (the Luniz), B (Shep) Shepard, Scott Moran, Eddie Sumlin, Chris Kelley, Danica "Peps" Ratjovich, Anastasia, Alfie, "Da Noses" (all of you!), Craig "Porkchop" Christensen (thanks for sitting with me in Tampa), Mack Dread, Chris Allen, Davey D. Cook, Limo G, and Chris "Young Hump" Clarke. If I missed you, please know that he did not and your words and spirit live within the color and folds of these pages even if my word-count ration failed to note it.

To my own circle of support: *Sam, my partner-in-everything, who kept the kids laughing and the coffee coming. Thank you for that first table you bought me when we met, so that I could spread out all the Post-its, photos, and artwork, and for believing in me through all the years of late-night edits and contemplative conversations as I brought this book to completion. Anaïs and Lennox, who remind me daily of what really matters and the importance of storytelling. Your joy, impromptu dance breaks, and fierce hugs are proof that art and family run on a similar vibration. You are always my "why." My mom, dad (it has been so much fun to connect with you about the publishing world—and your lake house was ideal for those long writing days), Mike, Lauren, Terry, Cam, Mac (hey Mac, thanks for wading through Shock's world in early edits), and to the whole extended and blended crew, for every flight, every babysit, every pep text, every "you got this." It means more than you know. Friends who fed my spirit throughout—you know who you are. I needed you and you were there. Love you, thank you.*

To my agent, Robert Guinsler, *who said yes when this looked more like a record crate than a book and who understood, respected, and stayed true to my vision from the very beginning.*

To my amazing editorial team at Clarkson Potter/Penuin Random House and beyond: *Porscha Burke, who first said yes to the manuscript. Thank you for believing in this book, and letting Greg's vision and legacy shine. Angelin, who took it from there and never flinched at my random emails full of hieroglyphics and bizarre wording from 3 A.M. thoughts. Danny Vazquez, your edits felt powerfully in line with Greg and his style. Thank you for your care with the book, and for letting me bounce so many funky ideas off you. To Ian Dingman, Ashley Pierce, Kim Tyner, and the entire team at Clarkson Potter, thank you for turning Rackadelic art, piles of photos, and spoken-word fragments into print that actually lines up clearly on the page while holding true to that scrapbook feel—true magic.*

Finally, to every single reader who picks this book up*—may Greg's whimsicality, tenderness, and boundary-bending art spark your own creative vision.*

Keep it beautiful.

PHOTO CREDITS

All photography copyright © 2026 by Alexis Wolfe Mbassa, except for the following images:

Copyright © 2026 by Brian "B+" Cross for Elemental Magazine: page 16, 137

Courtesy of Ronald Brooks (aka Money B): pages 148, 152, 154, 177 (bottom)

Copyright © 2026 by Kathy Crawford: page 121

Courtesy of David Elliot (aka DJ Fuse): pages 74–75, 81, 160, 175, 177 (top)

Courtesy of Reggie Gibson (aka Saafir): page 82

Copyright © 2026 by Lynn Goldsmith via Getty Images: page 198

Courtesy of Atron Gregory: pages 7, 149

Copyright © 2026 by Victor Hall via Tommy Boy/Reservoir Media: page 141

Courtesy of Gregory Jacobs: pages 9, 72–73, 76–77, 112, 124, 166–167, 185, 207 (right)

Courtesy of Gregory Jacobs and the Rackers: pages 212–225

Courtesy of Shirley Anne Jacobs: page 208

Copyright © 2026 by Pat Johnson via Alamy: pages 110–111

Copyright © 2026 by Jeff Kravitz via Getty Images: page 78

Illustration copyright © by Overton Lloyd: page 147

Courtesy of Cleetis Mack: pages 117, 173, 176

Copyright © 2026 by Kim Shady via Gregory Jacobs: pages 190–191

Courtesy of Tommy Boy/Reservoir Media: pages 71, 163

Copyright © 2026 by Alexis Wolfe Mbassa via the Rackers: pages 226–227

CLARKSON POTTER/PUBLISHERS
An imprint of the Crown Publishing Group
A division of Penguin Random House LLC

1745 Broadway
New York, NY 10019
clarksonpotter.com
penguinrandomhouse.com

Photography credits can be found on pages 238-39.

Library of Congress Cataloging-in-Publication Data is on file with the publisher.

ISBN 978-0-593-79632-0
Ebook ISBN 978-0-593-79633-7

Editors: Porscha Burke and Angelin Adams | Freelance editor: Daniel Vazquez
Assistant Editor: Darian Keels
Designer: Ian Dingman | Production Designer: Christina Self
Production Editor: Ashley Pierce
Production: Kim Tyner
Copyeditor: Amy Smith Bell | Proofreaders: Diana Drew and Miriam Taveras
Publicist: Felix Cruz | Marketer: Brianne Sperber

MANUFACTURED IN CHINA

10 9 8 7 6 5 4 3 2 1

FIRST EDITION

THE AUTHORIZED REPRESENTATIVE IN THE EU FOR PRODUCT SAFETY AND COMPLIANCE IS PENGUIN RANDOM HOUSE IRELAND, MORRISON CHAMBERS, 32 NASSAU STREET, DUBLIN D02 YH68, IRELAND, HTTPS://EU-CONTACT.PENGUIN.IE.